To: Chuck & [...]

As you read this, always remember:

"It's not how much dog is in the fight ... Rather — It's how much fight is in the dog!"

R.C. Mueller

8/23/96

LIES in the FAMILY ALBUM

Paddy Joe Miller

LARKSDALE

LIES in the FAMILY ALBUM

Copyright © 1995 by Schuromil Productions, Inc.

———————

Production Coordinator — Marilyn Overcast

Senior Editor — Mary Margaret Williamson

Cover Art — Costner Graphics

Computer Typography — Laura Couch

Book Design — Charlotte St. John

———————

Cataloging in Publication Data:
  Lies in the Family Album / Paddy Joe Miller.
     p.   cm.
  ISBN 0-89896-291-9
  1. Saint Clair (Schuylkill County, Pa.)--Social life and customs. 2. Miller, Paddy Joe, 1954-   --Childhood and youth. 3. Saint Clair (Schuylkill County, Pa.)--Biography. I. Title.
  F159.S13 B55   1994
  306.87'092--dc20
  [B]   94-43183
                                                  CIP

LARKSDALE

Printed in the United States of America

DEDICATION

TO THOSE WHO SEEK THE TRUTH

AUTHOR'S NOTE

This is a true story. Some situations which appear are presumptions made by the author due to his inability to ascertain the truth. Also, many of the names have been changed in order to protect the identity of the person.

"THE GREATEST DISCOVERY"

Peering out of tiny eyes
The grubby hand that gripped the rail
Wiped the window clean of frost
As the mid-morning air laid on the latch
A whistle awakened someone there
Next door to the nursery just down the hall
A strange new sound you never heard before
A strange new sound that makes boys explore
Tread neat, so small those little feet
Amid the morning his small heart beats
So much excitement yesterday
That must be rewarded, must be displayed
Large hands lift him through the air
Excited eyes contain him there
The eyes of those he loves and knows
But what's this extra bed just here
His puzzled head tipped to one side
Amazement swims in those bright green eyes
Glancing down upon this thing
That makes strange sounds
Strange sounds that sing
In those silent happy seconds
That surround the sound of this event
A parent smile is made in moments
They have made for you a friend
And all you ever learned from them
Until you grew much older
Did not compare with when they said
This is your brand new brother
This is your brand new brother.

PROLOGUE

"THE DAY OF DISCOVERY"

I AM MY SISTER'S SON. Hard to believe, yes, especially for me. But I'm getting much too far ahead of myself in this story already, and I've just begun.

In the early 1900's, the borough of Saint Clair, Pennsylvania, was booming due to the discovery of anthracite or "hard" coal in the region. It burns cleaner and longer than "soft" coal, known as bituminous. However, since coal has lost its emphasis in industrial America, Saint Clair is now simply a "strip mining" operation. The precious coal which still remains is being blown out of the mountains by those few who are still able to hold jobs related to the industry. The land, in most cases, is then left barren and stripped of its beauty. On all sides of the town, all one can see is huge coal banks with pine trees dotting their surface. There is one main road into the town and one main road out. The principal source of income, as far as I can remember, is unemployment. For once the coal was gone and all the land stripped clean of its black fruit, the only thing which could survive were people who knew nothing but survival.

My childhood memories deal mainly with the subject of survival. I was the youngest of ten children, and the year 1954 saw very hard times in a small coal mining town where the world was learning about the vast and cheap uses of electricity and oil. Whatever bed I chose to sleep in (there were four for the children, divided by ten), was always cramped with somewhat larger and somewhat lumpier bodies. It wasn't bad in the winter. It was always so cold we would huddle and snuggle together to stay warm. But the summers—they could be devastating. The heat and humidity, combined with brother Frank, who often threw farting concerts for anyone who would listen, were unbelievable. The heat and sweat of a Pennsylvania house were too much without the modern luxury of air conditioning.

The backbone of the Miller family was Victoria. A proud Irish Catholic woman who decided early in her life that things such as sex were bad, and the only person who could practice it was Victoria. Peter Miller was the man who provided the seed—a tough, old-fashioned man of German origin who rarely, if ever, lost his cool. When Peter got mad or thought things were getting too hot with Victoria around the house, he always had the recourse of walking up to Melnic's bar on the corner and tying one on. It never ceased to amaze me, whenever Peter took me on these alcohol missions of his, how he could walk into Melnic's with fifty cents change in his pocket, drink beer and whiskey all afternoon (along with soda and chips for me), and still come home with thirty cents. Everybody liked Peter and knew him to be a good, hard-working man. At this young age, I was sure proud of my Dad!

Peter worked as a laborer for Brokhoff's Dairy for as long as I can remember. Before that, he worked in the mines. The unforgiving mines. Mines which could kill instantly, with bodies never recovered. Mines in which a man inhaled black dust every working day of his life, black dust that eventually would become a medical nightmare—"Black-Lung Disease." Anyone vaguely associated with coal mining knows what causes it. The fact that he brought home only $88.00 every two weeks and fed twelve people at one time, will always remain a mystery to me. True, my oldest brother James helped out with his check from his civil service job, and this was essential for survival. A simple trip to the grocery store would most times net one bag of groceries per member of the family. This was half of Peter's pay. The other half went to the necessities of keeping the family together.

To appreciate the size of the Miller family, one would have to visit for a typical Sunday dinner. It was mandatory to be present for Sunday dinner right after church. I have often reflected on why I looked so skinny and malnourished in the few pictures I've seen of myself as an infant. Imagine dinner with twelve people, seven women and five men, at which only the strongest and quickest would survive. Mounds of potatoes, I believe, kept me alive. This, because any meat served was usually gone by the time brother James delicately picked his choice pieces. Frank, the sports hero at the time, had his huge portion, and a much smaller portion for everyone else.

Peter didn't much care about his portion—he was happy. He had already stopped in Melnic's on the way home after church for a shot and a beer. As a matter of fact, I was always the designated runner to get Peter on Sunday. Everyone in the bar knew that once young Paddy walked through the side door, Peter had roughly fifteen minutes to drink. They wouldn't see him again that day until at least four o'clock, when he would go back up to watch a ball game on TV and shut the world of the family out for a few brief hours.

Peter knew that six o'clock the next morning he would be hauling huge sacks of cheese or milk, or whatever it is a laborer at a milk plant was expected to do. Anyway, Melnic's was Peter's favorite bar. He knew and visited them all, but Melnic's was his favorite. One of the incredible features of this small, predominantly Catholic region was the ratio of bars to churches, 2 to 1. Or 26 to 13. All this for 4,000 people. What individual could ask for more?

It was 1958, when I was four years old, that I began to comprehend some things. One of the things which always boggled my family's mind was why, at the age of four, I was still taking a bottle to bed—a beer bottle with a nipple on the end of it. This was filled with the nectar of the breasts, "milk." I never tried to explain because anytime anyone would bring the subject up to embarrass me, the whole room would break into a thunderous roar of laughter. Truth is, I believe this was my security blanket. You see, some children have silk blankets, some suck their thumbs, but I had a beer bottle with a nipple on the end of it. Whenever I was perplexed because one of my sisters suddenly came home with her boyfriend and announced unexpectedly they were getting married, I fixed a bottle and waited for the show.

Victoria would proceed to throw every dish in the house against the wall and watch it shatter to pieces. "Where did we go wrong, Peter?" she would ask. "A good Catholic girl like this, raised in the ways of the church and this is what she gives us in return?" Smash. Peter would simply stand in the background wondering how they were going to replace these dishes and hoping Victoria would get out her phenobarbital to mellow her. One good shot of that stuff would put her in a super mellow mood. Combine it with a brandy chaser, and Victoria was super gone. This would buy Peter the time to sneak up to Melnic's and think the whole mess out over a shot and a beer. Pretty soon he would get a good snort on, start talking with one of his friends, and proceed to ask him for his opinion. The friend, having satisfied Peter's ego that he was a good man and father, would give Peter the impetus to go back to the terrible quandary at the house. It wouldn't be until the next day, when he got home from work, that he would have to deal with Victoria and the fact that half the town already knew that one of the Miller girls was pregnant. As for the bottle, I believe it may have been a reaction to how Peter would solve problems—with a bottle. These are some of my earliest and fondest memories of Peter.

Around the year 1958, various members of our family began moving out to begin a new life on their own. James, the eldest, was still single and was the sole occupant of the front bedroom, a room which he believed he deserved because of the heavy responsibility placed on him. The fact James donated money to the cause entitled him to, he believed, first dibs on the meat at every meal, first in the bathroom every day, first parking spot at church, first to leave church after mass, you name it. James was first, "Top Dog," as he would say. Definitely a legend in his own mind.

The only bathroom in a family of twelve can be a harrowing experience on a Sunday. The earlier you arose, the more likely it was you would get in. If you were real lucky, you even had the privilege of hot water. However, if you arose late, you risked a long line, cold water, and the chance of being late for church. If this was the case, you didn't bathe (there was no shower), you didn't comb your hair, and you got your ass up to the altar! After church you bathed. Missing church was a mortal sin, you can bathe anytime. To be sure, we were poor, but we were raised in the "eyes of the church," according to Victoria, and always were clean cut.

To be devious, sometimes I would come in after playing in coal dirt all day long and plot my strategy. On certain days, James played softball for Kulhic's bar. After the game, he would always come home for a bath before going up to the bar for some drinks with the team. My game plan was always to come in just in time to use all the hot water and leave a nasty black ring around the tub. I'd watch for the hero's entrance and split, just in time to take cover from the shouting to ensue. You see, when he couldn't find me to bitch at, he'd grab his nearest sister and tear into her. This, because she didn't make sure I had cleaned the tub—another must. Then he would make her scrub it clean, because James just didn't do tubs.

Because James decided to stick around and be co-man of the house, it is not hard to understand why some of the girls started leaving. Ellen, the third oldest daughter, decided to pack up and get a civil service job away from home. She left when I was three so I never got to figure her out. She had good looks, a good personality and a life of her own to get on with. With the impending pressures building in the house, she used her looks, personality, and smarts to leave. I always knew she'd do all right. It's too bad I never got to know her well.

Rose Mary was the next to go. She met a hard-working German and was gone. Through all my life she was the one sister who always remembered my birthday with a card and some money, and at Christmas always had a present under the tree for me. After marrying Tom, she moved to Harrisburg, which she still calls home. Within a year, she had her first of five boys. The oldest, Mike, would become one of my few acquaintances outside my small world of Saint Clair. Every year, once a year, Victoria would allow Rose Mary to come pick me up to go to her house for a one-week stay. It was during these visits that Mike and I became friends.

They lived in a three-bedroom apartment complex which sat directly across the street from a little league baseball field. I thought this was just dandy, since the closest thing for the eye to see from my house in Saint Clair was the Reading Railroad. This conglomerate of tracks and huge rail cars loomed as a constant threat to my life. Anyone seeing me near the tracks had instant approval to test the size of their hand on my rear. This, however, never seemed to stop me. I could always find some kind of action over by the tracks. Anyway, every year, once a year, Rose Mary would put me on a bus back home. My yearly vacation was over and I got to spend it with the same person.

Once back home, I immediately headed for the railroad tracks where all the "boys," as we called ourselves, were planning our next venture. Here I would tell all kind of great lies about my week's vacation with my "rich" sister while five or six young kids just like me stood with open mouths trying to put themselves in my shoes for one hour of that week. You see, this was action and news in this slow-moving, depressed town.

Sister Clarice was next to go. She met a smooth-moving, smooth-talking lad named Rob. Everyone who knew him called him

Cookie, and that he was. Cookie and Clarice soon began having children of their own. They saved money and bought a small farm complete with barn, chickens, the whole works. This would soon become my favorite vacation spot since the stories I could tell all my friends would stretch far beyond the normal imagination. Riding a horse, feeding the chickens, milking the goats and cows was a whole new ball game for me. And to think, the farm was only ten miles away. Why, if I ever got pissed off at Victoria and Peter, I could just run away to the farm. This was one of my favorite fantasies when things weren't going quite right at home, something that at times happened often.

Clarice's first child was a son, Billy. Through all of my childhood I found it increasingly difficult to feature how I was only one year older than Mike and Billy and yet I was their uncle. I was soon to have the name "Uncle Paddy" dubbed on me by all the offspring of my brothers and sisters. My brothers and sisters simply called me "Paddy," and this would prove to become increasingly embarrassing to me in crucial situations. My high school coaches, close friends, etc., would agitate me by this simple nickname. Strangely enough, as I got older and achieved more maturity (if it can ever be achieved), I came to acknowledge this name being called me by my family and acquaintances.

My fondest memory of Cookie was going raccoon hunting with him and his friends in the cool autumn Pennsylvania night. Cookie was the proud owner of approximately twenty hunting dogs, and every car or person that came by their farm knew it. We would wait until pitch dark and head out with nothing but a bright flashlight, a rifle, and four of Cookie's finest. Cookie would entice these dogs with the scent of a raccoon skin from a prior hunt. The dogs would be set free and from that point on, our job was to keep pace with them.

The Pennsylvania countryside is a maze of trees, small creeks, thorns, you name it. We would struggle through these conditions for miles. Suddenly, we would happen upon all four dogs surrounding one particular tree. The sensation hit, after all this running, that we would finally witness the thrill of the fight.

The spotlight scanned the pine tree and, without thinking, I asked Cookie, "What the hell ya lookin' for Cook?" He took the light off the tree and put it on me. What a sight it must have been for him to look at.

I had been up to my waist in water, thorned near death, and freezing. Did the sight of this poor bastard appeal to Cookie's sympathetic side? Not on your life. When the spotlight left the tree to look at me, the raccoon jumped the tree and we were off again. Needless to say, my raccoon hunts for the rest of my life were few and far between, to the distress of neither Cookie nor me.

Frank would be an unexpected heartbreak in Victoria's life. I think by this time Peter didn't give a shit. Frank was, up to this point, Mr. Jock of the family, an all-American guy—good looking, smart, excellent football player. He managed to keep his head above water with our family through some of the worst times. Overall, through thick and thin, Frank Miller did the Miller family proud.

I recall going to watch him play high school football in the early sixties. He played halfback and was damn good. I could tell that by how tall Peter and James would sit at the games. Nativity High School was a big name in football back then. Although they were Catholic, they were the best. Frank once scored five touchdowns in one game, and it was then and there that I decided this was the brother I wanted to pattern myself after. I wanted the people and all my family to look up to me. But Frank was muscular and already popular. How could I top that? After much thought, I decided humor was the answer. I would humor people into liking me. Through most of my life, I've used this technique. Sometimes it works great—helps you get out of some real tight jams, acting the fool. Sometimes, however, it can be a dismal failure. My humor, however, really started to blossom much later, in college.

Throughout all of high school, Frank dated Betsy. She was pretty, intelligent, the type of woman for Frank. He kept dating her through most of his college career. I'll never forget the night Frank came in the house and sat down with Betsy in the living room. Right then I knew something was up. That, coupled with the fact they tried getting rid of me right away. Not this time, however.

Both Victoria and Peter had half a snort on and gave me their blessing to stay. When Frank realized I was part of the furniture, he decided to go for it. "Mom, Betsy and I are getting married, she's pregnant." Hush. The room was totally silent when suddenly I blurted out, "Does that mean you won't put the Christmas tree up for us anymore, Frank?" Right then and there I got my exit sign. I went no farther than the next room, however, where I heard the whole conversation. Victoria obviously was pretty well spent, because she didn't believe them. Betsy said that they had told her parents already, and Victoria didn't believe that, either. Immediately she went to the phone and called Betsy's mother. Similarly, Betsy's mom thought they were only joking, since Victoria ended their conversation abruptly.

It had seriously dawned on her that Frank would now be leaving her life and she was heartbroken. It was sad—Peter even cried. (However, it was definitely not the reaction which Peter and Victoria had when finding out one of THEIR daughters was pregnant.) Frank gave them a lot of happy times and he was now leaving this once packed house. After they left the house, Victoria went through her usual "Catholic-upbringing, by the eyes of the church," routine. Peter dished out the phenobarbital and brandy. However, before she became mellow, Victoria went through another set of dishes, probably to keep her in shape.

C. J. was to be a unique story of her own. Carlene Janice was the female apple of Victoria and Peter's eyes. All through her life she worked hard around the house, helped out whenever possible, and helped keep some semblance of order. The joy could not have been more profound in the Miller household than the day, in her senior year of high school, that C. J. announced she was going to devote her life to God. She wanted to join the convent and become a nun. Finally, someone in our house had helped to answer Victoria's prayers. No one, however, realized the financial burden this would eventually place on our house, especially C. J. Many sacrifices would be made by many people, all to help C. J. achieve what she thought was her calling. This was all immaterial, however. What was important to the Miller family was that someone in their domain was going to become an immediate servant of the Lord.

C. J. was not without her faults, however. Many was the day I would be playing in front of the house and see the flaming ash of a cigarette butt coming down at me from a third-floor window. After careful investigation I decided it had to be C. J. up in the third floor acting very liberated. I had even known her to take a hit or two off a cigarette while she was confined to her convent stay. You've come a long way, baby.

In the year 1963, when I was nine years old, Susan first met

John. He was home on leave from the Navy, staying with a buddy of his who was from Minersville, another coal mining town just nine miles from Saint Clair. Right away, from seeing and watching John act, I knew trouble was brewing. It was evident Victoria was against this drifter from the Navy courting one of her daughters. First, and always of importance, he was not Catholic. Second, John carried himself in a way that made one dare to guess he was a hustler, somewhat of a flim-flam man. In any event, and against the wishes of anyone concerned in the family (except me), Susan kept this flaming romance up.

One particular day in 1964 while I was sitting on the porch watching cars go by, a bright orange Ford Mustang came to a screeching halt at the stop sign next to our house. In it sat John with a big macho grin. John thought he would show me what this machine had by putting forty yards of rubber in front of the house before parking. He was two weeks shy of getting his discharge and received some "early out" pay. He also had a whole wad of fifty dollar bills rolled up. Needless to say, Susan was smiles from ear to ear; and John—I could tell what was on his mind after being at sea for an extended period.

In truth, the car was really sharp. It was a four speed and perhaps the fastest machine I had been in. John took me for a ride around town, and, of course, I thought I was a bad dude. I sat shotgun while Susan sat in the back. At that time John looked like he was barely 17. "This guy is all right," I told myself. Little was I aware that John was to be the next person who would be on the hotseat with Victoria.

John finally received his discharge from the Navy. It had been two months since I first saw the Mustang on that hot, summer day. I remember it well because a rinky-dink circus had come to Saint Clair and the town was getting primed.

During the two month interim Susan had been fidgety, on edge, short-tempered. Living with six sisters, this was not uncommon. Menstrual periods were common. Tampons were not in then, especially with the staunch Catholics. Thus, we had the ubiquitous napkin. They dotted our house waste cans' landscape. In any event, Susan was tense. I was aware, through process of elimination, that she was not making her monthly napkin donations into the bathroom garbage can, which was open for all to see. Right before I left for the circus with the boys from the neighborhood, I noticed her puzzled look. She was near tears.

"Susan, are you in trouble?" Although I was only ten, I could sense it. She burst into tears and, rather than telling me what was wrong, asked me to pray for her. I felt bad, close to tears. In fact, when I did walk away, I was crying. I loved her, just as I loved all the members of my family. This included the ones who moved out early and I never really got to know. But Susan and I had a deeper, fraternal relationship. I think we both realized that we were going nowhere fast in this town. We also realized that sooner or later we had to get out of here. Susan, it turned out, would go much sooner than I.

The circus was uneventful. A lot of elephant shit and gambling booths. Besides, I just realized Susan could soon be leaving and she was a good buddy of mine. I'd gone through this before, and it got tougher each time. Also, we were down to eight plastic plates and were on a very tight budget. One more bad tirade from Victoria and paper plates would've had to suffice.

Upon getting back from the circus, I realized that the real "main event" was yet to come. John and Susan were out for a drive. I suppose they were plotting how to go about the monumental task confronting them. Also, I suppose they were both nervous as hell. Quickly, I decided to try and get Victoria hammered since I knew there was no way she could've handled this straight. Peter was watching a ball game and savoring his favorite drink, beer. "Nectar of the Gods," he often said to me. I knew if I could work on Victoria, Peter might have a chance to control her.

I remember it well. It was 7:30 p.m. when I saw the headlights. Victoria saw them too, for she was quick to state that she wished he'd "stop driving that damn motorcycle so fast." I was convinced I had done a good job. I was wrong.

It was also evident to me John had had a couple to settle his nerves. After extending phony pleasantries all around, John wasted no time in getting to the point. "Peter, Victoria, I would like to ask for your daughter's hand in marriage, she is pregnant and due to have our baby." Holy shit! The place was a mad house. All Victoria could do was yell, "Jimmie, Jimmie," not "Peter, Peter." James came running down the stairs with his potbelly dangling and underwear on. By this time Susan was crying and Peter kept on saying, "Jesus, Mary, and Joseph; Jesus, Mary and Joseph; Jesus, Mary and Joseph." I don't think even they could have helped at this point.

James, whom we all called Jimmie, asked what was wrong. Victoria for once remained silent, fully intending our young intruder to go under a double hotseat. John once again relayed the information to Jimmie. "Oh, no, John, I'm sorry. You and Susan are not getting married. We'll send her off to Philadelphia and have the baby, but you are not getting married. You can just be on your merry way now." It seemed the speech had been preplanned or, he may have had to say this on several other occasions. The party of screaming had made its way to the kitchen now, and things were getting heavy. John, realizing that he was in trouble, quickly split town. Not, however, without the stern commitment from James again, that they would never get married.

Susan had to remain behind for the assault that was about to ensue. This time, Victoria didn't stop with just the plates, cups, and saucers. Oh no, she outdid herself. Corningware, water glasses, everything was flying. I was under the kitchen table trying to avoid glass. James took off up to his castle and, I assume, took a Valium. It was around this time he started enjoying Valium as a release. Peter stood around saying, "Jesus, Mary, and Joseph," over and over. As for Victoria, not phenobarbital, brandy, or any other drug known at that time, could have mellowed her. I split for the railroad tracks to let the boys know another of my sisters had a loaf in the oven. They didn't seem to be phased by this, since this was a story I had told before.

I suppose Catholic pride had Victoria thoroughly rattled. Yet another of her children had taken a bite of the rotten apple. "How could it be such staunch Catholic family members would shun their beliefs about virginity," I constantly wondered. Virginity at marriage was definitely a short suit in our family. My belief is that, since sex, or its subject matter, was never discussed openly in our house, all involved in its premarital act in my family took it upon themselves to find out on their own. They all seemed to do a good job too, including me.

Remaining in the house now were Victoria, Peter, James, myself, a pregnant Susan, Jocelyn, and Hugh. C. J. had already entered the convent after her graduation from high school. She was still one bright spot in the glum picture which was beginning to unfold.

Still, impending situations had to be handled at home. What to do with Susan, where to send her to have this child? It was common knowledge that she and John were still seeing each other and, according to Victoria, "supposedly" in love. I was the moral minority who believed they really were. Also, at this time, Victoria was beginning to worry about Jocelyn. She was out of high school and dating a guy from Minersville on a very serious level. Victoria had to figure out some way to keep Jocelyn's virginity intact, since the percentages were increasingly going against her.

Victoria was getting older beyond her years, and her affliction with liquor was increasing. Her health was poor. She was, perhaps, the oldest 51-year-old woman alive. Peter also was growing older. The many hours of thankless hard labor were taking their toll. He was losing weight and the happenings over the past five years were crushing him inside. He was never a man to express his feelings, no matter how hurt he was. It was at a point for him, however, where the physical and mental pain were equal.

With Susan and her soon-to-be child, Victoria seemed guarded in her few conversations with me. I was old enough to understand what was going on, and yet she was genuinely concerned that I never overheard any conversation concerning Susan. After all, "what harm was I?" I thought to myself. Susan insisted frequently, and cried many hours trying to persuade Victoria, that she truly loved John and he was a good man. Victoria, however, would have no part of it.

I don't think anyone in the family was prepared for John's bold decision concerning his child. It definitely shook the family tree. It seems Victoria sent Susan up to see Father McHenry for counseling and, while there, she saw the writing on the wall. Susan was convinced she would soon be married to John. This time, she would not allow Victoria to determine her future, her family, or her life.

Eventually, everyone in the house realized that Susan had been gone a long time. So much so, that Victoria instructed Jimmie to contact the Pennsylvania State Police and put out a missing persons report. "It certainly couldn't be hard to spot that ugly orange car," Victoria was thinking. Wrong, Victoria. The one thing that everybody knew about John was that no one knew anything about him. His background, that is.

Approximately a week went by before the phone call finally came. It was Susan calling. Since there was only one phone, Victoria got on. Susan informed her that she and John had eloped and were married by a Justice of the Peace. Victoria went into a tirade. She went absolutely berserk over the phone. I could just imagine Susan having to listen to this on the other end, alone and pregnant as she was. Victoria instructed Susan that she was not "married in the eyes of the church," and that she would have the marriage annulled. Jimmie got on with John and informed him he was in a lot of trouble, he was going to have John thrown in jail for kidnapping. This was unbelievable. Imagine being in second grade at a Catholic school and having this melodrama unfold before you. The story of Adam and Eve couldn't touch this one.

Susan informed Victoria that they were at John's stepmother's in Pittsburgh. She also told Victoria that she was going to have the baby and raise it as her and John's child. This was totally flipping Victoria out because she was in a position where she could do absolutely nothing. Susan was of legal age and they had a marriage license to prove they had indeed tied the knot. "The eyes of the church" definitely lost out on this one. Victoria had lost at her own game which was to strike the first resounding blow. Susan would be ridiculed for years to come for this unforgivable move, and was never forgiven by Victoria, even on her death bed.

****

I wrote the introduction to this book on July 11, 1978, my 24th birthday. I decided to stop with the story of Susan, since there were so many other stories which needed to be told and a myriad of questions which I wanted answers to. Therefore, there is a fourteen-year-lapse between the time I wrote this prologue and when I finally decided to complete the book. I now have enough answers, or most of the important ones anyway, and decided this is a story that anyone living in America who believes in truth—and will stop at nothing to find it—will surely like to read.

CONTENTS

LIES in the

FAMILY ALBUM

PADDY JOE MILLER

SECTION ONE

CHILDHOOD

CHAPTER ONE

"SAINT CLAIR—THE LAND THAT TIME FORGOT"

It was July 11, 1978, my twenty-fourth birthday, when I was hit with the realization that I was adopted at birth. The day of discovery for me was never meant to have been. However, one unfortunate person made an error and sent documents to me that, until that time, had never crossed my eyes. *My "sister" Rose Mary was really my mother.*

As you can imagine, so many emotions went through my mind and my body when confronted with the truth. At first, I laughed, thinking it was funny. Then, a myriad of questions started to run rampant through my mind. Considering this was my birthday, and I was feeling no pain, the emotions intensified themselves. However, when you finally get to the point in your thought process where you realize that your whole life was a LIE, your emotions turn to frustrations and tears. Oh, so many lies, so many times I should have noticed things as they really were. Not only was my entire life, and everything that was told me about my birth a lie, but in this town of 4,000 people, how many of them knew and maintained a strict vow of silence when dealing with me? How could I be so stupid, and yet, when finding out, realize it should have been obvious? One thought which kept crossing my mind during those first hours was I knew I wanted to find out the truth, and I knew I wanted to write about it. I realized there are perhaps millions of other people who are currently, or have been, in this situation. I believe all of these people, if they don't know yet, should be told the truth. To understand the truth, and how situations like mine can evolve, one must first look at my background and the philosophies of the anthracite coal regions of southeastern Pennsylvania. For these towns which make up "coal country" have a unique, unbelievable story of their own.

The borough of Saint Clair is much like any of the towns which make up Schuylkill County, Pennsylvania. It is the remnant of a once powerful region whose dynasty was built around what was referred to as "Black Diamonds," or coal. Most historians will agree that the start of the industrial revolution truly did arise in these coal regions of Pennsylvania. Further, through discovery of the anthracite coal, or hard coal, many wealthy people became wealthier.

However, another fact is also known: those people who had to do the work, go down into these mines, never found wealth. The miner's life was a continuous struggle for survival. In return for his back breaking work, he never made more than it would take to feed and clothe his family. Housing was intolerable. Most houses were built by the coal companies to keep a work force located in a central area. They were built in row fashion, and became known as "patches" in the region. The housing was not free, and upon termination or death due to an accident, the family would immediately be evicted. Every miner's dream was simply to have a piece of land with an adequate building which he could call home.

A diverse cross section of nationalities make up those towns in the coal region. Poles, Lithuanians, Germans, Irish, Slovacks, all immigratted to the area in the 1800's and early 1900's because of the immediate availability of work. In most cases, they arrived at Ellis Island and within days found themselves located in one of any number of towns where a coal mining operation could be found. The men usually arrived alone, gained their employment and housing, and through thrift were eventually able to save enough money to send for the remainder of the family. Most nationalities were clannish, and housing was usually in quadrants, whose boundaries were decided by ethnicity and religion. The single strongest element of the family unit was religion. There are numerous religions in these coal regions, each with their own beliefs, traditions, and superstitions.

In the Roman Catholic religion, sex, or the mere mention of

anything pertaining to sex, was taboo and never to be addressed, not only in our household, but in every God-fearing family who chose Catholicism as their religion. Therefore, with the theory of "sex by ignorance," one eventually found out the facts of life. Much more so for females, since males learned from talking amongst themselves.

Victoria fully planned for each of her six girls to be a virgin at the time she and Peter allowed them to marry. A member of the church indulging in premarital sex and possibly becoming pregnant had extremely far-reaching implications. Any person falling into this category, male or female, had to answer not only to their parents, but also to an entity higher than they, their Priest. Therefore, God. I just happened to be the first casualty, in a very long list of casualties that plagued the pride of Peter and Victoria Miller. With religion being the foremost priority in a situation like this, Victoria made several decisions. First, and what I found to be very interesting as I began looking for the truth, she absolutely refused to allow a marriage. "Shot-gun" weddings, as they were called, were only for Protestants. The mere thought of exposing the fact that her eldest daughter, Rose Mary, became pregnant before marriage, disallowed any possibility of a wedding.

Victoria sent Rose Mary immediately up to see Father McHenry, who had been the priest of Saint Mary's Church since time immemorial, for guidance in this matter. She sent her with Father McHenry already having full knowledge that a marriage was not going to be permitted. Basically, the counseling from Father McHenry was simply a continuance of the ass chewings she had already taken from Victoria, since she was always much more vociferous than Peter. Rose Mary was placed on a major guilt trip not only by her parents, but also by the Catholic Church.

Another thing about which Victoria was certain, Rose Mary would have the baby, away from our town, and I would be brought back to be raised as the youngest member of the Miller family. Therefore, Victoria would have ten children that she and Peter would call their own. Unfortunately, she realized that some of her children might realize something was amiss, even considering their basic ignorance of sex.

Certain members of our family would have to know the exact circumstances. James, as the eldest son, would be needed to ensure that the father never came near Rose Mary again, and that he never tried to make contact with me. Those brothers and sisters of Peter and Victoria would certainly need to know since they were part of the glue that would be used to hold this magnificent lie together. Several "valued" friends, all Catholic, would have to be informed in the overall scheme to keep this lie intact.

However, with this many people being told, and in a town of so few people whose complete land area would take up only several major city blocks, many people eventually had to have known. If Peter or Victoria ever got wind of this information being publicly discussed by someone who should not have had it, the person or family responsible for the fuck-up would be ostracized from ever getting any information on the Q-T again. Not only by Peter and Victoria, but by the whole town. For in a town that small, where lives intertwine daily, a man's word was what he lived for. The worst possible situation for someone to be in was getting caught not living up to their word. In this case, their word was a vow of silence about the circumstances surrounding the birth and continued life of Paddy Joe Miller. When I look back now, it is truly amazing that so many people would hold strong on their knowledge of me, people I interacted with on a daily basis as I was growing up.

For those who have never had an opportunity to visit this region, even before acknowledging the poverty which exists due to the failure of coal as a major commodity, there is no way to avoid noticing the distinct dialect of the people. A large majority of the people living here can still speak the original language of their ancestors. When talking to someone who was born and raised in this area, there is no denying the brutality done to the English language. They speak with intonations of voice and various phrases which are common only among them, speech the movie character Rocky couldn't touch. Virtually everything comes out as a question. In many ways, the dialect used by Archie Bunker parallels this, but there is still a noticeable difference between New York City dialect and that of the anthracite coal region of Pennsylvania.

For authenticity, I have used common words and phrases of a person from this section of the country. These are spelled the way they are said. Yooz guyz, deez guyz, doz guyz, or what?? (often used at the end of any sentence), whatz zup, dem, and yo, just to name a few. Most people have a nickname they go by rather than using their real first name. Or they may be called "yo."

For example, in a local bar the following conversation would be very likely among comrades regarding the Bush, Clinton and Perot race for the Presidency in 1992.

#1 "Yooz fuckin guyz followin dis fucked up delection, or what?"

#2 "Of course, ya goofy fuck. It's all dat's been on TV lately, whadda ya think we're fuckin stupid, or what?"

#3 "I'll tell ya dis. Jest let the crazy fuckers in dis country elect Perot and watch da shit fly. He'll have deez congressmen and senators and every udder fuck who has anyding to do wit politics goin to confession every week. And he'll be da fuckin priest. I'll tell ya what, dis is it right here. Just as George Orville or whatever-da fuck his name is sez—"big brudder is watchin. Or what?""

#4 "Yeah—well, ya shudda seen what I saw on TV the udder night. Bill fuckin Clinton was playin a trumpet or saxaphone or some fuckin instrument. I just knew dere wuz somethin I don't like about him. Hez in da band or wuz in school. Dat makes him a pussy in my book no matter how da fuck ya slice it. Ain't?"

#1 "Dat's no shit. Perot's a mini-Hitler waitin ta blossom, and Clinton's a pussy. At least wit Bush we know wat we're gettin—nuttin. He ain't done nuttin for four fuckin years and if dats the worst dat can happen, fuck it—I say reelect dim. Or what?"

#2 "Oh, so you're sayin dat us goin over to Iraq was nuttin. We went over dere and kicked fuckin ass and your sayin he ain't done nuttin? Are you fuckin nuts, or what?"

#1 "Fuck you, or what? If you can't go over dare wit as much money as we spend on our fuckin military and not kick fuckin ass, den we shouldn even be in da fuckin game. Why da fuck didn we take fuckin Hu-Sane out if he was so fuckin bad, or what? Mark my fuckin word right here and now, Hu-Sane will come back ta haunt all of us. That psychotic fuck shudda been takin out—case closed. And don't give me no shit on dat or I'll kick your fuckin ass—or what?"

#3 "Ain't you feelin froggy, or what? It don't matter who da fuck gets elected, were all fucked. Dare all fuckin crooks. Taxin us out da ass an dey live like fuckin kings. You wait and see—da day will come when we see a black president or worse fuckin yet, a fuckin woman. It don't madder, were all fucked no madder wat we do. Ain't?"

****

And this conversation can go on for hours. Another strikingly odd fact about these coal towns is how few blacks there are. All through my childhood in Saint Clair, not one black family ever lived in the town. The closest city, Pottsville, had several black families, but none I can recall in any of the small towns, such as Shenandoah, Frackville, Ashland, Mahanoy City, Minersville, Port Carbon. We never knew of prejudice as it has been exposed today. Due to the various ethnic background of all the families, the word "nigger" was seldom heard and, indeed, never used in our household. These coal people realized what it was like to be viewed as different, to hold a low position on the totem pole of esteem. Therefore, they would definitely not judge anyone by their color or use a negative term to identify them. As a result, neither I, nor any of the people I knew, were taught to look down at anyone—black, yellow, short, tall, or deformed. For this I am truly thankful.

The lack of racial prejudices which existed in this region was an oddity, considering the way women were treated. Many of the women from the coal region were there for various reasons, none of which was that they wanted to be. Many marriages were arranged well in advance, often by bringing them over from the old country, where they were promised at birth. Or, many marriages were the product of two families agreeing that their son and daughter were good for each other—were of the same culture and religion, and should be married. In any case, many fathers of daughters realized their only redeeming value was for the dowry that would one day be received for them. There was no mistaking the fact that when a birth was to occur in a family, the expectant father anxiously hoped for a son. A son meant eventual revenue into the family along with the taking on of numerous chores at a very early age.

The only work was going into the mines for coal, and boys started working in the coal breakers (where the coal was broken down and sorted out) as early as seven years old. Women never went into the mines, and it seemed a daughter's only redeeming value was helping her mother with the chores. However, a baby boy born into a family was always an answer to the prayers of the expectant father.

This view of women lasted only as long as coal reigned as king. Once it lost its potency, the women were the ones who, in most cases, picked up the slack—finding work, doing anything it took to keep the family fed and a roof over their heads. Foolish workingman's pride absolutely forbade anyone from applying to the government for food stamps, unemployment, or other relief. Now, however, many of these once proud people have had to accept aid in order to get by. With no major cities supplying jobs for the people, Saint Clair and all the towns like it are doomed. The only hope for the people and their survival is to commute a great distance to work, accept the government aid available, or get out—someway, somehow. As one views inhabitants of Saint Clair today, the realization that they have never gotten over the Great Depression is painfully obvious.

Growing up in Saint Clair, a person's options were very limited. Most of us who were lucky enough to escape, did so either with a college scholarship due to intelligence, or sports, or both. Or we had the fortitude to work our way through college. The rest found a menial job locally, and lived with their parents, even after they got married and started their own family, resulting in several families living under the same roof. The parents simply pass on their worldly belongings to their offspring, who live in the same row house for the rest of their lives.

This is still happening in a very small section of our country today. Since the house has been paid off for many years, one only needs to feed, clothe, and find the means to get heat in the winter. Most houses in the area still use coal today and the cost is still substantially less than gas or oil. Several people with menial jobs all contributing to the continuance of the family actually works, and it has been working like this for over two hundred years. The majority of the people born and raised here would rather be part of the regeneration process than have the courage it takes to break away.

One of the finest traditions passed down through the generations is a true coal region wedding—a ceremony steeped in tradition. Each of the ethnic groups has its own rituals which are still followed today. Coal mining families also passed down from generation to generation the ability to organize and enjoy a party of magnanimous proportions.

Due to many of the miners working on different 12-hour shifts, a wedding usually lasted three days, with Saturday being the actual wedding day. The parents of the bride and groom usually had a great number of friends and relatives whom it was mandatory to invite to the wedding. This enabled all invited, who wished to attend, to be present at sometime during the celebration. Friday night was always reserved for the bride and bridesmaids to get together and reminisce. Simple pranks and games were played on the bride-to-be while both families (minus the males) got to know each other better.

The males followed another tradition that still carries on today. The groom and all of the groomsmen celebrated the traditional bachelor party. However, a lot of them went well beyond the bounds of sanity. The groom often went to excess, and it got him in trouble every time. A cousin of mine had to be bathed by his friends two hours before his wedding and then dressed while he was in a semiconscious state. However, after the service, as he was being driven around town with horns blaring, he once again was able to start drinking. A wedding reception was no place to be with a hangover, or if you were a tea totaler. Fortunately non-drinkers were almost nonexistent and did not last long at a "hunky" wedding. ("Hunky" was a name branded on those immigrant coal miners by the locals who watched the influx of them over the years.)

The wedding reception itself is truly unbelievable. I have been to receptions with upwards of 600 people, most heavily intoxicated, and everyone, including children, having the times of their lives. Unless a family was extremely well-to-do, most weddings had the basics— excellent food, excellent drink, and good company all around. There is always a polka band—at the real hunky weddings anyway—which would play all day Saturday. There were unlimited barrels of draught beer and the only mixed drink usually served at receptions is called a seven and seven, half Seven-Up/half whiskey. There is also a shot of "Boilo," homemade whiskey to be had at any time for any willing participant, for which there were usually many. All day, during the entire event, there was unlimited food, dance, and drink. At a point during the reception, the band plays a simple dance song continuously as the bride dances with everyone there. After the allotted time, usually thirty seconds or less, a donation is placed in an apron which the maid of honor wears. After the dance and the donation, you are handed a shot of Boilo and a cigar—a long known tradition. You could go through the dance line as many times as you liked, as long as you gave a donation, did your shot, and took your cigar. I have also seen many a woman, because of the buzz she had worked up all day, puffing away at that huge cigar.

After the dance with the bride, the groom performs a mock fight with his groomsmen. Then the bride has a final dance with both parents, and the couple vanishes to points unknown.

After the band stopped playing late in the evening, all who were willing and sober enough went to either the residence of the bride or groom for an evening of partying, which did not stop all night and went well into Sunday. Weddings are the most interesting cultural ceremonies of the coal region.

Steeped in tradition, togetherness, and deep secrets, these rituals can hide the facts of a person's birth for twenty-four years. How many more cases like mine are out there, not only in the Pennsylvania coal regions, but all across America? How many people are living a lie about adoption secrets because they would be ostracized if the situation were exposed? I firmly believe it is every person's God-given right to know if his or her situation is not exactly as it appears—to know what the truth really is. One of the many emotions I have constantly dealt with is the hurt when I realized that so many people had compounded the great lie.

When and if such a lie is ever discovered, it can cripple an individual emotionally. Unfortunately, I did find out the truth and have had to deal with all the emotions raised, something I am not good at doing. There have been many times I wanted to cry but my macho, hard-guy upbringing prevented it. Growing up in the coal region taught me never to cry in public as a man. I have carried this philosophy with me through life and, several times I simply could not, as hard as I tried, control a waterfall of tears. But, I have realized over time that it really is okay for a man to cry, to show true emotion without feeling like a sissy, where the situation warrants.

The people of this area have always been survivors. Over the years, families have learned to endure in all situations. Terrible demographics, weather, an extremely low income based on the types and availability of work in the area, and extremely high unemployment forces one to become a survivor. So it was that the Miller family, with eleven already living under one roof, decided that an even dozen was the best remedy for this immense dilemma.

I can picture the scene upon my arrival at the Miller residence on Patterson Street. We had three entrances—the front door, the back door, and the side door, which, due to its parallel availability to the street, would be the quickest entrance. James drove; he pulled up alongside the side entrance which faces Third Street. Peter got out first from the back seat, followed by Victoria who was holding me. Rose Mary, who was sitting in the front next to James, was instructed to go immediately to her room and not to come downstairs until sent for by Victoria. The ride home from Philadelphia, after her recent childbirth, probably had her exhausted and she was in no mood to protest. However, the tears were still there for she was aware of what was about to happen.

Since she had already graduated from high school, the simplest, easiest explanation for her hiatus was that she was looking for work in Philadelphia. She was, in fact, staying at a Catholic home for unwed mothers just outside of Philadelphia until my birth. Victoria went directly to her and Peter's room, and laid me in the bed. James went around front to park the car. He had been instructed to round up all the children for an immediate family meeting with Peter and Victoria. This in itself is no easy matter, gathering eight children, excluding Rose Mary, for a family meeting which would last no longer than three minutes, with no questions taken from any inquisitive Miller family members afterward. Victoria would be the only one to speak and it would be in simple, coal miner language. "As youz kidz know, Peter and Di went wit Jimmie to pick up Rose Mary din Philadelphia. Uncle Billy tried, but dey jez couldn find her no jobs down dere."

With everyone packed into the little bedroom and a baby laying in the bed, the question had been answered as to why Rose Mary was back up on the third floor laying in bed, but who is this laying here in the middle of the bed? Once again, Victoria would speak.

"Oh, by da way, while we were dare, your fadder and I had anoder baby. Dis is your baby brudder, Patrick Joseph. He was born tree dayz ago, on July elevent, so now I guess we finally got da ten we always wanted. Ain't dat right, Peter?" Peter could do nothing but nod his head and marvel at the newest member, thinking, "Jesus, Mary, and Joseph; Jesus, Mary, and Joseph; Jesus, Mary, and Joseph."

Once again, it's a little late for their help, Peter. There I was. And there were eight other children ranging in age from six to 22. Remember, sex, conception, and childbirth were not discussed in our family, but now there were definitely some perplexed young faces in the room. James, age 22, was in on the whole scheme. There would be no possible way he could ever deny knowing the truth, or would there be....????? After all, he was in the Navy and had a good alibi if ever needed. Rose Mary was exempted from this meeting, due to her travel weariness. I have often thought what was going through my 20-year-old sister/mother's (smother's) mind when I was taken from her by Victoria both physically and legally. Were her religious convictions so strong, that she thought this was right, and that this was the correct thing to do? "This was what Father McHenry told me was best for everyone. This is what my parents want. Can they really pull this off???? Oh God, what should I do???" she must have often thought. Was she ever convinced in her mind that she would defy the family and all it stood for, the church and its almighty word, and just want to say, "To hell with it. He's mine. I want him, and I'm going to do whatever it takes to keep him?" Oftentimes, I look at the situation objectively and can definitely see the quandary she was in. Was she in love with my father, did he love her, was she making the mistake of her life?

Clarice, at age eighteen, knew it was coming and was just waiting for it to happen. Try as she might, Victoria could not control those facts of life which kids learned in school, and Clarice knew plenty. She knew Rose Mary had a boyfriend she really liked, she knew he got her pregnant, and she knew both Rose Mary and the boyfriend disappeared simultaneously, like magic. Exactly why he disappeared, she never would get out of Rose Mary. She did know that the baby lying in front of her was Rose Mary's and that Rose Mary was heartbroken by what was happening here today. And because of that, Clarice was also hurt. She knew Rose Mary loved the man who impregnated her, and that whatever was said to him by Jimmie must have been strong and left an impact. More importantly, she knew all decisions made here today had been done by Victoria, and it would be foolish to make any statement which would be construed as negative by Victoria and Jimmie, who, of course, were backed by the silent Peter. What Clarice was wondering, more than anything else, is what the younger children were thinking right now. "Were they truly grasping what was happening here?" "Did Dad and Mom really think this was going to get by our neighbors, relatives, and friends?" "What the hell are they doing this for?" For right now, she was sure of one thing. She would hear Victoria out for whatever she had to say and get the hell out of there. Her number one concern was Rose Mary and maintaining a semblance of compliance and ignorance around Mom at the same time. That would not be easy to do since Clarice always had been viewed as a malcontent by Victoria. Of course, as I look back now, everyone was viewed as a malcontent radical to Victoria. She trusted no one, and never showed any open love in front of any family member. Victoria went through life viewing it as a CIA conspiracy to overthrow a poor Irish-Catholic family. Unfortunately, these traits have ways of permeating themselves through others.

Ellen, being sixteen years old, surely must have been doing cartwheels in her mind. She knew it was not proper to speak, and, she was naive sexually, but some things definitely were not adding up here. "Why was Mother not showing or talking about having another baby to her?" Why, she'd seen Mother on five separate occasions with child, and each time she could definitely tell a child was coming. Even for Frank, when she was only three, she knew Mommy was having a baby by how big her belly became. "Why hadn't I noticed a long time ago the sure changes in Mother when a child is due?" But wait, could it be that Ellen, even at the tender age of 16, and, to Victoria, definitely not versed sexually, knew more than that blank stare on her face was showing. Could it be that Clarice had filled her in on the necessities by then? I've often wondered if Victoria ever instructed any of the girls what to do once their menstrual periods began, or did she let them figure it out for themselves, or learn it from their friends? In any event, when the time actually came, and Victoria realized another daughter could now bear a child, surely another Novena was said. "May the God of Chastity please look fondly upon my now mature daughter." Evidently, Ellen, at this age, was aware all was not kosher. She also realized this had to do with Rose Mary, and many more answers could be given by her than could be had in this room full of untruths.

Both Victoria and James agreed well ahead of time that Frank would be a difficult convert, due to his intelligence and the fact that he was on target as far as his maturity, adolescence, and knowledge of sexual explorations. Therefore, it was no shock to Victoria or James that a huge hairy eyeball penetrated both of them from Frank after Victoria made her announcement. Frank may have been only thirteen, but he knew he was going to get some answers. However, the sudden reappearance of Rose Mary quickly added up, and he figured his best, most honest avenue for information would be from the girls themselves. Besides, he knew James would have some horse-shit story about not

knowing anything—"he was away on a ship at sea." Through the
years, that simple lie, "I was away on a ship at sea," would come back
to haunt James.

I played this line over and over in my head the day I found out,
and eventually figured out he was lying. When I found out the extent of
James's real Naval duty, it cut like a knife. But, of course, "It was
what we thought was best for you at the time." Frank also realized
there was no sense to make an issue out of what was transpiring.
However, he would certainly retain it in his memory bank should he
ever need a marker to fall back on. Within ten years, his planning
would prove him right.

At age eleven, C. J. was susceptible to any fairy tale that came her
way. Although she shared the third floor with Rose Mary, Clarice,
Ellen, Jocelyn, Susan, and Hugh, she would have no idea of the truth at
this point. She assumed what was being told was fact and that God had
given Mommy and Daddy another baby for our house. She was just too
naive to grasp the picture, nor did any of her roommates wish to fill her
in for fear she would question Victoria, and then they would be in
trouble. Not only would they have questioned Victoria's judgment, they
would have also informed their eleven-year-old sister of a grave sin her
oldest sister had committed. The "sin factor" definitely played a large
part in this scenario.

Another factor which was vital was that C. J. had absolutely no
sexual knowledge. Therefore, the fact that I could very well be her baby
brother was, to her, very real. From C. J. on down the sibling line, the
story was a reality. From Frankie up through James, the lie would
remain sealed as tight as the envelope to the adoption papers in the
Schuylkill County Courthouse. In those days, knowing a few politicians
and calling a couple of markers in could get an adoption cover-up
handled easily. The beauty of the plan, as it was originally set forth,
was that no one would know, except the elders, whose personal vow of
silence was as good as a priest's vow of celibacy. Surely none of these
vows would ever be desecrated, would they????

Eight-year-old Jocelyn or Jo, as she was nicknamed, was another
child with total ignorance of the situation. In second grade, in a
Catholic grade school, she was only too proud to have another baby
brother. "God sure has been good to our family," she thought, as she
stared quizzically—first at me, then at forty-three-year-old Victoria,
then at forty-five-year-old Peter. Medically, it had been known to

happen, but certainly not in that region of the country, and certainly not to a forty-three year old woman who already had nine children. "Could Peter possibly be that virile?"

Poor Jocelyn, even to this day she seems to be caught in an identity crisis. She was never meant to be a Rhodes scholar or brain surgeon, and throughout her life has never done a single thing to hurt anyone. Never a harsh word, never a doubt about working hard for a living, she has maintained the true meaning of survivor as carried on by the Millers through the ages. Therefore, at age eight or forty-eight, Jocelyn probably would have had a hard time grasping the complexity of the whole situation. That is, until fate would deal her a blow which would surely decide her future.

Exactly fifteen months younger than Jocelyn, Susan, at age seven, was also very impressionable. Obviously, Peter worked hard and played extremely hard to keep Victoria impregnated. During a short span of his married life, Peter knew pregnancy to be the norm. Susan must have viewed me as par for the course, seeing the age variances already present in the room. She now had a baby brother she could treat like a little doll, which I remember is what she did. As I was growing up, Susan, of all the children, showed me the most open affection. Jocelyn, who was only fifteen months her senior, never did any of that. Susan, of course, would be the ultimate radical in the Victoria era. She has always been able to say without hesitation that she broke the hold, however strong it may have been, and did it her and her husband's way—right or wrong!

Finally, there was young Hugh, who, at six years old, was totally lost. When I introduced the Prologue with Elton John's, "The Greatest Discovery," I had Hugh in mind. Here he was, just six, the last Miller child, and he was viewing his new baby brother. Not unique under most circumstances. However, considering his oldest brother James was twenty-two, he must have been totally mindfucked. He had a brother who was twenty-two years old, and able to drive, and he also had one who was not yet quite sure about the ten strange faces he was staring at. However, Hugh would be starting first grade this year and he would have to learn to accept the responsibility of being a big brother.

When I look back on my childhood, there were very few clues noticeable to me. I do remember that around age six, Hugh being twelve, I was often puzzled by our distinct differences. Our appearance was totally different, and I was just as tall as he was. I asked Peter why this was, and he simply responded that he didn't know. As I would later analyze the distinct differences between the Millers and myself, my height was always a dead giveaway. They must have started getting nervous about it. And yet, the earliest years of my childhood are filled with fond, happy memories.

Frank's wedding was another fond memory of my childhood. Frank was marrying into a family that was steeped in religious traditions. Betsy's parents and family were from Schoentown, three miles from Saint Clair. They had always been hard working, and planned for their daughter Betsy's wedding. To be sure, the wedding was a bit impromptu, however, it would have happened eventually. I remember the large number of people, and the reception hall being very big. Everyone was snockered if they were over the age of fourteen. Boilo shots were everywhere. There was a live polka band. They were inebriated also.

Peter was bad drunk, and Victoria had resigned herself to this reality and decided to get blitzed also. The band did a "limbo stick" routine and Victoria fell flat on her back trying to go under.

The band, which had been playing virtually all day, took a break. I remember sitting at the drums and starting to play. Nobody was concerned, because everyone was too drunk. Even at that early age, I knew I liked music, especially playing it. Unfortunately, due to the local stigma given to playing an instrument, or playing anything except sports, it would be many years before I would finally try to develop my love for music. Once started, however, it is like a fire burning inside me which won't go out until my death.

At age seven, I was to begin attending first grade at Saint Mary's Catholic School. I never attended kindergarten since it was not offered by Saint Mary's and there was no way Victoria would allow me to attend a "public school." It would not be until much later, when C. J. became a nun and was teaching grade school, that I learned most nuns, and a number of priests, have not earned a certified teaching degree from an accredited college. They are simply taught the vows of Poverty, Chastity, and Patience, and given a classroom full of children to teach. Imagine, no prior training in school for any of us, away from the security of our little houses, and having to face nuns in total black and white who, it seemed, were wearing something akin to a modern day hard-hat. I was scared shitless and I cried unmercifully for several days. I really really didn't want to do this and I was making it perfectly clear. Eventually, I was dragged, by Peter, into the classroom and forced to endure the agony I was surely going to face.

My classmates, of course, were all Catholic and the majority were the offspring of coal mining families. Regular Sunday Mass was mandatory and the nun who was your teacher sat behind her class in church for disciplinary actions. Ties were mandatory, as well as uniforms for the girls. Your teacher taught every subject, qualified or not. If someone were to ask me to capsulize my grade school days and what was retained, I would have to say it would definitely have been the discipline, before any studies. We were always to keep our hands folded neatly on the desk. Not conforming could mean a knuckle slap with a ruler. Heads and eyes were to be kept straight at all times. Not conforming could mean a severe hair pulling to straighten the head out. All in all, the nuns got the point across quickly. Those students who couldn't or wouldn't conform, would more than likely be expelled and be forced to endure an education in the Saint Clair public school system.

Having never attended the public school, I cannot make any judgment about the quality of education. I can only go by those friends of mine who did attend, and the results speak for themselves. The percentages of continuance into higher education were much higher from the Catholic school system, mainly due to the discipline factor. However, most Catholic schools, as I remember them in the region, have dwindled considerably due to the extremely high tuition fees. Most all children attend the public school system in the region today.

In essence, I was fortunate. I began to know children from all over the Saint Clair area due to the private nature of my school. After school, I could always go home and hang out with the children living in my neighborhood.

Most of these crazies would stay friends and acquaintances for a great deal of my childhood and adolescence, since rarely did anyone get a chance to break away from the coal mining regions. There were no transfers for Dad to a bigger city for a higher paying job. There was only the constant, daily struggle for survival. Coping with that struggle was the essence of maintaining your sanity. Most anyone knows, in situations where you are left to "cope" with anything, those people whom you know and trust as friends are usually the ones who eventually pull you through. Therefore, those of us who lived parallel to Third Street, which ran directly parallel to the Reading Railroad, formed a unique conglomeration of personalities: over-achievers, dreamers, athletes, fighters, and survivors. Those other kids in town around our age group referred to us as the "Turd Street Gang." To us, we were simply, "da Boyz." We also were of a mindset, even at an early age, that there was nobody badder than us in this little shit-hole town. Therefore, it is only fair if I am to write an autobiography about the search for the truth and finding myself, to describe those friends of mine who made a very definite mark on my personality and the way I view life today.

CHAPTER TWO

DA BOYZ

David "Pretzel" Bender:

"Yooz fucks wanna go up ta da fishin hatchery today, or what? They ain't been fed in over a week. Ain't?"

Michael "Shot" Colna:

"Nah. We gotta open da gamblin' casino dis afternoon. We got a bunch a kids comin' over. An dey all got bucks. Remember da udder day when we told dem what ta do, or what?"

Michael "Peanuts" Bender:

"Yo. Don't yooz guyz forget we got ta go steal some wood for da hut tonight. If we don't get da second floor done soon, what wit da size of Eddie's head, we might das well sleep outside. It's jest too fuckin cramped in dere when we're all dere at the same time. Ain't?"

Eddie "Da Head" Hassenbein:

> "My head ain't dat big. Yooz guyz stop pickin on me about my head or I'm gonna tell my brudder. Or what?"

Mark "Scab" Ryscavage:

> "Will ya look at dis? Yooz guyz have been arguin back and forth dere an nuthinz gettin rezolved. If yuz don't get yer shit straight here, yuz are still gonna be standin' here at midnight. Anyway, we can't get da wood 'til night time. What do yooz crazy fuckers think, yer gonna steal da wood in broad fuckin' daylight? Or what?"

Paddy "Putt-Putt" Miller:

> "Yo, Yo, hold dit, hold dit, hold dit here. Yo, why don't we do dis: we go ta da hatchery right now, get sometin' ta eat, an den meet out back by da tracks when it starts to get dark so we can go raid da wood. Ain't! Or what?"

Billy "Binky" Wolfe:

> "Yo. Don't yooz guyz forget we were gonna go wreck da pussies from North Wards hut tonight. We might be able to get some good stuff from dem, but remember, nobody can never find out about id, or dale come after us too. What dey don't know won't hurt dem. Remember, nobody from North Ward never steps foot in our hut, or they'll notice dare own shit. Den, somebody will have da sleep in it every night soz dat dey don't try da hit us. Ain't?"

Bobby "Horse" Lowthert:

> "Well den, we gotta lot of stuff ta do because a whole new load da boxcars jest pulled din. Yooz guyz know we getta lotta good stuff in dez boxcars to help us. Only ding is, dose fuckin railroad cops

have been askin questions about dus again. Dey know it's us dats hitten dem. Nobody's gonna point da finger at dus dough or dey know dey are gonna get what's comin ta dem. Dey better never fuck wit us. Ain't? Or what?"

Now, I know some of you might be thinking that, as young Catholic boys, "raised in the eyes of the Church," we used the work "fuck" a lot. We did! Fact is, I have a hard time remembering where or when it was I first heard and began using it, but it was at a very early age. Unbelievably, one also learned to curtail the word in a necessary situation:

A) School (obviously);

B) Church (it was bad manners to say the word "fuck" in The Lord's House);

C) Anywhere near or around your or anyone else's parents (although your or your friends' father probably was saying it on a regular basis).

There were other situations where it was used an awful lot:

A) When talking in a normal conversation with one of your gang or anyone else near your age from another part of town;

B) When engaging in sports of any kind. Obviously, if it was a non-officiated, pick up game, it was used rather loudly. Once again, when officiated, one learned to use it within earshot of his opponents only. Never the referees. When they hear that word, they tend to take it personal;

C) When in a potential or real fight. In a potential fight, one might be able to "out-fuck" the other and back them down. In a real fight, the word "mother" is usually placed before the word;

D) When having drunk a lot of alcohol at a party. One might be heard going up to a woman he knows, or, for that matter, one he doesn't know, burp, and slur at the top of his lungs, "wanna fuck me?" You knew you were in for a big night if she burped, and slurred at the top of her lungs, "O.K., but ya gotta help me get undressed, I'm really bombed."

I don't want you to think all people in the region talk like this. They don't! But there are still an awful lot that do. And it's not only men doing the cursing. Go into any bar, even today, and listen to a basic conversation. It is simply an understood part of the language for any local. Today, I have greatly curtailed the word. However, in the proper setting it is still a common part of my vocabulary. It is also a large part of the regeneration process since we learned this from our mentors, those older "Turd Streeters" who were our brothers.

This was a very intricate conversation between young, budding entrepreneurs. Very early, we realized you had to have money to make money. Therefore, we devised numerous endeavors to make us money when it was scarce. Although we all were given the basics of shelter, food, and an education, few of us were able to carry any "luxury" money, unless we made it on our own. Between the ages of nine and twelve years, we were running a fish hatchery and a gambling casino. Not your ordinary gambling casino, and definitely not your ordinary fish hatchery. The casino was erected on the back porch of an abandoned rowhouse directly adjacent to the Reading Railroad. When gambling, customers would be within ten yards of the first row of tracks. Up until 1965, trains were still hauling minimal amounts of coal. Therefore, we had the noise and size of huge coal trains operating very close to our roulette wheel. The vibration often helped us move a number or two off the wheel, always in our favor, and always when one of us would divert our customers' attention. Our customers were those children directly below us in the regeneration cycle.

Our reign went into areas outside of the Third Street area. We also advertised! The advertising on the casino was dualed with the fish hatchery. And the hatchery was a bigger money maker than the casino.

About a mile up the hills directly behind Third Street, if you knew exactly where you were going, you would come across an area dubbed "Seven Wells" by us and several generations behind us. It was a freshwater, ice-cold spring emanating from the base of an abandoned coal mine. The water was crystal clear and the flow of the water rising up from the ground never ceased. However, the rise of the water was very slow, yet constant, and eventually overflowed the banks of the wells and worked its way downhill. I believe it was Pretzel Bender who originally thought of the idea of the hatchery. He proposed we dig a trench directly from the wells downhill into a dam which took us well over the course of one summer to build. The dam held water in an area of extremely large proportions and was at least four feet deep in the middle. It took over a month before the dam held enough water to stock fish.

These fish were all catfish and sunfish caught in a local stripmine reservoir. After capturing the fish, we would place them in a bucket and keep them alive until we got back to the dam. Since the water was the same temperature, the fish made a smooth transition and we eventually had a very well stocked pond.

Once a week we would hold a "fishing rodeo" at the hatchery and twice a week the casino opened. This would allow for the children whom we made participate in our investments to restock the money we told them to go steal from their parents small change. The hatchery would make more money because we charged a fifty-cent registration fee. We also charged a fee for each fish caught. We did, however, distribute the prizes we advertised being available and we also lived up to our advertising slogan of "everyone catches a fish." The prizes were usually a cheap game from the vending machines which could be found in the supermarkets and only cost us ten percent of our registration fee. The children would be made to register for fifty cents, pay us fifteen cents for every fish caught, then throw the fish back, since the rules of the rodeo stipulated that no one keep the fish they caught.

The Roulette Wheel was the back of a round dart board, the old type of dart board numbered from one through twenty. We hammered a large nail in the middle, and used a popsicle stick as the marker. There was also tossing pennies in milk jugs, and a ring toss on bottles that it was obvious the rings would not fit around. The profits, although not always large, were constant and over time were to build to a sizeable amount.

It was generally agreed that Shot Colna was our gang leader and spokesman, due to his age and the fact none of us wanted to challenge him. He was very tough and loved to fight. Pretzel Bender often came close—basically a "fuck-off fight," but no one ever really challenged Shot. Therefore, it was mandated by Shot that he would act as treasurer of our wealth. The wealth which we dreamed one day would make us all rulers of our own kingdoms, perhaps be our ticket out of here. Our general game plan, agreed upon by everyone at an overnight sleepover in the hut, would be simple, but it would take a lot of work and eventually all of us would be involved in our own business. Basically, we were going to try to save $200 at the hatchery/casino as quickly as possible, then spread out over various areas of town. Then, we would be opening hatcheries and casinos right in our rival gangs' neighborhoods. The key, of course, would be protection. However, we would have one thing going for us—capital. A certain percentage of our take would have to be for the health and wellbeing of each other. United, we stood solid. Separated, we were definitely vulnerable since there was no love lost by any of the other "quadrants" of town toward us.

In Saint Clair, one eventually had to decide to declare allegiance to one of eight "quadrants" of town. You were either a Third (Turd) Streeter, Fourth (Fort) Streeter, North (Nort) Warder, South (Sout) Warder, East Mines, Dieners Hill (Deeners Hill), Arnouts Addition (Are Nuts), or The Patch. The Patch was an area of housing located at, or very near the coal breaker where the "black diamonds" would be sorted out. If you were living somewhere in between one of these quadrants, such as Scab Ryscavage on Second Street, you had to make a big choice at an early age. Either make a commitment to one of the eight quadrants, or risk being an independent in a town where dependency is a given. The latter did not fare well.

Therefore, you can already understand the magnitude of what we were going to attempt. Capitalize on our rival gangs' own area of town—from finding a spring for a dam to finding the right garage or necessary area to open our gambling casino. We would ask for the protection from the age bracket directly above us (12-16) in the various quadrants. Since our businesses were working so well, we reasoned, with enough backing, we could literally enhance our profits sevenfold, since there were seven total of "Da Boyz." Fall and winter would be coming on, an excellent time to scout for wells in the hills, build the dams, and have them all ready to go by next summer.

We were also adding another room (upstairs) to our already large and well-furnished hut. Each gang had their own hut to hang out at, always with door and lock. When we decided to build ours, we knew Pretzel Bender would be working the hammer. Pretzel literally hammered thirty nails into every section of this building. Destroying ours would be very difficult since it was located within forty yards of a house, and it would take a crane and wrecking ball to tear it down quickly. It was also very well-hidden amongst the many trees. It lay within twenty yards of the railroad and trains would frequently rumble by all night. However, those of us who lived on Third Street became immune to the loud roar, since it has always been a part of our sleeping habits.

For the addition, we would need a lot of wood, nails, and the furniture and appliances which would be needed in any shelter. We "borrowed" the wood from a large machine shop, although we had to borrow it at night since the owner was never there to ask permission. On two occasions security guards spotted us and, believe me, the spill one can take when running directly down a coal bank dotted with pine trees in the middle of the night can be disastrous. Bad cuts, combined with coal dirt, made for a night of agony. However, they never caught us until the very end, when we wrecked the hut ourselves. We decided to make an outfield fence for our personal baseball field, and we were dead in the water. The only thing to do was tell the police what any good, law-abiding children "raised in the eyes of the church" would. We lied.

"Officer, we have no idea. We found it out back by the tracks, and decided no one wanted it. Please accept our apologies. Please feel free to take it." Notice how the grammar cleaned up a little. Also, we realized the wood was too old and beat up to be claimed by the owner. They had no evidence, we had our fence, and the owner realized we were guilty as hell.

When we did eventually finish the second floor, with an extra large entryway to the upstairs for Eddie, it was a good, safe place to hang out. It slept eight easily. Heat was provided by small Bunson Burners, and we also had lights hooked up to a small generator. It was in the hut where most of our brainstorming sessions would be held on how we would become wealthy, what gang was ripe for knocking off, or who would be the first of us to get laid. Obviously, at our age, we tended toward talking about making money much more than the other two—although knocking off another hut was always in the cards. Usually, we had to have a reliable tip from someone before attempting it since, if we ever got caught, we would have to either fight or apologize. Of course by apologizing, we would be giving up our honor. This we would never do. Most raids would also have to be done during a week night, since weekends all huts were usually occupied.

One of the thoughts which often went through my mind during this period of my life was how much older my parents were than all my other friends. When I was ten, Victoria was fifty-three, Peter fifty-five. They were extremely worn, with many hard miles placed on both their lives. The Bender boys' father was young and he was one of those men who chose to make the sacrifice and travel out of town so he could adequately provide for his family. Al Bender would drive to New Jersey every Sunday night and return on Fridays to be with his family. Al was a line worker in a General Motors plant and eventually retired after thirty-plus years of service. Imagine, thirty-plus years and spending every week of it in a different state and residence. That's sacrifice, no matter how you slice it.

Scab Ryscavage's father was the town doctor. This came in especially handy because we would always go with Mark and his dad to the sporting events where we would be ushered to the sideline in football, directly behind the bench in basketball, etc. We went to some classic games thanks to Doc Ryscavage. Another plus was that Bill "Binky" Wolfe's dad was the town football and basketball coach. Thus, we were always allowed to go into the locker rooms before the games and hear the pre-game pep talks. Coach Wolfe, before his career was over, would win a State Basketball championship and came within one win of a State Football championship. We learned an awful lot about the desire to win from listening to and watching Coach Wolfe. At an early age, that had a profound effect on all of us and still does today. However, above all, we learned about the discipline it takes to be successful athletes. This would definitely come in handy when it would be all our turns to show what we had. There was not one of us who could not compete adequately in each of the three major sports.

****

After a vigorous summer of digging and maintaining the hatchery, combined with the success of our casino, we were definitely seeing our plan coming toward fruition. We advertised weekly, always to the same children, in a brochure we printed up. One Christmas, I was given a small beginner's printing press. At the time I received it, I had no earthly idea what I would possibly use this for. Two years later, fate would find a way to make this apparatus useful. It took an awful lot of painstaking work to lay all the letters, one by one, on the press. Also, learning proper doses of ink took time. However, the end result wasn't bad and it got the message across. "Come to our hatchery/casino. Win BIG—CASH and PRIZES. CASH ONLY ACCEPTED. BRING A

FRIEND—EVERYONE IS WELCOME.

OK, so the Hearst family we weren't. However, for nine-year-old kids, with a wealthy future in store, we were all sure we had the world by the gonads. At the end of August, we had amassed one hundred sixty dollars which would eventually be multiplied several trillion fold. There was no doubt in our minds the world desperately needed and demanded fish hatcheries where you not only had to pay to catch the fish, you also had to throw them back. Also, we'd only had vague notions of what Las Vegas was like, but we definitely knew we were headed in the right direction.

****

We weren't exactly sure how long it had been since we had seen Shot, but one thing was certain: he was avoiding us. During school, he would remain distant. After school, he simply wasn't coming around the tracks, to the hut, or anywhere we would frequent. We had shut the casino and hatchery down for the winter, and were waiting to go stake our claim on some other turfs' wells so we could begin the work on the second dam, this one to be overseen by Pretzel Bender. We were all kind of scared to go down to Shot's house and yell "yo" for him, simply because we weren't sure how he would react. One thing was certain, we all agreed it should be Pretzel Bender since he, in our estimation, stood the best chance of holding his own should Shot want to fight. It was a chance we had to take, since many things, to say the least the money, were hinging on Shot putting the Howard Hughes routine on hold for awhile and getting back in sync with da boyz.

When Pretzel returned, he was holding two shoe boxes in his hands. "I have some bad news, and I got some really bad news. Which do yooz fucks want first, or what?" We asked for the really bad news first. "Shot said his dad found da money and spent dit all. Hadta buy coal and food and shit. We're fucked big time fellas!" "Wow!" "Devastation."

All the work we had put into that summer, all our plans for wealth, stardom, and a ticket the fuck out of here, SHATTERED! I remember how we all looked at each other and thought, "Nobody has ever been able to fuck with us, beat us at anything. And here it is, one of our own beating us from within."

When the shock wore off, the thought finally hit us. "Whatz da bad news, Pret?" "In return for da money, Shot said we could have his collection of baseball cards. He sez it's gonna be worth a lotta money someday.'' Pret opened the boxes and showed us approximately one thousand vintage, extremely old baseball cards. We were so pissed off, we simply left them at Pret and Peanuts' house. The last I heard, Pret said he had given them to a young neighbor boy who got run over by a car and was undergoing a long convalescent period. If he kept those cards, I promise, Shots' prophecy of long ago would have come true. They were probably worth mega-times what Shot's dad "borrowed" from us. We did, by the way, find out that Shot's dad went on a four-day drinking binge with our money, and made a helluva lot of friends over that four-day period. This setback, however, was only temporary since we were constantly finding ways to make the "luxury money" most kids from a poor family could only dream of. A lot of times, we found that simply "borrowing" something was a heck of a lot easier than digging a dam or running a casino. By the way, I am proud to report that as of 12/92, our dam is still standing, verified by Pretzel Bender. It has completely dried up, and is overgrown with trees and greenery. However, Pretzel states he can still walk directly up the hill to it, which would be no easy feat even for someone like myself who used to be able to find it in his sleep.

****

When we weren't building, maintaining, and operating a fish hatchery, running a Vegas gambling casino, or convening in our hut, we could more than likely be found playing whichever of the three major sports was in season. The majority of us had a football, basketball, or baseball placed in our hands at an extremely early age in the hopes we would one day be a star athlete, with a college scholarship and, with any luck, a professional contract. In this way, the family name would be known throughout the region and, of course, they would brag considerably about the accomplishments of their offspring or siblings.

Each of us, to a degree, was a natural athlete in all the major sports —baseball, basketball, and football. Soccer and tennis were still not big money sports. Although thick ice formed in the winter, hockey was not played or understood in the region. We all knew, however, that if we excelled in baseball, basketball, or football our chances of "getting out" increased considerably. With this philosophy ingrained in us, and with the many talks we heard Coach Wolfe give his teams about desire and the "want" to win, we took to sports the way most grown people strive for perfection in their jobs. The team we fielded against all the other areas of town was not only blessed with God-given natural talent, but was also extremely disciplined for our age.

When we were pre-Little League, basically seven to nine years old, Joe Muldowney, one of the local elders who worked in Port Carbon, three miles south of Saint Clair, was asked by one of his co-workers if he knew of anyone who could play against the Port Carbon Little League All Star team for practice. They were soon to begin the tournament which decides which teams will eventually represent the region on the climb to the Little League World Series, held yearly in Williamsport, Pa. Mr. Muldowney had a son, Joe. Jr., who was our age and lived near. Although we let young Joe occasionally play sports with us, he never did quite make it all the way to become one of "da boyz." His father did, however, volunteer us to play against the All Stars, as long as his son was on the team. Therefore, we all gathered our baseball gear and headed for the Port Carbon Little League field. Just the anticipation of playing on a real baseball field, with a real fence, had our stomachs doing cartwheels. Up until this time, we played on our own dirt field, or on the field of whatever local team challenged us, never a real baseball diamond.

There we were, in tattered baseball jerseys bearing the name "Honnicker's Dairy," getting ready to play against kids four years our seniors, who had made the All-Star team, and on a real baseball field. We were in beat-up sneakers and jeans with a jersey five times too large, and they were suited from head to toe, to the nines. Our first ever, real officiated game and we must have looked like something out of an old "Keystone Cops" movie. Pret Bender was our pitcher, Denny Hughes (another "tweener") was behind the plate, Horse Lowthert at first, Scab Ryscavage second, Peanuts Bender shortstop, Putt-Putt Miller at third, Shot Colna in left, Binky Wolfe center, and Eddie-da-Head in right. We figured we would place Eddie in right since he ran extremely slow due to the weight being placed on his body by his extra large cranium.

We also figured Joe, Jr. would be our reserve since he wasn't really one of us, and he wasn't really very good in baseball. If his father hadn't put this whole event together, he would not be involved at all. As it was, we didn't have a clue where we would put him when his dad decided it was time to put him in, although our only logical move was replace Eddie-da-Head in right.

From the very first pitch Pret threw, I realized that several things were inevitable. First, it was our destiny to kick the shit out of this All-Star team, something neither they nor any of their coaches were prepared for. Secondly, I knew deep inside me that most of my teammates on that field would one day be All Stars and it would take one helluva team to beat us. Finally, because of the final score, 15 - 6, I knew it would be virtually impossible for any of us ever to play on the same team on the Saint Clair Little League, since word quickly spread around the area of our athleticism. No matter which sport we tried out for, rarely were any of us on the same team because we were usually the first picked by the coaches. Consequently, in any sport with more than six teams, we ended up playing against each other. Even in grade school and high school events, we ended up playing against one another because half of us went through the Catholic school system, the other half public.

It can be very difficult sometimes, lining up to play against someone you grew up and were friends with. Especially in high school, when all our desire to compete would come out. It certainly is sad that never during our childhood or adolescence did we have a chance to compete as one team, to show the fierce competitive spirit we learned at a very early age, EXCEPT ONCE. And that one time, none of us will ever forget.

I can honestly say that I can only remember once, as youngsters, getting beat by another local team in any sport, be it baseball, basketball, or football. The sport was football, and we traveled to Arnouts Addition to play an away game when we were approximately ten years old. We always played tackle, no pads. The Arnouts field was unbelievable, rocks everywhere, and we knew this one was going to be tough! Arnout's was led by Dave "Studs" Delenick, who would one day become a Saint Clair High School legend. They literally kicked the daylights out of us, the first and only time I can remember us, as a team of youngsters, getting thoroughly manhandled in any sport.

The one time we would have a chance to play competitively as a team, as I had predicted roughly five years earlier, would be when we were all voted to the All-Star team ourselves. Of the seven "Turd Streeters" playing Little League, each playing for a different team (except Pret and Peanuts Bender), five of us would be voted by the coaches to represent Saint Clair on the 1966 All-Star team. We were only eleven or twelve, but we knew we had the talent it would take to go far. Of the five of us picked, Pret, Scab and myself would be starters. Binky and Peanuts were reserves, although they were good enough in my estimation to start. It would also be a unique experience because, for the first time, many of us who competed against each other as rivals in town, would join forces to see how far we could go.

Others that were on the starting team were Studs Delenick (representing Arnout's), Dennis Davies (South Ward), Joey James (North Ward), Harry Schultz (East Mines), Russ Sabados (undeclared), and Eddie Colna (Deeners Hill), all comprising the starting nine. Dennis Davies and Pret Bender would alternate pitching between games, with Joey James available as a reliever, if needed. Due to the way I was growing, combined with the fact I had a gun for an arm, I was the catcher, a position I played for three years of my Little League tenure.

It was single elimination, playing first against All-Star teams from around the state, then proceeding onward to a possible invitation to the World Series. Although I can't remember all of the games, some of them will forever be embedded in my mind.

Our first game was against Shenandoah, a tough coal mining town ten miles north of Saint Clair. This was the first real ''big'' thrill of our young lives since it was being played in front of a large audience, many of them drinking hard, and both towns playing for what was purely a case of coal mining pride. I remember standing on the field, while the National Anthem was being played, my hat across my chest, my knee pads and chest protector on, wishing my parents were there to see me. In all the organized sports I ever played, I can only recall Peter seeing me once, and Victoria the same. Peter to see a Little League game and Victoria, much later, at a high school basketball game. But I understood because Peter worked late at Brokhoffs, and Victoria simply had no interest in sports. She was, by this time, already experiencing numerous illnesses, combined with the mental anguish of what was happening with her family. Although Peter and Victoria would not attend any of the All-Star games played, Hugh, Susan, Jo, and James attended many of them. It is possible James attended as an undercover agent to ensure my real father didn't try to show up and claim any ownership in the young athlete.

We shut Shenandoah out 4 - 0, with two homers by Pretzel Bender, one by Dennis Davies, and, unbelievably, Pret also pitched a no-hitter. Only two walks away from pitching a perfect game his first time as an All-Star. It was also a prelude of games to come, and our audiences grew larger each time and with each win. We won two games at home, one more on the road, and finally had made it to the local finals, against the team from Frackville, just four miles to the north of us. In a first-time-ever decision, the site of the game was changed from Frackville to Saint Clair, due to the terrible condition of the Frackville field and limited area for spectators. Saint Clair, to this day, has always maintained a beautiful Little League field for all of the kids, with meticulously manicured grass, and a well-kept fence (always a necessity for any ballfield). Frackville had breezed through the playoffs led by their star athlete George Johnson. George was unbelievably big for his age and had amazing power with a baseball bat. The coaches who scouted Frackville for us came back with what we thought were far-fetched stories of power by a Little League player. True, he had hit three home runs against one team, but hell, Pret hit two against Shenandoah with several more after that. All the bullshit we had heard about George up to that point was simply that to us, "bullshit."

That is, until he came to the plate for his batting practice before the game. I recall I was down in the bullpen warming up Dennis Davies, who would try and carry us this game. Behind the left field fence lies approximately twenty yards of parking space. Farther beyond that is the fence which surrounds the Saint Clair High School football field, a distance of approximately forty yards. The distance from home plate to the left field fence is sixty yards (180 feet). Therefore, the total distance from home plate to the football field fence is approximately 300 feet or, the size of an actual football field.

George and the coaches for Frackville made a grave mistake in batting practice when, on the first swing, George cleared the football field fence, easily the farthest ball I had ever seen hit by a Little League player. All I can remember as I watched it sail way over my head, the left field fence, and the football field fence was, "Holy Shit!" And he continued to do that for about ten more practice swings. All the people from Frackville were going nuts and cheering like crazy, and the game hadn't even begun. I looked at my starting pitcher and he was, as the song states, "A Lighter Shade Of Pale."

Had George not taken batting practice, we would never have completely revamped our game strategy fifteen minutes before the opening pitch. After his batting display, our coaches, Jerome Dempsey and Joe James (Joey's father), sat down with Dennis and me and told us to do something that was, to my knowledge, unprecedented in Little

League history. We decided to intentionally walk George. Even if the bases were empty with two out, our strategy was going to be to walk him. Since we were considered the visiting team due to the change of locations, we batted first and scored two runs. Scab Ryscavage was always our lead-off man. At maybe four feet, five inches, and putting himself in a crouch position, Scab has a strike zone of three inches. Nolan Ryan would have a hard time not walking him. Therefore, we always had our lead man on base every game. Another asset which Scab possessed was blinding speed once on base. Due to his lead-off walk and several key hits, we took an early lead.

In the bottom of the inning, their first batter popped out, the second hit a double, and the third grounded out to the infield. The next batter was to be George. Calmly, I called time out and walked out to talk with Dennis. The field was surrounded by the largest crowd ever to witness a Little League game in Schuylkill County. Half were for Frackville, half for Saint Clair, many were drunk, and the place was filled with the electricity of the moment. I told Dennis to relax and be prepared for what was going to happen the moment I stood up from my crouch and put my arm out for the intentional walk signal. Even I wasn't fully prepared. The contingency from Frackville went berserk, screaming at us. George looked back at me after he realized what I was doing and said, "Yooz guyz are fuckin' kiddin me, right?"

Wrong, George, it's really happening and right here in little old Saint Clair, Pennsylvania. Not only that, after the Frackville fans started harassing us, our fans, with pride of their own, got into the act. Pretty soon, fights were breaking out everywhere around the field, the place was absolute bedlam. We walked George, got out of the inning unscathed, and regrouped for our next go-round. I had no earthly idea of the commotion walking someone in Little League baseball would have until, all during the next week, I could pick up the sports page of any local newspaper, and there would be a full-blown picture of the umpire standing, me standing with my right arm out, and George looking at me with his, "Yooz guyz are fuckin' kiddin'me," face on. I was an instant celebrity at eleven years of age.

In the third, we picked up a run. However, it was still a competitive, highly-charged atmosphere. In their at-bat, Frackville had two down, two on, and the number three man up. It was trouble because if this man got on, we would be forced to either walk in an intentional run, or pitch to George the potential leading run. The next play will forever stay engraved in my mind—even should all my senses fail me—above all moments in any sport that I ever played. I still see it happening like it did twenty-seven years ago—only it plays on 78 instead of 33—very slowly. The third batter, a right-hand hitter, got jammed on a fastball, and grounded the ball directly at Joey James, our shortstop. The runner on second, upon the sound of the ball on the bat with two out, "barely" nicked Joey's uniform on his glove side, but, he did touch him. Joey proceeded to bobble the ball, and everyone was safe around.

However, Joey immediately appealed to the second base umpire who saw the play clearly. I saw it and turned around and told the home plate umpire, George Machamer, who said nothing to me. "I KNOW I SAW THE FUCKING GUY TOUCH HIM, UMP," I was pleading inside of myself. But Machamer, also being the crew chief of the four umpires, was a smart, crafty umpire. He immediately convened them into short left field, away from everyone. The difficult call was that, unless you were keyed on the runner, like I was, instead of Joey, like 98% of the people, you would have missed it, like they did. I know I saw it, but I don't really think George behind me, or the third base ump saw it clearly. You see, I was already taller than the umpire by then, and I was standing. The umpires also had to figure on getting out of town alive, because there were a lot of rowdy people there—for both sides. However, the Frackville fans were still mad about us walking George in the first, and here was an opportunity for them to see if we were really pussies, like they were calling us openly, or to see if we had the real deal here—balls.

I know one thing, I had a large knot in my stomach getting bigger every minute the umpires were convening. There was one other person also aware of the brush by the runner. He would have to stand against the three other umpires, who really didn't see the play, and convince them it happened. After fifteen minutes of convening, and the entire stadium basically silent and growing restless except for the occasional person who would scream, "Yo, yooz guyz make a decision here. We got drinkin' ta do when we get outta here," the umpires finally decisioned us to our dugout—"interference on the runner." By this time, George had been standing by me waiting to bat, really trying to rattle me. We were about the same height (he was tall also), but he was much stockier. While the umpires are standing in left field, George is saying to me, "Yo, puss, I hope I get a chance ta lay ya out comin' home.

Yooz guyz are really chickenshits an' I'm gonna take it out on you.''

This was going on for about five minutes, with me trying to be cool, because I knew there was the distinct possibility the scenario he was painting could happen. Man, he was big! When the umpires made their decision, George slammed his bat on homeplate, looked back at me and says, "DIZ IZ FUCKIN' BULLSHIT! YOOZ MOTHER FUCKERS ARE KIDDIN' ME?" Of course, I was the only one able to hear him since the stadium was going absolutely bonkers. When I saw George's reaction and his remark to me, I yelled back to him, "Yo, George, ever get the feelin' your gettin fucked, or what?" Man was he pissed. I mean, there was cursing and fights began starting everywhere. All I needed was for George to decide he'd had enough, and try to put my head in the football field with that bat. It was hell for the umpires to pay, too. The Frackville contingency were mother-fucking them bad—no, really bad.

In those days, when your hometown was playing sports against a rival, fist fights were common. For neutral umpires to come into our region and make that call, it took a lot of guts. But, it was the right call. I bet the umpires couldn't recall the last time they had to fight for their lives after officiating a Little League baseball game.

In the fourth we added another run on a blast by Pretzel Bender. Dennis Davies, who was still pitching, was starting to have terrible control problems. In the bottom of the inning, the leadoff man, George, was intentionally walked. I knew deep inside he wanted a piece of me real bad. So did the Frackville people. Later, many newspapers would show various photos of me with my arm out, and the piercing look George was giving me. The Saint Clair people had witnessed over the years a lot of excellent sports. However, this was usually high school. This Little League game had the tension and excitement of a World Series game.

We finally had to yank Dennis with two on and no outs. When I went out with Coach Dempsey to get the ball from him, he was crying. This is what is truly amazing about how we were raised. A man was required to be strong through all kinds of circumstances—death, monetary problems, health problems. Almost nothing was worth crying over. Yet, I have seen, and done so myself, many people cry during sports, especially the agony of losing at them. When I saw Dennis (who was a very tough kid) crying, it made me realize for the first time that true teamwork, of any sort, is also being able to share in the losses.

When Dennis turned the ball over, and walked out to shortstop with tears streaming down his face, I felt for a moment what he was going through. His want to finish and win was so strong, he let his emotions overtake him, which is a rarity among the men of this region.

Joey came into the game with two on, no outs. Since Joey was on my regular team in Little League, I had caught him for the past three years. He had an excellent fast ball and a vicious curve that would break at the last second. During the regular season, if we had a big lead, Joey would cross me up when I called for a fastball and throw that curve. Forget the batter, he usually never came close. It was me who looked really silly. Joey struck out the side, a masterful piece of pitching. In the fifth inning, neither of us scored, it was still 4-0. In the sixth, we got two more runs, making it 6-0 and giving us some breathing room. The Frackville fans were pissed to the power of ten. They knew what we had done was bullshit for a Little League baseball game. Yet, they brought this strategy on themselves when they cheered wildly as George was launching the ball in batting practice. It would have been insane to pitch to him when the game was close, especially with men on base.

In the bottom of the sixth we began to feel our first-ever district championship was within reach. Just three outs away. Joey got the first man to ground out. The second batter was George, and the first thing he says to me when he steps up is, "Yooz pricks tink ya can pitch ta me now, or what? Or, are ya gonna walk me again soz I can get a shot at ya comin' home, or what? Eder way, I ain't goin' back to da dugout 'till I touch home plate. An' I hope you're in my way!"

"Dat's it, fuck dis," I thought. I called time and went out to Joey. "O.K. Joey. Fuck dis guy. Two more outs an' we're home free. One's a fast ball, two's da curve. If he blasts one, be ready, 'cause I'm gonna motherfuck him when he crosses da plate. Ya never know what dez crazy fucks from Frackville will do."

On the way back to the plate, I looked over and Coach Dempsey nodded his agreement, knowing full well we were going to pitch to him. I also knew that I was going to call nothing but curve balls. "One's a fast ball, two's da curve. Right? Right!"

The first pitch to George was the wickedest pitch he had ever seen until this point. It broke so quickly at the last second, I could swear I felt the air move when George swung his bat. Man was he ever red-faced and pissed. "How da ya like me now, Georgie?" I said.

"One's a fastball two's da curve."

Second pitch, George thinks is coming right at him, as if to hit him smack on his left ass-cheek, and he cringes away. "Strike two," shouted Machamer after the ball broke cleanly over the middle of the plate. This time, thank God, I didn't feel obligated to say anything since the whole town of Saint Clair was laughing at George. You could literally fry an egg on the back of his neck. I remember the slight grin on Joey's face when I called for what I thought was the curve. Joey had been wanting to throw the heat, and unbeknownst to me, I had given him the green light.

It was the only time in my years playing in that stadium that I could remember someone only getting a single after hitting the ball to the gap in right center field. George connected with the ball so hard it hit the fence on a line drive and bounced directly back to Studs Delenick who was shading him that way.

Reality sets in. George's at first, and he wants someone to get in his way rounding the bases. Next man up hits another shot in the gap, only much slower. George is off to the races. Studs relayed to Dennis in short left center, and George is already twenty feet down the line from third. Dennis had found a way to put his emotions aside, and threw a perfect strike to me, on one bounce, as I was blocking home plate. George and I had played against each other in midget football league and had also played against each other on the All-Star team for our region in midget football. I knew what tackling George with pads on was like, let alone having him coming full tilt at me while I'm concentrating on catching a baseball. He hit me, head first, in the chest and knocked me two yards back. The wind blew out of me faster than shit through a goose, but I still had that ball deeply embedded in my catcher's mitt.

The stadium went absolutely bananas when I held my mitt up in the air, showing the ball, while at the same time gasping for air. Joey took the ball out of my mitt and held the original batter at third. On the next pitch he scored, but that's how it ended, 6 - 1.

Your new division champions were headed for the elimination tournament toward the World Series. I recall people I never met or saw before were hugging me, the field was filled to capacity. We had done it! Proved how good we actually were when we put all our natural abilities together. I never saw George Johnson after that game, but I bet he remembers me today, if he's still alive, as I have remembered him.

****

We eventually lost to a team that we should have beaten easily, and we knew it. However, even in losing, we won something. As we sat in the dugout bawling our eyes out after the game, I became acutely aware of what the word "team" truly means, sharing in the losses, as well as the wins, and accepting defeat as gentlemen and athletes should. This would carry over into my personal life.

It is my belief that learning how to win and lose in any sport parallels those moments in life when we are confronted with good and bad news, positive and negative incidents. As youngsters, it was obviously very easy for us to win and see the other teams walk away with their heads down and tears in their eyes. It was difficult when it was our turn for defeat, but we learned to accept the fact that life goes on—either in a defeat from a sporting event, the death of someone close to us, the breakup of someone close to us, or, as in my case, having to accept the reality that I was deceived for many years.

The hurt that I would have to deal with and try to overcome would be not so much from finding out the truth as from dealing with the fact that virtually everyone who knew me was hiding something from me. Nor would my family volunteer any information about what really happened nor help in trying to locate my real father when I wanted so badly to find and meet him. Many of them still cannot understand that I am old enough and mature enough to absorb and accept the truth.

****

Throughout our elementary school years, "da boyz" were virtually inseparable. Because of the age variances, some went into high school earlier than others, some attending the public school system, and others, like myself, remaining in the parochial educational system.

Shot Colna went on to excel in both track and football for Saint Clair High School, but he never accepted any scholarships to further his education. Today, those boys I have been able to locate do not know what happened to him after that. Shot, wherever you are, get in touch with us since, when this book becomes a success, we are going to have a massive reunion.

Pretzel Bender and I would lose contact for several years. However, fate brought us together again at a party we both attended, not knowing the other would be there. Pretzel went on to excel in basketball at Saint Clair High, being an integral part of their state championship team. However, for reasons only he knows, he never accepted any of the myriads of scholarships to major colleges that were presented to him.

Peanuts Bender excelled in football for Saint Clair High, playing middle linebacker. Unfortunately he dropped out of school halfway through his senior year. He eventually realized his mistake and went back and finished high school, got a good job, and is raising a family in a beautiful home. Like his father, he is a line worker for General Motors and travels from his home in New Jersey to the Baltimore area each week, returning to his wife and daughter on the weekends. Today, he has slimmed down considerably from when I knew him due to his involvement in running marathons.

Although never being formally accepted as one of "da-boyz," Eddie-Da-Head still deserves recognition. Eddie has had to fight adversity and negativism all his life since he was born mentally handicapped. As kids, we never purposely tried to hurt his feelings, although by his nickname I'm sure we did. We always protected Eddie from rival gangs since he lived in our neighborhood. Eddie was also allowed to hang with us whenever he wanted, but it hurts me now to see how we treated him as kids. Unfortunately, when we were young, we didn't have the maturity and perceptions we develop with age. If I had a chance to go back in time and change situations, one of them would definitely be our treatment of Eddie. We never physically abused him, but the mental aspect of his handicap never dawned on us as youngsters. Pretzel told me he is still living at home and had been working in a local lumber yard until recently when he was terminated for telling one of the patrons to "get fucked." He was then hired on at a local beer distributor where he still works today.

Horse Lowthert also excelled in football for Saint Clair and, like Pretzel and Shot, elected not to pursue a college education on a scholarship. After much thought, I realize this may have been "burn-out" from sports since it was forced on us at such an early age. Or, quite possibly, they simply were not ready to break away from the regeneration process of the families in that region. The last I saw of Horse, he was working for a pharmaceutical chain, married with children, but his whereabouts now are unknown to me. Horse, wherever you are and whatever your situation, keep the winning attitude and get in touch with Pretzel for our eventual reunion.

Binky Wolfe, like his father before him, went on to become an Education major on the heels of a football scholarship. Binky excelled at running back for Saint Clair High and, due to his father being the coach, his future was predictable. He is currently teaching and coaching in Florida, although his exact whereabouts are unknown to me. Binky was fortunate to have an opportunity to play on his father's state championship basketball team, and was the halfback on the football team which came within one game of being state champions. Imagine, a town of four thousand people pumping out this type of athletic ability. If I have any major regrets about that period in my life, it is that we never played together on the same team, and that I had to play against my friends and was never once on a team that beat them. That's really hard to swallow. Binky's Dad passed away from a heart condition, but his memory will forever be etched in my mind. Not only for those basic principles of a winning attitude which he instilled in us, also because he truly cared about us as human beings. As for Binky, there is no doubt in my mind he is a successful teacher and coach today. Binky, wherever you are today, "Yo, I miss you. Get in touch!"

Finally, Scab Ryscavage has become a success in his own right. Mark was always my closest friend of "da-boyz" as we were growing up, and I managed to keep in touch with him throughout the years. Like myself, Mark attended Catholic elementary and high school. Unlike me, however, he possessed natural, God-given intelligence. He is someone who doesn't need to study to learn, he is just naturally intelligent. Therefore, it is no mistake that he went on to become the successful attorney he is today. Having to deal with various attorneys in the profession I have chosen today, I realize that the truly successful ones, like Mark, possess the "win at all costs" philosophy that was planted in our minds early in our childhood. Mark and I also had a chance to play together on the same basketball team, where he excelled as point guard. Small in stature but quick as a greyhound, he also possessed the skills necessary to dribble a basketball with precision and feared no one who may have been taller and stronger than he. Unfortunately for both of us, we were on a Catholic high school team that entered into the public school system league play its first year. Due to the limited availability for quality players in our school at that time, we learned to accept defeat many times, although the desire was always there to win.

I have very fond memories of Doc Ryscavage taking the time to treat all of us the way he did Mark—as his sons. The day I learned Dr.

Ryscavage had passed away was very emotional for me since through the years I became closer to him than to my father. That Mark would become successful was never in doubt from the perspective of all "da-boyz." I hope that when he reads this, he realizes how much he means to me as a friend and also the valuable lessons I learned from his entire family. For this I say thank you, and hope one day our children look up to us the way I did to Mark's family.

As for me, suffice it to say I had no choice but to break away from the regeneration process. This is always difficult for someone who is born in this region to do. However, with the philosophies that I learned from these individuals, it was much easier for me. Today, there are many people who live in this region who possess qualities that would make them extremely successful, but they are afraid to make a conscious decision to pack everything and leave; they live life on a day-to-day basis with an unrealistic view of how difficult it is to survive in our country today.

More than the "win at all costs, never accept defeat" attitude I inherited from my friends, I also realize that you get out of life what you put into it. I have learned that my physical and mental capabilities are what I decide to make of them, that the sky's the limit if I choose to pursue it. For the record, I hope to pursue that limitless sky until the day someone says a prayer over my final resting place.

To Pretzel, Peanuts, Shot, Eddie-Da-Head, Scab, Binky, and Horse, "Thanks for the memories." As Eddie Money said in his song, "I Really Do Miss My Friends," and I cannot wait until the day we're all reunited.

CHAPTER THREE

GROWING UP
(IN THE SCHOOL OF HARD KNOCKS!)

Possibly by now you have snapped to the fact that the prologue of this book was written by a very young, immature person who received news that literally shook him to the core of his very existence. It was written in a single night, when emotions thoroughly riddled my body, and I chose writing as my way to lash out at those people who deceived me. Hopefully, to give back some of the hurt that I was having to endure by the lies. If it wasn't for having friends like I grew up with for support, I am sure I would have been a problem psychologically, and emotionally. I also hope that you've snapped to the fact that the remainder of this book is written by a semi-intelligent person who is trying not only to exorcise those negative emotions once and for all, but, to make a plea to all those people who know someone in a situation like mine.

I have analyzed for hours how Victoria came to have so much power over Peter in a region and era when women were considered to be virtually powerless. Peter Miller was working in the coal mines around the tiny town of Girardville when he met Victoria Hill and impregnated her out of wedlock.

Victoria's father, whom I only knew as "Pop," was a man of

strong political influence in Saint Clair, one with direct connections in the "Ancient Order of Hibernians." When Pop Hill discovered that his daughter was pregnant out of wedlock he sent for her to come home immediately. Peter Miller could follow if he wished. He did follow his new bride and became part of the Hill regeneration process, living in Pop's household with his wife and newly arrived son, James.

Pop lived until I was two years old and kept complete control over the domain. While Peter eventually added nine children to the household, he was an afterthought when it came to any decisions. Pop Hill probably was the one who made the ultimate decision regarding his first granddaughter's pregnancy, while Peter looked on as a foreigner in the home he was forced to share with his ever-increasing family.

Upon Pop's death, Peter would not assume control of the house. James, as the first grandson, was trained by Pop and Victoria to be the male spokesperson for the Miller household. Peter, unfortunately, never saw the day he was the true ruler of his own household. Victoria would ensure James's *coup-d'etat* upon Pop's death. (Victoria's mother had been dead for several years at this time.)

Peter had no say in whether he wished to accept me as his child. It was an edict from above—meaning Victoria and her father—with full involvement of James. It had always been a puzzle to me why Peter was so distant toward me, never showing affection, rarely taking an interest in my childhood evolution. True, he worked hard and had lived a tough, demanding life. However, he never really took time to be with me the way my friends' fathers did. My friends' parents tried to include me in those plans a young boy might be interested in doing. They were, in fact, much more of a father to me than the man I believed was mine. As for Victoria, she never became close to me, as was also the case with her nine children. Perhaps, in her thinking, there were simply too many children to show preference to one over the other. Except for James, who, with his new-found role as the breadwinner, was granted the tacit love of the first-born. Never, however, by hugging or any physical encounter.

When Pop died, Victoria assumed all decision making, with consultation from James. If any arm-twisting was necessary, James would be the person called upon to fulfill this function instead of Peter. Peter was simply too nice a guy, with absolutely no say in any decisions. It is no wonder his free time was spent in a bar instead of at home. His orders were simple. Work, bring home a check, and please stay out of the way. Victoria assumed full tyrannical control over the upbringing of her children, with direct involvement in any and all decisions regarding me. Victoria's views on everything would be accepted and any orders given within the household were to be carried out without question.

Fortunately, at that time, I preferred spending as much time as I could outdoors, away from the bedlam. I began to understand that my parents were not the "loving" type, although I assumed they did love me because I was their son. They put no real demands on me to perform in school but I had enough natural intelligence to feel my way through. Although nowhere near what would be called a brain, I was able to get through mainly on common sense and logic without studying. My steady friendship with Mark Ryscavage since we entered first grade together helped me learn enough to get by. Mark would often explain what we were learning in school better than our teachers did. He helped me learn various subjects by simply talking about them. Since I usually listened to him 75% of the time he was talking, I maintained a steady "C" average. Never a brain, but never a trouble student either.

We often stayed outdoors until well after dark, especially when school was out. I virtually controlled my own schedule early in my life with much of my time spent in various activities with "da-boyz." During school the only real time I saw or spent with my parents was on Sunday, when attendance at dinner was mandatory. This seemed the only time the entire family spent together, under direct orders of the powers that be. Otherwise, in the mornings Peter was already gone, while Victoria was seeing that everything and everyone was going as scheduled. She was an excellent cook and was able to make a little bit of something go a long way. Not only with food, but clothing, furniture, everything. That's one compliment I can truly give her. Through all of the poverty they had endured over the years, her children never wanted for food, clothing, or shelter. I honestly don't know how they did it on Peter's meager salary.

By the time I was in sixth grade, Rose Mary, Clarice, Ellen, Frankie, C. J., and Susan had moved out of the house. The previous summer we had won the All-Star tournament, and I was feeling good, positive about myself. Then one weekday I came down for school to find something was definitely wrong. James had already left for work, and Jocelyn, Hugh, and I were the only children still around. My Dad was sitting at the kitchen table with my Mom standing nearby, and he couldn't hold his head up. He couldn't even look at me across the room.

"Mom, what's wrong with Dad?" I asked. I remembered this past year when Victoria had suddenly taken violently ill, and Doctor Ryscavage literally ran to our house to save her life. I never knew or understood what was wrong with her. She eventually recovered but it really had scared me, my mother almost dying in our house, right in front of my eyes.

"I don't know. I woke up in da middle of da night and he was moanin'. I taut he was dreamin' in his sleep, so I didn turn da lights on. I tink he's pretty sick dough."

He was definitely sick. When I went closer and looked at him, the entire left side of his face was contorted, as though in pain, and he was salivating heavily out of the same side of his mouth. With James not around to help get him to the hospital, Victoria was in a quandary over what to do. Normally she would have put him in James's car and taken him up to Doctor Ryscavage. Without James, she was afraid to call the town ambulance. Either from fear of drawing attention to herself, or the fear of what an ambulance ride would cost. I moved closer to Peter to get his acknowledgment of my presence in the room. When I moved to within a foot of him at the kitchen table, his downward gaze caught my shoes. His attempt to look up toward me resulted in a regurgitation of saliva, blood, and a greenish phlegm.

Immediately I panicked and started crying at this sight of my father. In between crying I begged Victoria to call Doctor Ryscavage, which she decided to do. Unfortunately, Doctor Ryscavage was at the Pottsville Hospital doing his morning rounds and would have to be paged. Victoria left a message to call us, but I knew something had to be done immediately. I virtually screamed at her, "Mommy, call an ambulance and get Daddy to a hospital. There is something bad wrong with him." This is the only time I can ever recall Victoria paying attention to anyone other than herself or James when making a decision which would affect this family. She made the call and, of all things, I remember she tried to straighten the house before the people with the ambulance got there.

Although not close to my father, especially in terms of physical contact, I remember putting my hand on his shoulders and telling him everything would be O.K. Interspersing this with uncontrollable tears.

Tears which came regardless of how hard I tried to hold them back so as not to alarm the person I was crying about.

An ambulance at any house in Saint Clair was never a good sign. They became known as "death wagons," from carrying the miners to the morgue after a cave-in, when they were already dead. Therefore, anyone near the house where the ambulance was would stand and watch, trying to determine the fate of the fallen occupant. When the attendants arrived, Peter was so confused he could not understand that they needed him to lie on the stretcher. He was utterly reluctant to let them load him. The ambulance drivers had no patience with him. It was becoming a complete fiasco. Eventually Victoria realized Peter did not want them to take him because he had on only his underwear. When we finally got his pants on him, he was loaded into the wagon and whisked away. I did not know what to do. Victoria had gone to the hospital in the ambulance with Peter. Hugh and Jocelyn were gone. I was left there scared and afraid I was going to lose the father I still didn't get to know.

In the meantime, Doctor Ryscavage called and I was able to tell him that they would soon be arriving. Extremely afraid, not knowing what to do or who to call, I decided the best thing would be to go to school and hope the entire episode was a figment of my imagination, a dream so to speak.

When I got home, Hugh and Jocelyn were already aware of the situation. Victoria had filled them in, and James was en route from Harrisburg to pick us up and get us to the hospital. No one showed any concern about the psychological implications this may have had on me, seeing the entire illness and having to deal with it on my own. Even today my family still doesn't understand the emotional impact seeing my father in that situation had on me. Today there would be help for a child with such a trauma, but not then.

On the ride to the hospital, I tried to comprehend STROKE as the word applied to my father. Not one of the kids I knew had a father who had suffered a stroke. No one was able to explain it to me so that I understood. I had no one to turn to for understanding and physical consolation.

When we got to the hospital, the specialist Doctor Ryscavage had called in on the case told my family to prepare me for what I was to see. But I was still thrown into complete turmoil emotionally by what I encountered. Peter was hooked up to machines, tubes, air masks, and the left side of his face and body were so contorted it didn't even look like him! This, along with his glazed eyes and inability to recognize me, let me believe we were in the wrong room. The confusion combined with a lack of physical consolation from my family put me into complete denial of what was going on in front of my eyes. Not one person noticed or cared about me at this moment. To this day, they have no idea of the psychological scars this has left. Nor will they ever understand any of the philosophies about illness and death that I undertook at this early stage of my life.

****

It took two months of intense rehabilitation and convalescing before Peter was able to come home. The stroke had left him virtually paralyzed on his left side and his speech was limited to no more than twenty understandable words. Those which he was still able to mutter clearly were: "yes, no, goddamn, son-of-a-bitch, goddamn son-of-a-bitch, and, I'll get you, you son-of-a-bitch." Anything else was virtually unintelligible. Besides the stroke, the doctors found that Peter's lungs were completely infested with the cancer of a coal miner—Black-Lung Disease. His years inside the mines inhaling the coal dust had caught up with his lungs, and he would frequently regurgitate a tar-like substance upon coughing. Although able to walk, he required a cane and virtually half of his body was useless. At this point his mind was still functioning somewhat, although his body was unable to understand the commands being sent to it.

This compounded his frustration. Fortunately, although the family's income had been severely hampered, Peter now qualified legally for those disability benefits available to people with Black-Lung Disease and who could prove it was the result of working in the mines. Hugh and I also received benefits since we were dependents under the age of eighteen. The income derived from the Black Lung for Peter, Hugh, and myself added up, oddly enough, to more than Peter was making working at a dairy farm. The only positive this terrible disease had was that Peter would no longer be a slave for Brokhoff's Dairy.

I made a conscious decision at an early age that this would not be my fate. There was no way I would follow in the footsteps of my father like so many of my friends were already planning to do. It is only now that I realize how tough Peter Miller really was. He had nothing all his life, yet I can never once remember him complaining. Never once did he say, "This is bullshit. I want my family living in my own house." He accepted what he was confronted with because, I believe, he truly loved Victoria. I never once saw the man blow his stack, lose his cool, ever get into a fight with any man—or Victoria—until after he came home from the hospital when the stroke had completely overtaken all major thought processes of his brain.

Victoria was increasingly losing touch with reality through her consumption of nerve medicine and alcohol. When Peter took sick with his stroke, it seems her intake of both of these drugs increased to the point of her being, at times, totally uncomprehending. She was, however, still trying to maintain control over her children, even those who had already married and moved out of the house.

I remember one Sunday when we went to visit Ellen, Edgar, and their daughter Michelle at their apartment in Fredericksburg, Pennsylvania. Edgar had recently resigned his commission as a Captain in the U.S. Army, and they were settling with some difficulty into a middle-income lifestyle. It was the weekend of the assassination of John F. Kennedy, a time before Peter's stroke. Victoria was already in a very bad mood because of Kennedy's death. Because it happened in Texas, she firmly believed all Texans were as despicable as Lee Harvey Oswald. I was watching the black and white television when Jack Ruby jumped from the crowd in the basement of the Dallas Police Department and shot Oswald.

At the same time, Victoria and Edgar became embroiled in a nasty verbal altercation centered around how he was caring for her daughter and grandchild. Edgar had always done his best to better his family and became extremely offended. Finally he asked, no told, Victoria to leave his residence—immediately. This had never happened to Victoria. I have the utmost admiration for Edgar; he stood up for himself and his family.

Of course Peter and I left in Victoria's wake. This incident caused a major furor in the Third Street residence. Edgar was verbally hung out to dry. James decided to keep his distance on this one since Edgar was an intelligent, proud, bull of an Irishman. Peter also knew this was none of their concern anymore, although he had to appear to side with Victoria. This was the first sign that Victoria was beginning to lose her complete control over her family.

The stroke would leave Peter with a new perception of me. Before, I was the youngest of his family, now I was an outcast, someone who didn't belong. I had no idea this was going to happen and I was not prepared for it.

Victoria also became increasingly hostile toward me since the stroke and I couldn't grasp exactly why this was happening, or if it really was happening and not a figment of my imagination. Peter became hostile toward me from the moment he would see me walk through the door. If I wasn't totally cognizant of his whereabouts, he was wont to slap his cane across my back. The hurt in my heart was much heavier than the physical scars this would leave. Pain was something I could absorb; abuse I did not understand at all. "Did an illness really affect his mind like this, or was I doing something wrong?" I had to maintain my composure because he was, after all, very ill.

However, Victoria simply could not handle the strain which was placed on her and began also to physically take it out on me. There were times when I would be sleeping on the couch downstairs, while she was watching television and drinking, that I would be abruptly awakened by her pulling ferociously on my hair. Clumps of hair were yanked out by the savagery of her pulling. I became increasingly involved in an abuse which according to today's standards and laws would warrant a thorough investigation by the authorities. Then, it was simply something I learned to accept. The thought of being afraid of your parents at age twelve rather than intensely involved in a loving relationship was something I had extreme difficulty dealing with. Most of the members of my family had long since moved out. Therefore they had trouble understanding the severity and complexity of my situation. The warmness and acceptance shown to me by people like Doctor and Mrs. Ryscavage, Mr. and Mrs. Wolfe, Mr. and Mrs. Bender, and so on, helped me through the increasingly difficult periods I was enduring.

Peter's stroke would now keep him bound to the house at all times. I found myself seeking more often the companionship of my friends and their families. When not in the hut, playing sports, or in school, I more often than not could be found in any one of "da-boyz" houses. They rarely entered ours since Peter viewed me the same with or without my friends present, and never had any trepidations about giving me a good whack of his cane in front of them. They were aware of what I was facing and helped make my situation better when I traveled with them. Even with the open, visible physical abuse, I was never offered help by my family. I became increasingly dependent on my friends, who would take the place of the parents I never knew.

****

During the seventh and eighth grades at Saint Mary's, several things became apparent in our home. First, both Peter and Victoria were physically and emotionally ill. Second, they finally realized that I could not continue to deal with what I was going through without a breakdown of some sort, somewhere along the line.

The problem was what to do with me. There were no government programs to deal with child abuse, nor any counseling available for the abused child. Things that under today's laws would be considered child abuse were seen back then as normal discipline. "Dysfunctional" would take on a new meaning when applied to my family situation.

Another factor to consider was James's growing power. With Peter's stroke, James's hold on the family became open and he was more verbal in dealing with any situation that arose. He used his control to enforce Victoria's facade and denied the truth even years later when confronted with written evidence.

There were already several factors that should have made me aware of the truth: the disparity in age between my parents and my friends' parents, my height, and most glaring, Peter's treatment of me after his first stroke. He was a man who would never hurt a soul. Now, I was the only one he would hit any time he felt the urge. The scars left by this abuse are the most difficult emotion I am now having to deal with. I hurt very badly while enduring the abuse and thinking I had done something wrong when in fact, I hadn't.

****

It was my natural father, whom I found in November 1992, after searching for him for fourteen years, who would solve the mystery of Peter's reaction toward me. I have the physical characteristics of my real father. When Peter looked at me, he saw the man who had first broken his heart.

****

The first stroke was while I was in sixth grade, the second at the beginning of the eighth. This one would yield even more deterioration of Peter's speech and his entire left side. However, he could still rattle a clear "son-of-a-bitch." This stroke scared me also, although I wasn't present at its inception. Just the sight of this broken-down man, my father, brought a very uneasy feeling to my stomach. Many more of his motor nerves seemed to be depleted. His cane was now needed more for support than anything else. He was constantly having to wipe drool from his distorted mouth with a handkerchief held with his good hand. He also took another step backwards in his view of me. Although not able to swing the cane as he once had, he was still able to communicate with me through verbal intonation. Even though hard for a trained ear to pick up, I could still clearly understand Peter in many verbal assaults toward me.

The physical abuse was not as constant, however, the verbal abuse increased to the point where I set Peter off whenever I entered a room he was in. Hugh and Jocelyn, who were still at home, also rationalized that it was the illness which made him react this way toward me. However, I believe they were becoming aware that it was definitely wearing on me. I became more withdrawn at home, in school, and even around my friends. I had a mental monkey on my back and I could not understand what was making it happen. I believe Hugh and Jo also made Victoria aware of how this was affecting me because she even began to ease off me, understanding the difficulty I was having dealing with Peter. It was extremely odd because James, Hugh, and I would frequently be called upon to help Peter bathe, shave, and dress, among other things. During those times I helped, the verbal abuse never let up. Sometimes I thought it was just the frustration he was feeling from having to be helped to do these things. Other times, I knew it was a direct verbal assault on me due to those intelligible words which I could make out plainly. It was obvious to me at this point that my father simply did not want me around or love me any longer. If only I had known or been told, the hurt would have been diminished drastically.

Due to my feeling that I was unwanted or unloved, I made the conscious decision that it was time I took action against Peter's tirades. Although this man was ill, there is only so much a person can take before it becomes time to defend himself.

During the summer before I entered eighth grade, "da boyz" were initiated into that "nectar of the gods," beer. The first time we each drank two quarts apiece and almost killed ourselves falling down the hill. We had become totally inebriated before entering the eighth grade. Unfortunately, it was also unanimous that we liked it, not unlike those

older "Turd Streeters" above us. It gave me a sense of power unlike I
had ever felt before. It gave me the strength I never had before to ward
off any physical or verbal assault from either Victoria or Peter. There
were times, beginning in the eighth grade, when I would come home
drunk and Peter would lash out at me and I would come right back
with, "What did you say?" Or, "Do you have something you want to
tell me?," in a threatening voice. One particular time I'll never forget.
Peter balanced himself against a cabinet and whacked me with his cane
when I walked by. This would be the last time he ever attempted this
since I turned and said as threateningly as I've ever said anything
before in my life, "You do that one more time to me and I'll break it
over your fucking neck!" I could not believe I said that, but what
bothered me most is that I didn't feel bad for saying it. I also made it
clear to Victoria that I had had enough of her. If she attempted to grab
me, I would stand up and hold her at arms' length at the top of her
head. She would often try swinging at me when I did this and hit my
elbow, at best. It was not only when I had been out drinking with
"da-boyz," that I would not take the abuse. I now had enough fortitude
to stand up to both of them physically or verbally, which ever they
chose. This anger which I thought was going away through my
retribution was, without my knowing it, actually building to a
crescendo.

It happened on Christmas Eve of my eighth grade year. C. J. was
home from the convent as were several others. I was going to attend
midnight mass and take care of my duty as a Catholic before the
crowds the next morning. Hugh was also. It was cold and a light snow
was falling. There was a Christmas tree, although with few presents
under it. Everyone seemed to feel pensive and uptight due to the nature
of the season and the obvious degeneration of both Peter and Victoria.

Hugh had already chosen one of his two suitcoats to wear to
church. Since I did not have one to wear I naturally assumed Hugh
would not mind me wearing his other because it was sitting idle. When
I came downstairs with it on, he immediately told me to take it off and
put it back where I got it from. I thought he was kidding and shrugged
it off good-naturedly since I knew it was a one-time borrow due to the
shortness of the arm length on me. Once again, Hugh demanded I take
it off and replace it in the closet. The only thing I remember from that
point forward is that C. J., Victoria, and Peter were present. Both my
pride and anger blew sky high at the same time, and I can remember, to

this day, saying to Hugh two simple words, "Make me!" Once again, that old 33 R.P.M. started playing on 78 and things happened in slow motion, just like in the Little League all-star game. He attempted to grab my shoulder to strip the arm off and I let him have it. I took him off guard and landed a right directly to his face. The pace increased dramatically although the record stayed the same. I hit him again and again and, by this time, had completely lost my conscious mind. I pushed him into the bookcase which had a glass covering, completely shattering it. All during this time, Peter, Victoria, and C. J. were screaming for help. None came, and I was involved in the biggest adrenaline surge I had ever had to this point. I grabbed Hugh, who was lying by the bookcase moaning, and forced him to stand up. I then punched him again, this time into the Christmas tree which went tumbling down. James finally arrived and tried to hold me off, but I still wanted more. I wanted some of his action, too.

Had it not been for C. J., who was alternately screaming and crying hysterically, I might never have stopped. When she finally stepped in between James and me, her nun's habit brought me back to reality. Strange how something to do with the Catholic religion was able to immediately bring me to my senses.

James went over to help Hugh, who was lying in the middle of the Christmas tree. The old-fashioned large, glass Christmas lights were shattered everywhere, including shards stuck in Hugh. C. J. got me into the kitchen where I was sobbing and shaking uncontrollably and tried to calm me down. I had lost control of all my senses. This is the first time that happened to me although, unfortunately, it would not be the last. It takes an awful lot to anger me to the point of physical retribution. However, when it happens, I lose all sense of control, even to the point where extreme pain may be inflicted on me and I would not know it. The worst part of this incident was that it involved Hugh. He had always been a friend to me as a brother should, since he was not aware of my true circumstances. I cried for hours because of what I had done to him and because I was scared, being this young and totally losing control of all my faculties.

Hugh eventually got over his hurt toward me and his wounds also healed. But I never got over it—that is, until now when a lot of the pieces of the puzzle are coming together.

The Christmas Eve debacle was the single incident which awakened the powers that be in the Miller family that something had to be done for me. It had finally dawned on them that I was crying out for help. However, what to do with me would be difficult, since they still thought it necessary to continue with the deception rather than finally telling me the truth.

****

I believe it was March, two months before my graduation from St. Mary's, that a sixth sense was telling me something was up. Twice, during class, our nun had left the room and was standing in the hall talking to a priest who was wearing a brown robe, rope belt, and sandals. Although he was Catholic, I had never seen this denomination before. He appeared to be looking at me, as though sizing me up. Little was I to know he really was evaluating me. To say I was surprised when Sister called me out of the room to meet him would be an understatement. He was tall, handsome, and had a ruggedness about him, even with all of his clergyman garb on. When he asked me if he could speak to me a few moments in private, I was definitely baffled. All I could think, since I was an altar boy, was that he probably wanted me to act as server for him at a mass he would say for someone.

We went to the Mother Superior's office (principal), where she excused herself so that we could be alone. He explained that he was from Saint Aloysious Junior Seminary in upstate New York. He also told me they were having a week long "workshop" this summer and would I be interested in attending? It sounded and looked great. The pictures depicted large, cathedral-type buildings set behind three massive lakes which made up the entrance to the seminary. They had a pool and an indoor gymnasium. The workshop would feature numerous religious-oriented projects with other individuals my age, with various sports and swimming interspersed. Little did I realize that the very first type of recruiter I would meet in my life would be one sent from God—a Priest. Without hesitation I told him I would love to go, feeling like I had been chosen above and beyond my other classmates. It never even dawned on me to ask him why he was choosing me, of all possible applicants, for this workshop. He simply told me to keep my grades up until my graduation and he would see me in the summer. That was the last I saw of him until the workshop.

I could hardly wait to get home that day to inform anyone who would listen of my good fortune. My mom and dad would be so proud of me because I had been asked to attend a week-long workshop this summer at a seminary. Victoria and James both acted delighted that I had agreed to accept the invitation, and the anticipation was already beginning to surge through my body and consume me. Since Hugh was a senior in high school, he thought I was crazy. However, since it was a seminary, he also accepted and liked the idea. Amazingly, they even took me into Pottsville that weekend and bought me my first suit. This was unbelievable, all these good things happening to me at once. I realized they would eventually have to buy me a suit before I went into high school, but that was still five months away. For now, I was starting to feel good about myself, and a trip out of state, to New York, was only ten weeks away.

Graduation day finally arrived. Our teacher asked us to stand up and announce the high school we had chosen, and I, of course, said Nativity, like all my brothers and sisters before me. However, the anticipation of an actual vacation in New York state, away from home and all its inherent problems, was foremost in my mind. It never dawned on me to investigate why I was the one chosen for this event when there were several smarter classmates of mine who would probably have loved the chance.

****

It was like nothing I had ever seen before. Kids my age from all over the country, particularly the New England states. The junior seminary, which accepts students from all over the country, went from grades 9-12. Then two additional years of college spent there and off to Theology school, the last stop before being ordained a priest. The school, church, dormitories, and all school-owned facilities were beautiful, at least by this coal miners backward standards. We slept in dormitories. Each large room in the dorm had enough space for seven bunk-beds, fourteen total "vacation occupants." We awoke at seven each morning, with mass starting at 8:00. At mass, it was very lively, unlike St. Mary's. They played guitars, drums, pianos, all kinds of music, and I was in heaven. It was one of the first times I could ever recall enjoying going to church. Mass was followed by breakfast. This was made by real cooks, and served to your specifications. All during the day softball tournaments were held, mixed with swimming events and evening sing-alongs done to guitars. "If I had to script a perfect scenario away from Saint Clair, this would be it," I thought to myself.

All through the week it never dawned on me that I was here for a reason. My name wasn't pulled out of a hat by the bishop as a lucky contestant to appear representing the Roman Catholic Church for the diocese of Allentown. I was, simply put, in "hawg heaven."

Most of the kids there were really cool, since they were from New York City and surrounding metro areas. There was definitely no one there from the coal regions of Pennsylvania although I was acceptable due to my "keen" accent and sports prowess. In fact, I asserted myself as one of the leaders, definitely not a follower. During the week I befriended a kid quite like myself. His name was Robert Jacksta. He had a good personality, sense of humor, and, like me, was very athletic. He was from New York City and listening to him tell stories about this urban behemoth held my mouth open in awe.

One evening as we were lying in bed, Jacksta yelled over to me and asked what day I was reporting. I had no earthly idea what he was alluding to and told him so in no uncertain coal miner terms, "What da fuck are ya talkin' 'bout, Jacksta?"

At which point he replied, "Boy, are you keen Miller! Coming to the seminary in two months time and cursing like you do. We're gonna room together man!"

I still wasn't grasping it. Jacksta finally told me we are all meeting here this week as an "orientation" to our actually coming to school. This had nothing to do with me since I was enrolled at Nativity for my freshman year. Or was I?

"Wait a minute! What da fuck is goin' on here?" I actually jumped out of my bunk and ran to the nearest pay phone. Only problem was, believe it or not, with my sheltered life in the coal regions I never learned how to use a pay phone for long distance calls. Come to think of it, this is the farthest I had ever been away from home. When an operator finally made me understand about a collect call, I told her that is exactly what I needed. Since it was only about ten o'clock, Victoria answered.

"Mom, one a da kidz jest told me dis is a camp for students who enrolled here for school next year. Dat's not why I'm here, is it?"

Fully expecting her to say "No, not at all," I was exasperated when she said, "Yes, Patrick, it's what we tink is best for you."

When I finally regained my composure I told her I didn't think I would be cut out for the life of a priest. "Hell, what will da boyz tink when dey hear dis?" I thought. Honestly, being enrolled in a seminary was the absolute last thing or place I could possibly think of being at.

"Man, I'm gonna miss a chance ta play sports against my friends." A lot of weird emotions were going through my mind, and my friends were at the core of them rather than my family.

****

When I returned home after my week-long vacation at the seminary, several things became clear. My going to Saint Aloysious was an edict from above, nothing could be done to stop it. Also, all the paperwork necessary had been processed without my ever having witnessed it. I was six weeks away from a world I had no idea existed, let alone me being part of it. My family was hoping I could stay long enough so as not to endure the inevitable that would happen in Saint Clair. I would be alone in a strange state, strange environment, strange people, and definitely different from the high school of my visions. To me, this wasn't the end, just the beginning of the end. No friends, no future, no money, no class, no life!!!!! I had to convince James and Victoria this was a drastic mistake.

My immediate future had been planned for me. It would be spent away from the physical anguish and alcoholic delusions of those people I knew as my parents. The theory of the junior seminary and the facilities of the estate were very good. But the people there were an awful lot different from me—in all aspects! Money, social status, etiquette, you name it.

About the only thing I would have on my side would be street smarts—since I had been around the block a time or two already—and my fierce competitive nature. If I had to, I would accept this challenge and do my best to win. If winning was the priesthood, the Catholic Church would have to prepare for the horse of a different color, a left-of-center-priest-kinda-guy.

It would have been a whole lot more fun going to Nativity and meeting women from all around Schuylkill County. I knew at that early age the scent of a woman would definitely be more appealing than the scent of 150 men. Although not having lost my virginity yet, I was definitely in that grey area bordering on adolescence in full bloom. The thought of losing it was sounding and feeling more attractive with each passing day. This venture into the great, frozen, snowy north was something I would not have dreamed of in a million years.

To make the situation seem right, Victoria decided that the element of surprise would allow me to believe this was good for me and my family. Since my mother already had a daughter who was a nun, wouldn't it be wonderful if Patrick would get "the call" and become a priest? Therefore, my departure for the seminary 250 miles from Saint Clair would be a wonderful place for them to ensure my safety and well being.

The only person from "da boyz" with whom I would have entered freshman year at Nativity was Mark Ryscavage. All the others would go through the Saint Clair Area Public School System. Shot Colna was a sophomore at Saint Clair. Pretzel Bender was also a sophomore on his way to becoming a legend in Saint Clair basketball folklore. Binky Wolfe was entering his freshman year at Saint Clair. Horse Lowthert was in the same class as Pretzel Bender. Peanuts Bender was a year behind us, just entering eighth grade. Eddie da Head was going to a special education school in Port Carbon. I rarely saw him after that.

Everything would have been as scripted in a movie. Mark and I against Pretzel, Bink, Peanuts, and an assortment of other quadrants we had got to know over time. The new scenario being presented to me was leaving me in a win/lose mode. I win if I leave the tragedy unfolding at the Miller house. I lose if I stay and have to endure the pain and sadness, even though staying would see some of my visions coming true. The thought of competing against our friends made Mark and me excited. We would like nothing better.

I was in a quandary. The path of least resistance was the seminary. The path of most fun, albeit emotional sometimes, would be going to Nativity. However, since I had never seen any of the paperwork from either place, my gut reaction placed me in New York state. For some reason, I realized my fate had been sealed the first day I turned around and saw the priest looking at me. Of course, it would be win-win for Victoria if I went. I would no longer be around the house in a very static-filled environment. The various areas of miscommunication among all of us would cease. Victoria, Peter, and I would be taking a mutual hiatus from one another. However, it was Victoria and James's decision from the outset. I would attend the seminary and the family would take pride in my "calling."

****

"The Priesthood. Father Patrick." I kept running it through my mind and nothing was there but blanks. Although an altar boy, I was by no means overly religious. I knew in my mind and in my heart I was meant to be with women, many of them if possible, and this was not the avenue to take to achieve this. Also, I knew I was not of the same cut, class if you will, of these other boys. Their parents were all young and vibrant. Very religious, very gung-ho. My parents wouldn't even be able to accompany me on the day we were to report. I had about four weeks left to do something.

The simple fact of the matter is that I was ready to leave. Even in my immaturity, I realized this was a way out of Saint Clair. It wasn't the glorious way I had hoped for: lining up against my friends in sports, meeting other kids from my region living in other towns.

Now I would be meeting kids from all over the country, every one of whom had grown up to know a better standard of living than me. Also, these kids would be going to this junior seminary because they wanted to.

There was no doubt in my mind that I was destined to be a "rebel with a cause." Now as I analyze it, the cause would be a simple word, "time." I was buying time until I could return home. I had to make a decision which would be best for me under very peculiar circumstances, and I had ultimately no say in the decision. James had become my pseudo-father and would make the decision in this matter. Victoria had made her opinion known long since.

None of my friends knew about the plan until shortly before I was to leave. When they found out, the shock never wore off them either.

My biggest concern was to get James to listen to reason before I was to depart. Hell, I'd even apologize for something to him. Just what, I don't know. Or Victoria. Although ill, she surely would understand me wanting to stay. I was sure we could work things out with a little communication and understanding. I truly believed things would turn out for the better, although there was no denying Peter and Victoria were deteriorating rapidly.

In retrospect, James made the correct call. There was just too much illness in our house on Patterson Street for a thirteen year old boy to understand. I know I sometimes portray James as cold and calculating. However, this one time I believe he truly had my best interest in mind. Peter was becoming increasingly unmanageable and his mood swings were erratic. Victoria, on the other hand, became more mellow and subdued due to her alcohol addiction. She was actually becoming a fairly easy person to deal with. All considered—good call, James.

Many emotions flowed through me when I realized I would be

leaving home, my parents, and all my friends. I had firmly believed I could be a star in all sports my freshman year at Nativity. Also bothering me was the thought of not having any female classmates to lust after. I was definitely hitting a period of my life where the question of losing one's virginity was no longer a choice, it was a necessity. A school full of boys in dorm rooms was really not registering at this point. And I wasn't even thinking of the true, full-blown picture: early morning rise for mass, rigid classroom requirements, regimented study halls, definite bedtimes (which I never had before in my life), and no alcohol. Ouch! No women, no booze, church every morning and studying every night. Talk about discipline. Where were the sports, swimming, and sing alongs?

After realizing I would be going to this school I became very apprehensive. Other than the "vacation" this past summer, I had never been this far away for more than a week, let alone a full school semester. To break away from this region after a college education or a lucky break was unique. To break away during one's freshman year in high school was unfathomable.

I only had about three weeks left, and all my pleading to James and Victoria went for naught. My next course of action would have to be to inform "da boyz" of what I was about to embark upon. How to do this and what time was appropriate was another question indeed. I decided it could be done best when we were all drinking quarts, pontificating about the world in general. Besides, when people are drunk they tend to shrug off ridiculous statements such as I was about to make. However, when you are supposed to make the proclamation and you yourself are drunk, sometimes it backfires. Such was the case with me.

We were all at a beer party held at "The Catty," the fish hole where we caught the catfish to stock our dam with. When all "da boyz" were real tanked I decided to lay it on them. "Fellas, I'm not gonna be goin' ta Nativity dis year; I decided to enroll in da seminary."

Silence, glances exchanged, then extreme laughter like I had just told the best joke of my life. It was like a dagger had just been thrust through me because no one was buying what I had to say. They didn't even realize seminaries like this existed. They figured priests were born like grapes on a vine. Finally I convinced them I was not kidding, this is what I truly wanted to do. They thought I had lost my battle stations.

Next thing I remember, Pretzel Bender made the truest statement of his life. "It's jest as well yur gettin' outta dare, cause the next couple years are gonna be hell ta pay." His prophecy would come true.

Another of my concerns was a simple matter of survival. I had terrible sleep habits already. Trying to conform to a 7:00 A.M. wake up call could be hell on a person like me. On regular school days I got out of bed at 7:30 for 8:30 classes. Now I would have to get up a half hour earlier and make my bed. In short, I was about to embark upon a totally different type of discipline, and it would have to be done with no family or friends around. I felt it was right and my duty to go, but I really didn't understand why. I also would have to totally readjust my nighttime habits since I was sure they would have a curfew. "Probably 11:00," I thought. "'Nough time ta take a dip in da pool, listen ta some guitar playin', then catch some Z's." Also, being accountable for my laundry, bed, personal items, all this would be new to me. I constantly lost sight of the fact this was a place where one went to become a priest, that there were bound to be some sort of prayer meetings. There were new clothes which would need to be purchased, new shoes, ties, a whole "new" look. I was still having a difficult time accepting the fact that there would be no women around since I was about to take the leap into puberty.

I also had concern about their sports program. With only 150 total students enrolled, what kind of sports teams would we field? What's my chances of makin' the varsity my freshman year? I was having delusionary thoughts about where I was going since the only time I had been there was a vacation of sorts, a big party.

The thought of the total culture shock I was about to encounter never entered my mind. Although what was about to happen to me would certainly test all the mental, physical, and emotional boundaries of my masculinity, it provided two things that were definitely lacking in my life—guidance and supervision. I was about to encounter what the words "work ethic" truly meant.

Since "da boyz" and I had started drinking beer fairly regularly that summer (nightly), I would also be kissing my inebriated fulfillment away. I could see why everyone in town seemed to drink. It was really fun to be with your friends and walk back down into town totally spent. I could actually go back in to the confines of home at night now and ignore all the goings on around me. Unfortunately alcohol was all around me, widely accepted, so it was much easier for me to rationalize. Fortunately it was only alcohol back then, for if drugs had been popular (marijuana was just becoming the counterculture thing to do), I am sure I would also have resorted to them as a "quick-fix" to those problems going on inside of me. Even if I had gone to Nativity, drinking would be widely accepted although it was a Catholic school. This new pastime and way of release would diminish just when I was really getting into it. What I didn't realize was that seminarians are regular people, too. In New York state at that time the legal drinking age was eighteen. Therefore, the seniors in the school could go into a bar and get beer for us. Although I was not aware of this at the time, it sure would come in handy later.

I had no tests which needed to be taken for my admission, only a week's vacation to look the place over. Suddenly I began to feel as if this deal wasn't all it appeared to be on the surface. More than my appearance at this school would be needed for my survival. I would have to learn a whole new skill: gaining acceptance in a group where absolutely no one knows your credentials. Just being tough was not going to scare anybody in this case. One would also have to be smart.

****

When I was within one week of reporting and all of the town seemed to have learned my destiny, I felt very awkward. Kids my age were making jest of my situation, the thought of me going away to a place where priests are bred. To the elders I was revered. Most were treating me like all their Rosaries and Novenas had been answered. Victoria was especially proud because she would have both a daughter and son "receive the call."

Peter was able to comprehend very little at this point but he did seem able to perceive that I would be going away. I was starting to feel very sorry about the way I chose to lash back at him, threatening him at times. After all, this was still my father and inherent manners bred in me stated I respect him for that. I was beginning to get a bad case of the guilts for the way I treated him since I was within a week of leaving home for an extended period of time.

At this point a girl I had a terrible crush on in grade school moved into the house directly linked to ours. Her name was Janice Culbert and I was bonkers over her. She was entering her sophomore year at Nativity, but we had known each other while attending Saint Mary's. She was tall, thin, and beautiful. Just the smell of her when she would pass by our stoop sent a unique feeling through my body. She was the first woman I can recall having any physical feelings toward. I didn't understand the feelings but I did know they made me feel good. For some reason she always took the time to stop and talk with me and would eventually become a very valuable person to Peter and Victoria in my absence. Over the course of the years I was to be away she became an ear piece to Victoria, someone to listen to her since everybody except James would be gone.

Hugh had graduated and was to be drafted into the Army. Jocelyn got a job in Pottsville. Although she was still living in the house, she was rarely there. Over the course of my visits home I would increase my thoughts of lust for the beautiful Janice. I did sense she was keen to my thoughts toward her, and she never dissuaded me from my obvious interest.

The day before I left, a party was held in our back yard. Most of "da boyz" had a chance to stop down and a lot of the Miller family attended. I didn't know whether to feel like a hero or a scapegoat. Most could not believe I was doing this. My family kept ribbing me about it being the first time I'd ever be away from home. No friends, no sports, no booze. "No life," is the way I was already beginning to feel.

****

The next morning, James and Hugh drove me the four hours to New York state. Jocelyn gave me a hug and wished me the best. Victoria was interspersing crying with praying due to her latest coup of getting me away from there. Also, if I liked it and became a priest, kudos for her.

The absolute toughest goodbye of my life however, would be the one between Peter and me. Not only did I already have the guilts, I believe he was feeling sorry for all he had done to me in the past. I also felt like he believed it was his fault I was being sent away. His head was bent down toward his lap when I reached down and took his strong hand in mine and shook it. When he looked up at me saliva was dripping from his mouth and he had tears coming out of the eye where the ducts were still functioning. Peter was crying. I couldn't figure out if it was because of all the tough roads we'd been down and he was showing respect for me, or if it was because he knew he would never see me in this setting again. His condition would deteriorate to where he would barely recognize me on my trips home. In any event, I truly believe it was also Peter's way of saying simply, "Sorry, son."

As we drove away with me looking out the back window and waving to everyone, I returned Peter's tears with my own. For it was at this moment of my departure we learned that we truly did love and respect one another.

SECTION II

PUBERTY
ADOLESCENCE
EARLY ADULTHOOD

CHAPTER FOUR

Father Patrick?????

"Welcome to Saint Aloysious, Patrick. My name is Father Nicholas and I am your dormitory captain. I will be in charge of your health and well-being while you are here at school and, as such, will inform you of our rules and regulations. First, let's get your belongings put upstairs and I'll show your father around."

"Geez, tanks Fodder, but dis ain't my dad, he'z my brudder, James. Dis is my udder brudder (sounds like a candy bar), Hugh. I don't have a whole lot a stuff so we can get da tour outta da way quick. My brudder's got a long drive back ta Saint Clair."

I told him the name of my home town like it was a major metropolitan area, and by the quizzical looks I was getting from this priest, I felt like he thought I was the consummate country bumpkin. I had no earthly idea that Father Nicholas would become my worst possible nightmare—a priest with a huge ego and an attitude. Father Nick would be the first martinet I would ever be exposed to, but definitely not the last.

James and Hugh took the "quick tour" and were on their way within an hour. I didn't even have a chance to feel lonely before Nick explained the rules. After being told what they were and the seriousness which should be shown them, desolation immediately set in. A normal school day would begin at 5:45 A.M. with mass beginning at 6:30.

When the bell rang, I had 45 minutes to shower, shave, make my bed, and be in church. If late, or the bed was not made to the satisfaction of Fodder Nick, one was penalized and given extra detail which would cut into one's free time. After mass, breakfast. Study hall went from 7:45 to 8:25, classes beginning at 8:30. Lunch at noon, classes until 3:30. All intense—both students and teachers. Monday, Wednesday, and Friday were for activities: sports, fishing, whatever the student was interested in. Tuesday and Thursday were for work details. Dinner was at 5:30. By 6:30, everyone had to be at study hall which lasted until 9:00. Lights out at 10:00, except Friday and Saturday, 11:00.

I was dead in the water. I had never been exposed to this type of regimen, especially the time changes. I'd never disciplined myself on how to study. I'd never worked at any manual labor except building a two-story hut and a dam to accommodate fish. Now I was going to have to be accountable in a militaristic type of setting. It was unfortunate that Fodder Nick and I would never see eye-to-eye. I wasn't in the mood for an intimidating personality after what I'd gone through at home. If any of us under ''Nick da Prick's'' (what a majority of us came to call him) supervision became too extreme a discipline problem, he was wont to give us several extremely hard licks with his thick leather belt. I even witnessed Nick punch Izzy Velasquez, one of my dormmates, in the face because he believed Izzy was lying to him about something.

My educational experience at the junior seminary left me with a strong animosity toward the Catholic Church. Don't get me wrong, I believe in God and that there is definitely a force which controls our destiny. However, after my seminary experience, I would not be attracted toward any denomination. I want the person who is preaching to also be a motivational force in my life, and there are very few out there who can do this.

In a matter of a few short weeks, I managed to hit rock bottom emotionally. My life seemed to be going exactly opposite of what I'd hoped for—doing things to make my family, especially my parents, proud. Now I was in a totally different environment than I was accustomed to, with no understanding of why.

The second day I was at the seminary a young man introduced himself as Mike Broderick, my designated big brother. ''Brod,'' as everyone called him, will never know the role he played in getting me to understand what I was up against and what it would take to beat the system. From day one I was extremely lonely, and Brod realized this within two weeks. He was from Long Island and could not possibly visualize how I grew up. His life was as strange to me. I wasn't used to expressing myself to anyone other than my friends or family. This guy was trying to figure me out and help me conform to the system. But I didn't know how to open up or express myself. Anyone trying to get close to me would have a very difficult time. I had gone into a shell.

All my free time was spent in the gym, shooting basketball. The gym was a dungeon beneath the dormitory, the perfect place for a lonely kid to hang out. If I was alone, I would fantasize games against teams I would be playing this year if I'd been at home. I did not have a clue what they were teaching in school nor did I care. I knew that I was totally different from these kids both intellectually and socially. Brod, fortunately, would help me a great deal. Each night, when I went to the gym, he would come down and challenge me one on one. During the games, and over the course of the first several months, he would ask questions. Eventually, he realized I did not want to be there, and tried to help me. He was a junior, very mature for his age, and I was a freshman. He did a great job in bringing a scared, lonely kid from the coal region out of his shell. Brod was extremely good in sports and we played on the same football and basketball teams. For a school of only 150 boys, we had extremely talented athletes. I decided to completely ignore all studies in lieu of sports. It was easy for me to rationalize flunking as an easy way out.

There was no Junior Varsity team like most high schools had. I was fortunate to make the varsity as a freshman in both sports. This also helped in bringing me out of my shell. However, this was from a sports angle only, definitely not scholastic. I had no idea that playing sports for Saint Aloysious would open my eyes to a completely different culture. Due to our small size, the only teams we would play against were other seminaries in New York state, and, unbelievably, prisons, prisons which housed men sixteen years of age and older. The thought of having to play sports against convicts did not sit well with me, since it was apparent they were incarcerated for something other than stealing candy from the local grocery store.

Our second football game was played at a large prison. Fortunately, just the players and their families were allowed to the field, not the entire prison population. Since I was playing defensive back, I had a chance to evaluate the surroundings while standing on the sidelines. I couldn't help notice that one of the "chain-gang," those responsible for the first down chains, was a young boy who appeared to be my age. He was Caucasian, definitely the minority within these walls. It seemed to me he could not possibly belong there; he was too young and innocent looking. During the second quarter, while standing on the sidelines watching our offense not perform, he was right in front of me holding the first down marker. He seemed very similar to me so I asked him how old he was, and he replied seventeen. That is where my nerve seemed to end, but he could sense in me the need to ask why he was here. He volunteered the information that he murdered his mother and stepfather last year. They tried him as an adult and he got forty years. I was shocked to such an extent that on our next defensive series their wide receiver blew by me en route to a seventy-five yard touchdown reception. For the rest of the game I wasn't myself. This incident would help me put a lot of things in perspective. First, my situation was not near as bad as I perceived it to be. For the remainder of the game I was useless, however. We got the shit kicked out of us. Playing against convicted felons who had nothing to lose in hurting you was an intimidating situation. The things they would say in between plays and during time-outs had all of us wanting to forfeit and get out of there. Brod, for our team, was the only one willing to talk back at them trying to wake us up, but we were all scared as hell.

It crossed my mind what "da boyz" would say if they could see me now. Inside prison walls with guards and guns everywhere, playing football against criminals. On top of this, I meet a kid I think looks a lot like myself, and he tells me he murdered his parents. This had all the setting for an Alfred Hitchcock movie.

****

After one semester, due to help from Brod, I was finally acclimating myself. The first month was mental hell, but I'd developed a personality and realized I dealt easily with people. All I had to do was be myself. I now had many new friends and a chance to see most of New York through visits to their homes. It was easy for us to take a bus or bum a ride with one of the priests who were going out to Long Island or into the City. The first time I stood at the base of the Empire State Building I felt like I'd finally made it to the mountain. That, and the inside of Madison Square Garden made me feel like a world traveler although I was only three hours from Saint Clair. I was learning that there was a whole different world than I was used to. I had been sheltered in the coal regions of Pennsylvania where repetition is the norm and had no idea that visiting cities in other areas of our country was a possibility.

Unfortunately, by my Christmas break my first semester grades were horrendous. I had gotten an F, two D's and two C's in the major courses I was taking and was placed on probation already by Father Robert, the principal. What the powers that be didn't realize is that I didn't care. It was in my best interest to get an early exit by flunking out. The only real problem would be explaining to James and Victoria how I'd only made one year in what was supposedly "my calling." By the time I went home for Christmas break, there was also a noticeable change in my character, a positiveness about me. It was in the way I walked and in how I presented myself verbally to others. I was no longer afraid to say what was on my mind. Although my grammar was still a nightmare, I was sure of myself and what I was discussing. Being away these four months helped me mature immensely. Sadly, the trips to Saint Clair would become increasingly more difficult due to the continuing deterioration within the household.

****

Although I was terribly lonely for home, being there was a very difficult situation to deal with. Only Jocelyn and James were still there, and Peter was becoming increasingly difficult in all aspects. These were difficult times since Peter would frequently need help with bathing and other necessities. Victoria was too weak, and alcohol had totally taken her over. Therefore, Jo and James were being forced to deal with the difficulties in handling Peter. Although very ill, his mind had not totally deteriorated because he still recognized me when I entered the room and actually seemed to perk up. Shortly, after the Christmas break, Peter would suffer yet another stroke in a series which would span a six-year period.

I could also sense static involving Victoria and James, but I could not figure out the root cause. They were not going to volunteer this information to me. I asked Jo if she thought anything appeared weird and she was quick to answer no. If she knew, she wasn't going to volunteer anything either.

All of my friends were currently involved with their respective basketball teams, as I would be when I got back. My stories about playing football against convicts blew their minds, as did the stories of traveling around the state of New York.

I saw Janice Culbert frequently during Christmas since she was wont to spend more time in our house with Victoria. Her mother was single, living with another man, and was abusive to her. Janice drank tea while Victoria would go through her daily bottle of brandy. I became increasingly attracted to her and there was no hiding this since Jo sensed it also and commented about it. Although I was becoming adjusted to seminary life and its disciplined ways, there was something about a pretty, long-legged young woman that appealed to me a whole lot more. It would be difficult for me to explain to Victoria why her son who got "the call," was going into heat over her young friend from next door. Therefore, I chose fantasizing as my immediate cure-all. However, I knew that this situation was not resolved. It all hinged on the extent of my tenure in the seminary. I decided to do whatever it took to terminate my stay in New York. It was a nice school with a great bunch of guys, but there is just something about when a young man in adolescence gets the scent of a woman and all the urges that go with it for the first time. There is virtually nothing that can be done to stop him from his mission!

****

We were now into another semester at school, and the weather had changed noticeably. I was used to cold and snow in Pennsylvania, but nothing can compare to the freezing conditions of New York state. No amount of clothing can possibly be worn to protect you. Due to my poor grades the first semester, Nick da Prick was riding me hard. I was consistently pulling extra work detail and he was always in my face about one thing or another.

Although I was maturing in a lot of ways, I still didn't know how to study, and I was not grasping any of the difficult courses which were being taught me. My negative attitude toward being there didn't help the situation either. It was becoming obvious that Father Nick and I were headed for disaster. I don't deal well with constant negative reinforcement. Although dressing someone down is necessary some-times, it should be carried out in the proper manner and in a private setting. It should not be done on a consistent basis like Father Nick was doing.

Although my grades were deficient, I was still allowed to play basketball. The powers that be realized sports was the only release I had and believed it would be best for my mental attitude if I were allowed. Nick da Prick, who believed the only way to discipline someone was hurt them in such a way that it affected their mental attitude and, by intimidation, wore the person into conforming, did not approve.

****

There is nothing more awesome than playing against inmates of a prison in football other than visiting the prison to play them in basketball. At these games, they allowed the entire population of the prison to attend. The team and the spectator population was predominately black or Hispanic. I was very, very scared. I didn't know prejudice, but these people did. They were shouting insults at us like I'd never heard before. On several occasions, during warm-ups, fights broke out among the inmates, and the guards were forced to discipline them. I was thoroughly rattled and could not imagine even playing tiddlywinks under these conditions. On one occasion, I stole the ball from their guard and was en route to an easy break-away lay up. The player I stole the ball from became very offended and decided I would not score an easy two. He caught up to me upon my shot attempt and pulled a cheap, flagrant foul across my face, then landing on me. Why I let it affect me, I don't know, but I immediately got in his face. I was going to have no part of a cheap shot now, or ever. Apparently, this guy was a prison bad-ass, because all the spectators immediately rose to their feet to see what would ensue. He was at least eighteen and me just a tall, skinny kid. He'd probably been in a hundred fights and Lord only knows what he was in there for. However, I was about to go into one of those "loss of consciousness" zones where pain and time become irrelevant. Before that could happen, guards had pounced on him and my teammates on me. The place had become virtual chaos in a matter of seconds and I was the focal point. I was awarded three foul shots for his flagrant foul and he was tossed.

On his way out he told me, in no uncertain terms, he wouldn't forget me and would see me when they played on our home court. I was still pissed and told him I looked forward to it. I was obviously not in my right mind. This guy would just as soon kill me as have to look at me. I don't think he had your typical fist fight in mind. When I came out of the game the insults were unbelievable. They were spitting at me. It was the first time I felt true prejudice. If nothing else, this was enough reason for me to realize I never wanted to do anything that would place me behind walls permanently.

When that same prison did come to play at our gym, several of their spectators gained access to our dormitory rooms and stole virtually everything of value while the game was being played. I was one of the first to realize my valuables were gone, and their warden was notified immediately. There was a shakedown on the bus on the way back to the prison and everything was retrieved. We received a letter of apology from the warden but that didn't quite cut it for me. These people had violated my privacy and stolen the few valuables I had. I made a conscious decision at that moment in my life I would never "borrow" anything again. I vowed to earn every dollar that passed through my hand and that I would never take anything that was not rightfully due me.

****

Basketball ended and spring break was upon me. I had heard of Peter's third stroke by telephone and figured it would be best if I went home instead of to a friend's. There were other reasons for needing to be home. Susan just had her second child, a little boy, and I was anxious to see him. I desperately needed to see Janice to ensure no one had moved in on her. From what I'd heard, Peter was in a very weakened state although he was home again. He was able to stand for brief stretches. However, walking proved difficult. His sensory perceptions were all but dead, and his speech was virtually nonexistent.

Hugh was stationed at Fort Indiantown Gap, Pennsylvania. The base was only forty-five minutes from Saint Clair and Hugh was able to help out with Peter once again. This helped Jocelyn immensely, since she had a difficult task working and coming home to the stress there. With Victoria being so dependent on alcohol and pills in her day to day routine, Jocelyn became the female focal point of the house. She had to cook, clean, take care of Peter, take care of James and all the extras he demanded, and try to maintain some semblance of a life to keep her sanity intact.

Most of the family was home to greet me (or to see my reaction). Susan was bubbly due to her new child and his good health, and I would be his godparent for the baptism to ensue. This would be great, the future "Fodder Patrick" being a godparent for one of his nephews. As I walked toward the living room and the couch where Susan and

John's child was obviously lying, that slow motion record began to play again. Victoria was there, Peter was sitting in his chair by the window close to the TV, Susan, Hugh, Clarice, a lot of my family was standing in that one small room. I looked past them toward the couch where my new godson was lying. The record virtually died in my mind. All sound ceased. All people seemed to be staring—waiting and wondering. There were two children lying on the couch. One had a hospital name tag on which said Sims, Susan and John's, and the other said Miller. My first thought was, "Hmmm. What a neat surprise. I wonder which of my udder brudders had a kid without me knowin' it?" Words cannot describe the confusion I felt upon hearing the infamous sentence from Victoria's mouth: "Dis, Patrick, is yer new baby brudder, Adrian."

My head was spinning. Although going to school to become a missionary for God, I had learned enough from "da boyz" and my seminary friends to know how children were born. I immediately asked whose it really was. Victoria was now in a real quandary, because she probably thought I would just accept this and believe it was theirs. I'm sorry, even naive old me was able to realize this could not be possible.

I was waiting for an explanation from someone. James finally spoke up: "Mudder and fodder have accepted responsibility for da child. Itz a close friend a da family's." I persisted, but no one was talking. (It was perhaps during this period that Susan was told the real story of me. Possibly Hugh, although to this day he swears he didn't know until I found out and questioned him about it.)

It was obvious that no one was going to tell me. It was not until the day I found out about myself, many years later, that I also demanded, and was told, the truth about his parenthood. However, I would not be told by James. He would continue to repeat the lies. I finally would elicit the truth from Susan, whose guilt on her conscience would be just too much to bear.

I'd even pumped Janice about Adrian. She knew as little as I, since everyone realized I would probably turn to her for the truth. If Victoria did tell her during a stuporous moment, Janice never informed me. She was now dating a sophomore at Nativity and, as she was relaying this to me, I could sense she was aware of how it was tearing me apart. She knew I was her toy and she could play with me as she pleased. She also knew if I left the seminary due to her, she would never be forgiven by the Miller family. Therefore, the game would continue with me always on the losing end.

When I questioned the friends I still saw on my rounds of the town and bars, they knew nothing either. One of them even suggested the possibility of him being Janice's. Believe it or not, this theory actually made sense until Mark Ryscavage informed me she was definitely not pregnant, since they shared some of the same classes at Nativity. It never dawned on any of my friends to question my existence, either. With them seeing my parents and the condition they were in, they certainly could have been aware that something was wrong. In Saint Clair, we naturally accepted things for what they were.

****

I went back to the seminary for the last portion of my freshman year with a new brother at home. Fortunately, none of my fellow students were aware of my home environment, so explanations would not be needed. I had decided not to play baseball in order to try to bring my studies up to an acceptable level.

In New York state a student could not progress to the next level without successfully passing the State Board of Regents Exam, a comprehensive test which covered all major areas of subjects we had taken over the course of the year. It was by no means easy and I had to pass this for movement into my sophomore year. I still had never learned how to study and was afraid to ask for help. The school tried tutoring me but nothing seemed to stick. From a scholastic viewpoint, I was in way over my head. No matter how hard I tried, I was just not grasping the complexity of the subjects I was taking. Over the course of a two-month period, I retained virtually nothing. I failed the Regents exam miserably and was not in good standing with Nick da Prick, nor Fodder Robert, our principal.

It was right before I took the Regents Exam that Nick's path and mine finally collided, the night he punched Izzy Velasquez in the face. When Nick punched Izzy, I immediately got in his face. First, to inform him that Izzy wasn't lying to him (I believe I was yelling at him), then to tell him if he wanted someone to blame and punch, I'd prefer he do it to me. Due to my past with Peter, I don't take well to people being abused, especially when the abuse is due to something they did not precipitate. When Nick hit Izzy, he basically tried him without a jury of his peers. He became the judge, jury, and executioner. Although Nick had at least twenty years on me, I was ready to give him the fight of his life. With me, he wasn't going to get a cherry, rather, someone who was used to being hit and able to block out the pain until the incident would be over. Also, I didn't care if I got thrown out. Nick, unfortunately, came to his senses with the crowd of students all around us. I became somewhat of a hero to my classmates for standing up to Nick da Prick. What I had going for me is that Nick was wrong in what he did, and the hierarchy of the school was well aware of this. They severely chastised him for his behavior. They couldn't touch me since I was sticking up for Izzy. Nick would now develop a serious case of red-ass toward me that would continue until my departure.

After the results of the Regents exam, Father Robert invited me to his office to discuss my future. School would be out for the summer soon, and I had not successfully completed the requirements for advancement in the state of New York.

Father Robert was a no-nonsense type of principal who got right to the point. "Patrick, you have done miserably in your studies. On top of that, you are a malcontent. Your defiance of Father Nicholas has not been received well by the remainder of the faculty. It is my recommendation, due to your attitude and the grades you have received, that you be dismissed from our school."

Although I knew this was coming, the reality of having to leave school because I was a failure hit hard. Moreover, Nick da Prick would seek his revenge in the easiest way possible, getting rid of me. However, Father Robert informed me there was one other alternative available to me if I chose to do it: repeat my freshman year while my classmates and friends advanced. If I chose to leave the seminary, my grades were good enough to advance to my sophomore year at Nativity, they just weren't good enough for seminary school or the state of New York. If I did this, I would accept being a failure but I wouldn't have to explain to James and Victoria. If I chose to come back and prove to myself and my peers I could do it, I would have to explain why I would still be a freshman. Actually, the decision on what I would do was made years earlier when we were taught never to accept failure or defeat as an alternative. I would rather go through my freshman year five times than accept the stigma of being a failure.

****

Over the course of the summer, I was able to get James and Victoria to accept the fact that I was being held back. They were not pleased. However, since I was not walking away from "my calling," it helped to ease their obvious displeasure.

Overall, the summer was a total bummer since Janice had definitely found a boyfriend. We would talk daily, but each night he would pick her up, and it cut me down at the knees. Just the thought of her being with another man was eating me alive. The possibility of her doing anything else with this man was destroying me. I knew I was diminishing any chances of ever being with her if I went back for another year of seminary school. Although it was destroying me mentally, my pride was my main concern, even above my virginity.

I would run into many of my friends at the nightly beer parties in town. I was often the focal point for many a barb. It was ironic I was studying to be a priest while holding a quart of beer in my hand. No one found out that I would be repeating my freshman year. I was something of an enigma in my home town. They were aware of my religious education and stories about playing sports against prisons. Since none of them could possibly fathom what it was like, I was considered a different breed of cat.

****

On the first day of my next year at the seminary, several things were clearly obvious. I had changed in both appearance and maturity. I was facing this year as a challenge. I was going to prove the "Doubting Thomases" wrong. My goal was to excel in both my classroom studies and sports. I was resigned to getting through this year successfully and then getting out. After this past summer, I realized how much I missed home and my family. It was no longer a matter of simple immature loneliness. I had something to prove to myself first, and then I was gone.

I also became acutely aware that they needed me at home to help take care of Peter. I was becoming strong and strength would be an asset when assisting with him. Where before I was needed out of the picture, now I was badly needed. Peter was very frail and his body functions were virtually useless. The sooner this year was over, the sooner I would bid goodbye to these many friends I had made, and I could try to make a serious play for the affection of my first true puppy love. These were the short term goals I had set for myself upon my return from vacation.

Against Nick da Prick's wishes, I was allowed to move upstairs in the huge dormitory to the semi-private, upper classmen rooms. This atmosphere would make it much easier to incorporate study habits conducive to my night habits, since there was no lights out. The only rule was that we had to be in our rooms by 10:00 on a weeknight. Although I was upstairs, I was still under Nick's jurisdiction. I truly believe he was shocked when I decided to come back and repeat. He probably thought I would quit and go away. There would be no doubt that he would be gunning for me since the incident involving Izzy.

I would also be mentally prepared to play football and basketball against convicts. For some reason the young kid image had vanished over the past year and I now looked older, filled out in my body proportions. I now stood 6'3'' and weighed right at 200 pounds. No more the tall, skinny kid, I was now confident that I could handle myself in any situation—be it sports or personal. If an inmate wished to get in my face and talk trash with me, "lets rock" was my attitude. If Nick wanted to test me and see how far he could push me before I pushed back, it wouldn't take a lot since I'd already lost my respect for him.

****

The situation with my "new brudder Adrian" was constantly gnawing at the back of my mind. I often wondered whose child this was since it was obviously not Victoria's nor Janice's. The fact no one would discuss this with me piqued my curiosity all the more.

****

When I started my second year of seminary school I also became aware of other situations which I failed to notice the first year. When someone endorses a vow of celibacy, make no mistake about it, that's an awful big promise to live up to. It was during the initial semester of my second year that I learned that homosexuality truly exists in today's society. Throughout my childhood we frequently used the word "homo" as a form of expression toward another person we were trying to put down. This year the word "homo" would take on an entirely different meaning. This year a real "homo" would make a play toward me and awaken me to a counterculture of society.

It happened on a weekday when we were assigned to our various workcrews. On this particular day, I was assigned hauling dirt to various areas of the grounds. We got the dirt from an area that was approximately a half-mile away from the school buildings. The leader of our crew was a senior, David Buckner. David seemed to be a normal guy who was trying to follow his "calling." I should have been aware something was wrong when the bell rang to end our work shift and David released everyone back to their rooms but me. This would be yet another time when the record that was playing would go from 33 to 78 and time literally moved in slow motion. I was sitting atop a huge mound of dirt when David began his spiel.

> David: "Patrick, how old are you?"

> Patrick: "I just turnt tirteen dis summer David. Why?"

> David: "Have you ever had a woman yet?"

> Patrick: "What da ya mean, Dave?"

> David: "I mean, have you ever slept with and made love to a woman?"

> Patrick (sheepishly): "Trutfully, Dave, no. But I tink about it often."

> David: "Well then, since you haven't, how would you like a blowjob so you will know what it feels like when a woman does it to you?"

> Patrick: "Scuse me, Dave?"

> David: "What I'm trying to say is, I'd really like to suck your cock. I have a real safe place we can go to, so that no one will ever know or find out, if you don't tell them."

> Patrick (very worried): "Whatdaya mean a safe place, Dave?"

> David: "Follow me and I'll show you."

It hadn't dawned on me that I might be leading him on by asking him what he meant by a safe place, but my curiosity was getting the best of me. He proceeded to lead me to an old storage shed which was located on the grounds. He took me down into the basement and through a maze of junk—old school desks, chairs, abandoned religious artifacts, and the like. At the very back of the basement, well-concealed by this junk, was a single door. He opened the door and walked into a small room. He then screwed in a single bulb in the ceiling. After my eyes adjusted to the light, I realized David had created his own "masturbation paradise." The room was very small but immaculate. There was a single bed there and a chair, basically all that could fit. I noticed a book lying on the bed and was able to make out the title, "Lady Chatterly's Lover."

It was at this point I realized the trouble I might have gotten into by allowing him to show me his private sex cell. If I allowed him to do what he wanted, everything would be fine. Since I was not, I decided to do the only smart thing I could think of. I bolted from the room into the darkness of the basement, knocking everything down that was in my way. I never looked back toward David Buckner as I made my dash to the dormitory. I went to the only person I felt I could talk to about this without feeling like an idiot, my big brother, Mike Broderick.

I was very upset and Brod was trying to calm me down. After I related the story in an extremely hurried manner, he shook his head in disbelief. I told him about David's "blow job room" in the basement, and he had a hard time believing me. I asked him if he wanted to go see it right now and he said no, I better elevate this immediately. I should go to the principal, Father Robert, to do this since it was such a sensitive issue. Brod and I began wondering how many people David had managed to coerce, how many other students fell into his trap. In a world where very few females exist, homosexuality is bound to arise. However, why did it happen to me? What was it about me that attracted David?

Father Robert was out of town but I made it clear to Nick da Prick I needed to meet with him immediately upon his return. Nick seemed pleased by my request since he obviously thought I was ready to do my swan song, my denouement so to speak. In truth, I was afraid to speak to anyone except Brod about this, since it dawned on me I wouldn't be aware if I was speaking to another person who found males appealing. Now more than ever, I realized the need to finish this year successfully, prove myself to myself, and get to a world where interaction with women was a necessity. Women with beautiful faces, long legs, and huge American breasts. That's what I needed and this incident only deepened my desire toward achieving this goal.

Father Robert called me out of class so that we could have our meeting. I believe he also thought I was going to express my desire to leave the school. Twice during the previous evening David Buckner asked to speak with me alone, and both times I refused. After the second time, he realized that I was going to elevate this, not let it drop. I saw the fear in his eyes, the same fear he must have seen in mine after he opened the door to his room of perversions. This is the conversation that ensued between Father Robert and me.

Father Robert:

> "So Patrick, what can I do for you? Are you no longer happy with your situation here at our school?"

Patrick:

> "No, Fodder, it's not dat at all. I am happy wit da school. Somethin happened ta me yesterday dat made me extremely worried about my future here. It happened wit one a da seniors dat was in charge a my work detail."

Father:

> "Did someone say something to offend you or try to harm you in some fashion?"

Patrick:

> "Harm wouldn't be da proper term, Fodder, but he did try ta take advantage of me in anoder way."

Father:

> "Patrick, I don't know where this conversation is going so why don't you come right out and say what's on your mind. Who is the student and what did he do?"

Patrick:

> "Well Fodder, da student is David Buckner and yesterday he asked me if, well, ah, he asked me if, he asked if..........."

Father:

> "Patrick, don't be afraid, just say it and I'll respond."

Patrick:

> "Well, Fodder, he asked me if he could.......ya know, ah, well, he wanted ta...ya know."

Father:

> "Patrick, I don't know and I don't understand. Just come out and say it. I'm a grown man."

Patrick:

> "O.K., Fodder, I've never said anyting like dis ta a priest before, but here goes. He wanted ta know if he could, ya know, a...., he wanted ta know if he could suck my dick."

Somehow, after I finally said it, I got the feeling Father Robert thought I was making an issue out of something that could not possibly have happened. I felt he was trying to intimidate me into a recantation of what I'd just said, that I was greatly sensationalizing a situation, blowing it out of proportion.

Father:

> "Patrick, do you realize the severity of what you are telling me? Do you realize you are making a direct allegation against a student that has been here four years already, and this has never happened before? There is no possible way you can prove this since it is going to be your word against his."

Patrick (getting personally offended now):

> "Whaddaya mean, my word against his, Fodder? Dis guy wanted ta blow me yesterday and you're sittin' here tellin' me nuttin can be done? Da ya tink dat maybe he's done dis wit other students dat have been afraid ta tell ya, or what? Besides, it'z not my word against his because I do have proof."

Father:

> "What kind of proof do you have?"

Patrick:

"Folla me."

My attitude had suddenly gone from fear to anger. Unfortunately, I had no idea of the correct words I should have used during our conversation. The word "fellatio" obviously would have been appropriate, but I had never heard it. "Blow job" was what I thought the proper terminology was.

We proceeded to the building where David had shown me his private sex room the previous day. I now had Father Robert's attention since he became aware that I did have evidence of the allegations I was leveling. I knew immediately when we walked down into the dungeon that something was different from the way it was yesterday. Even with the clutter I had walked through, things were strewn about worse. When we got to the small room in the back I realized that David had, in fact, tried to cover his tracks because the single lightbulb was no longer in place. We had to go back upstairs in the building to find a replacement. After we secured the bulb and screwed it in place, it was obvious David had been there. The chair was now missing, "Lady Chatterly's Lover" was missing, and the mattress was gone. The bed itself was still there since it was steel with heavy springs, making it extremely difficult to lift and move without help, especially in a hurry. There were papers thrown on the floor, as well as newspapers. It definitely was not the impeccable small room I had entered the day before.

However, David underrated my intelligence. I could see the skepticism showing on Father Robert's face and realized that I still had not convinced him. I had to act quick. I pointed out that beneath the papers thrown about the room, the floor was virtually dirt free. After that, I decided to kneel down and inspect the papers and newspapers that were scattered about. I realized that David had made one crucial mistake. The color of the newspaper had not faded, which it normally will over time. Moreover, he did not take the time to inspect the dates on the newspapers, since they all fell within the past two weeks.

After I pointed these facts out to Father Robert, his skepticism seemed to cease and a look of genuine concern showed on his face. He also began to wonder how many young men David was able to coerce into his den of sin. Although not wanting to admit David's guilt to me, Father Robert thanked me for having the fortitude to come forward and promised he would investigate the situation further.

Over the course of the next week, various other students were brought before Father Robert for questioning as to whether they had ever been approached by any of the other students to engage in homosexual activities. No one except Father Robert, Mike Broderick and myself knew why this was happening. However, when word spread about what the private consultations were for, many students came forward on a voluntary basis. Apparently David had intimidated others into not coming forth with the truth. Now his entire charade was beginning to unwind. Within four days of the incident, David voluntarily terminated his "calling," and resigned from the seminary.

****

The first semester of my second freshman year was going much better than the previous year. I had conquered my loneliness and matured while learning many other aspects of what life and people were about. My grades were good, due in large part to my desire to prove I could succeed and then proceed with my life as I wanted to. I was not nearly as intimidated as I was my freshman year when playing against convicts inside the confines of prison walls, although every one of us there was scared to some degree, believe me. Football wasn't bad, because very few inmates would be in attendance other than players. However, it was still different when indoors playing basketball with an audience of their peers.

Since a prison game was not league play against other seminaries, survival was our ultimate plan. The final score, win or lose, was an afterthought. Even the priests who were our coaches or fans wanted to get out of these god-awful places as soon as possible. Guards were everywhere to protect us in the event something did go wrong. We played at two different prisons three times a year, and each time made us appreciate all the more the freedom we possessed, regardless of the strict rules we were subjected to.

Somehow, these visits put a lot of things in perspective for me. I was extremely jealous of all my friends back home being local sports heroes. Yet I was learning much more about life and this would be beneficial for the remainder of mine.

****

Christmas break that year was needed to try and lay the

groundwork for leaving my "calling." Victoria's health was deteriorating and Peter was virtually bedridden, except for his bathroom needs. Those family members who had already moved out would have no idea of the pain being endured within that house. Hugh, Jocelyn, and James are to be commended for their ability to cope, especially Jocelyn. She was always there, attentive to the needs of both Victoria and Peter and taking care of "brudder Adrian" at the same time. She had quit her job to do all this and remain at home, thereby giving up any semblance of a social life.

No matter how hard I tried, I could get no information from anyone regarding whose child Adrian was. Even Hugh and Susan would volunteer nothing, stating they, too, were unaware. I later found out they did know and were lying to me at Victoria's and James's insistence.

As I viewed Peter that Christmas, I became further convinced of being needed at home and decided I would use this as a selling point at the end of the school year. My "calling" would have to come to an end so I could be with my mom and dad where I was needed most.

It would not be an easy sell. How was I to know the more questions I asked about Adrian, the less my chances would be to return home? They truly believed, with time, I would accept the situation and proceed with no further questions. They would be right. For, like Pavlov's Dog, I learned that talking about Adrian brought negative reinforcement. For not talking, I would be rewarded.

Christmas time dealt a major blow to my masculinity as I witnessed Janice with her boyfriend. I rationalized all the reasons why she would much rather be with me than him. However, her commitment to my "calling" was much stronger than mine. If I was seen with her in a friendly manner, Victoria would surely chastise her. All the more reason I had to return home for good this coming summer. I was bonkers over this young woman, and the seminary was no place to be to try and make my move. I simply did not have a lot of bargaining power while remaining there. Lord only knows the David Buckner situation was enough to make me run home, from New York to Pennsylvania, as scared as I was.

****

The remainder of the year went without a hitch except that I had to be hospitalized with pneumonia. During the week I was in the hospital, the seminary staff failed to contact my family to let them know. James was very upset!

Actually, James did not have a problem with my withdrawal from school. Victoria put on a mild facade that she was upset. However, this did not last long. I informed the school of my intention and received no questions about my decision. I obviously was not meant to be a priest, but the time spent in the seminary helped me immensely. I learned how to conform to a set of standards and discipline that would help in the very difficult times which lay ahead of me.

My priority would have to be helping with the care of Peter. Due to my size, I would be extremely useful toward the end. Victoria had been through a lot these past two years also. Her priority was keeping Peter alive while ensuring her own health.

I would also be involved in an area I never considered until my departure, helping out with the raising of my "brudder Adrian." It was unbelievable that I had a brother thirteen years my junior and his parents in their condition. The really puzzling part of it all was that virtually no one would discuss him with me. One thing was certain, it had to be someone close to the family for us to do something so crazy as adopting a child with Peter and Victoria in their critical condition.

****

Through constant contact, I discovered things were not going well with Janice and her boyfriend. Daily, she would come over to talk with Victoria and help out where possible. I made it a point to be around the house during these times. I was really bummed out when I found out about their problems. There were so many things I wanted to say to her, yet it was her situation which now stood between us, so I thought.

I remember the day well. It was an extremely hot August afternoon. Very few houses have air conditioners, even to this day. Perhaps a window unit in the family room or master bedroom but, that's it. I was sitting on the front stoop when the phone rang. Upon answering, I realized it was Janice calling but her speech was slurred as if she were ill. She asked me if I could come upstairs and give her a hand, since she had been drinking and didn't want to be seen like that when her mother got home from work. My first thoughts were of her health in the event she had alcohol poisoned herself. However, after getting there and viewing her condition, her drunkenness was much more an act than a true buzz. She was intermittently weeping during her act about the final breakup with her boyfriend. That's why she had been drinking.

I took the opportunity to hold her hand and hug her and let her know everything would work out, she always had me as a friend to fall back on. Boy, was I nervous now that it seemed inevitable the time of reckoning was upon me. All the things I had practiced over and over in my head went for naught, since my number one concern now seemed to be "what happens next?" I had never kissed a woman before and, now that the time was upon me, I couldn't figure out if I should play the aggressor or aggressee. Thank God, she finally realized my hesitancy and placed herself in my lap with her head lying against my chest. After another short cry, she simply tilted her head to face mine and asked me to kiss her. There can be no doubt about the first kiss in a man's life being something he remembers forever. That was all the introduction I needed, and realized that I was a quick learner. It is, after all, a lot of fun experimenting when you're young and infatuated with someone, especially if everything you're doing is for the first time.

****

Things were looking up already. I had registered at Nativity the week school was to start. Janice and I finally let our mutual attraction for each other blossom although it was not destined to last long. Unfortunately, she would move shortly, and our time spent together would be less and less due to the distance. I often think back to that first infatuation and all I learned from it. Going to a Catholic school would mean I would have a chance to meet and date girls from all around the county. At least I now had a confidence about myself when going through the dating process and all that it entails.

The downside of the equation was the deterioration of my father. I honestly admired his willingness to live without any machines for support. He would lie in bed in his small room and stare. Yet, I felt as though he could still think, even if his expression was blank. Frustration with his situation often brought tears and confused mumbling from him. If he soiled the bed, he knew it and tears would come rolling from his right eye. Eventually though, I believe what Peter was thinking was the same as I. I believed Peter would now be better off with God, and I think he was also praying for this. Victoria, James, and Jo all seemed to realize the inevitable was near, yet no one seemed able to comprehend the strength within this beaten man or how long his body functions could hold out. It was extremely difficult to realize that a few short years ago he was healthy and working to support his family. Now, he was at our mercy to perform simple tasks such as those which were needed to keep him clean.

****

I have no idea if Saint Aloysious is still in existence today. However, it will always remain in my memory. The lessons learned there were a valuable stepping stone on the path toward becoming an adult. I learned to accept things which I could not change. I also learned to always keep my situation in perspective, regardless of how good or bad it seems. Finally, through a person I called Nick da Prick, I learned never to call a man a liar, since that means stripping him of his dignity. If you strip a person of their dignity, they literally have nothing left. Thank you to all those young men at Saint Aloysious whom I had met. I truly hope God has looked kindly upon y'all.

MORNINGSIDE

Morningside
The old man died
And no one cried
They simply turned away
And when he died
He left a table made of nails and pride
And with his hands,
he carved these words inside
'For my children'

Morning light
Morning bright
I spent the night
With dreams that make you weep
Morning time
Wash away the sadness from
these eyes of mine
For I recall the words an old man sighed
'For my children'

And the legs were shaped with his hands
And the top made of oaken wood
And the children that sat around this table
Touched it with their laughter
Ah, and that was good

Morningside
An old man died
And no one cried
He surely died alone
And truth is sad
For not a child would claim
the gift he had
The words he carved
became his epitaph
'For my children'

CHAPTER FIVE

SHATTERED DREAMS

Nativity, Nativity

We Hail Thee Alma Mater

Nativity, Nativity

The Green and Gold Forever.

The Shining Cross

For All to See

Beacon Bright Leads Us to Thee

O Mother Dear

To Thee We Pledge

Our Love and Faith Forever.

Nativity of the Blessed Virgin Mary. The school which I hoped would make all my youthful dreams come true. A Catholic academy which drew students from throughout the Schuylkill County area. A school that was perceived by all the local public institutions as that of aristocrats, although the majority of us were poor. No doubt about it, the school places many college-bound successful people through its doors. There is also no doubt there was much hell-raising among the class of '73 graduates. All alumni of one high school or another will tell you their class was crazed. Ask any person who has ever taught at Nativity through the years and undoubtedly they will be unanimous about the class of '73 being the one all were pleased to see leave.

My sophomore year would be the first that we were allowed to enter into league play with the public schools in the county. This would include playing against my own hometown, Saint Clair.

In a region steeped in secret fraternal organizations with religious and ethnic connections, attending a small private school had its downside. It is amazing how much prejudice based on religious preference can exist among people otherwise similar in race, social strata, and history. We and our supporters met a great deal of prejudice at every school we visited that first season. (Because of these experiences, today I understand those who are experiencing prejudice, a word synonymous with hatred.)

Although difficult, the courses at Nativity were easy compared to the seminary. While I had learned many valuable lessons about life in the seminary, I had now returned to my own element with people I felt comfortable with. This would include my teachers at the school who were all very good at what they did. Unfortunately, many private schools rely on tuition and fundraisers to supplement their budget. Due to this, the salary structure of these institutions does not complement the job done by the teachers. My teachers seemed to take more time with me to ensure I understood, not assuming I was grasping what was being taught. I would not blossom intellectually at Nativity, but it would begin to awaken my latent brain cells. With any intelligence at all and a scholarship, life would truly be looking fondly upon me. I now had an opportunity to prove myself to my family and make them proud. Understandably, things would never be for me like they were during Frank's glory years.

Peter and Victoria were both very ill. Stroke-ridden, Peter was now virtually immobile and carrying him was the only way for movement. Victoria also was truly licked. She had fought the good fight and had nothing to show for it. Her husband was a broken man, most of her children were married and gone. She was monetarily broke, and very, very ill.

The lack of physical contact within the family structure during our lives would now become an asset when dealing with the situation because love had never been shown openly between Victoria, Peter, and me. What I was about to undergo and deal with, I did because it was my duty as a son. Coming home to the parents who had once beaten and abused me, and now having them at my mercy, was very difficult. Now, Victoria was glad to see me walk through the door so that I could assist with Peter.

****

Although Peter and Victoria were rapidly deteriorating, I decided to play basketball that first year—more for a release than anything else. This meant that Jocelyn would have to continue to hold strong through the day, until Hugh, James or I could get home. Often times, I would return from practice late at night and have to help with Peter, then tend to my studies. I was also becoming more involved with female relationships, and it would be difficult to juggle all these balls at once.

Our very first game that year would be played at Shenandoah High School and would prove that prejudice is definitely not restricted to the confines of race. Although less than fifteen miles from Saint Clair, the ride up the steep mountains in a "Yellow Bird" bus can be an eternity, definitely time for meditation or concentration on the immense task we were about to undertake. We would be the first Catholic school in our region to enter league play with the powerful public schools. As such, we anticipated a heated, competitive affair. We never expected what we were to encounter.

Both school principals had obviously talked during the week and agreed it would be best if we entered through the rear of the school and went directly to our locker room. (It was uncanny how this reminded me of the precautions taken when entering the prisons.) Police protection was to be increased considerably at both the front and rear entrances to the school. The bus driver was aware of the location of the school and made his way down side streets as if he had done this many times before. Suddenly, we came upon a crowd of people standing outside an old brick structure. The crowd was mostly young, many drunk, and waiting as if for a show to begin. It suddenly dawned on me these people were waiting for us. We had a Junior Varsity game which was scheduled for a 6 o'clock start, with the Varsity at eight. Rarely is there a crowd for any J.V. game. "What were these people doing here?" most of us were wondering aloud. Out of nowhere came the first bottle, then a second, then more. We were sprawling on the floor with only our gym bags for protection. Fortunately, it was November and cold outside or the windows would not have been closed to block the initial onslaught. At one point someone yelled, ''go around back, quick,'' to which the driver responded, ''Dis iz da back. Believe me, yooz don't want me ta take yooz around dare.''

Finally, six police officers arrived and escorted us, four at a time, into the building. ''Hell, this place needs twice as much security as the prisons,'' I thought. The insults being levied upon us because we were ''rich Catlicks'' was twice as bad as I'd heard in the prisons, and I thought I'd heard it all there. At least at the prisons if someone in the crowd became unruly, it was squelched immediately, forcefully. In this atmosphere, even the police escorting us had to fear for their safety.

By game time, the atmosphere was a circus. Many in the audience were drunk, insulting and very hostile. We were all intimidated—both players and fans who had made the short ride. Pregame warm-ups and introductions made for a very hostile environment. What we, as players, would come to realize during the course of the game was how much hatred their players had for us. This wasn't to be a basketball game, it was a war fought over a simple ingredient, as many wars are today, ''PRIDE''!

The game went into overtime. Throughout the game, insults and trash talking were going on heavy and the refs were hearing it, yet ignoring it. ''OH NO, DOUBLE OVERTIME!'' By this time, both their team and ours were talking rather vociferously to each other. Tensions were running high, especially with the competitiveness of the game and what was really on the line as far as a victory.

It was bound to happen. I went up for a shot underneath the basket. The person guarding me simply leveled me with a forearm to avoid the easy basket. A cheap, flagrant foul which sent me to the floor with two men falling on top. I looked up to see ''Robo'' Robbins, our center, popping the guy who fouled me in the face.

What happened next is hazy. Both benches emptied while I was lying on the floor and bedlam broke out everywhere instantaneously. I remember their player kicking, while he was screaming something at me. He got at least three open shots at my ribs before I could get my hands free for protection. By the third kick, intense pain was shooting through my midsection. During this time, fights had broken out everywhere amongst players and spectators. I was carried, gasping for breath, into the locker room after calm was finally restored. Whoever he was popped a couple of ribs and enjoyed every kick of it.

We eventually lost in triple overtime that night, and I had to be escorted, heavily taped across my ribcage, to the bus. Upon leaving, we were once again deluged with rocks and bottles, with glass breaking everywhere. I was in so much pain and taped so heavily that I couldn't possibly bend over to avoid the onslaught. Fortunately, I didn't get hit by anything except a dose of reality. I was feeling an immense prejudice, this time from people exactly the same as me. We were all plain people with many similarities. Yet due to deep-rooted, generations-engraved religious beliefs, we were hated.

****

Shortly after Thanksgiving of my first year in a real high school, Peter suffered yet another stroke. Whatever was going on inside his body, it certainly wasn't being kind to him. Pain was no longer an exception, it was the norm. Nativity High School is within a half mile of the Good Samaritan Hospital, one of two hospitals in the city. Peter was lying in a hospital bed there, torn and dazed by the batterings his brain was enduring, within a stone's throw of where I was attending school. I had this weird feeling that Peter and I weren't a match; yet, in an off sort of way, we had many similarities. He was rejected for what he wasn't, and I was accepted for what I was; the opposite of the truth.

Peter was about the truth, yet he could never tell it to me, although I believe he truly wanted to, when it was too late. Looking at him, I oftentimes felt there was something he wanted to say. Yet, due to his inability to speak, he was frustrated literally to the point of a tear—never tears, since a whole side of his body was totally incapacitated. Peter realized the truth was best. He didn't believe in lies. However, it would be too little, too late. He'd never get the chance with me.

****

Playing basketball during this period was extremely demanding, yet it was the sport I would truly come to enjoy the most since I believe it requires the most athleticism. By the middle of the season, in late November, I was playing well and enjoying the accolades of my fellow students and the local press. Once again, my schedule would become regimented, much like the seminary. After school, basketball practice until 7:30, stop by and visit Peter until 8:30, then get a ride home from there with James. By this time, Victoria, James, Hugh, and Jocelyn were holding a continuous bedside vigil since Peter's condition was tenuous at best.

There was no true Thanksgiving that year, only prayers. I prayed daily for the life of my father and mother, while trying to deal with and accept the situation.

Each game we played that year, I privately commemorated to Peter. Each game, I played with more intensity and enthusiasm. When Shenandoah came to play at our home court that year, we beat them in double overtime. There was also a bench-clearing brawl in that game. It really doesn't matter if you're on home turf or away, hatred/prejudice can creep through the smallest cracks imaginable. That particular game was played during the third week of November, when Peter took a turn for the worse, with oxygen tents and machines seemingly everywhere. I had played a great game that night, but the reality of what was going down around me never let me feel right.

****

Christmas was once again upon us, however, circumstances dictated that it would not be a holiday where we would exchange presents, only hope and prayers. It is often a very difficult holiday, since its whole meaning is centered around joy and the birth of Christ. Due to its upbeat meaning as a holiday, it creates many depressions amongst people who are experiencing sadness, loneliness, illness, or a combination of all. Amongst the Catholic religion, Christmas is the epitome of holidays, since it truly embodies all the beliefs of their faith.

Through all the Christmas holidays I have participated in, the year 1971 and its happenings stand out in my mind. For it was during 1971 that I would take the leap from adolescence into adulthood, where being tough has absolutely nothing to do with strength. It would be the first time I experienced feelings for my family, yet I did not understand why I encountered difficulty displaying them openly. It was the first time that I would experience personally the fact that God takes people away from us, regardless of how bad we may wish it not to happen. Up until this point in my life, the norm for me with my family was additions to staff, never the opposite.

It was a cold December day with flurries falling all day, typical for Pennsylvania this time of year. Our coach decided we would practice

Christmas Eve, then have Christmas and the day after off before playing a game on the twenty-seventh. Since we did not have school that day, practice was to begin at noon, ending about 2:30. I decided to go directly to the hospital after practice, anticipating a ride home. When I got there, Victoria was standing by Peter's side, holding his hand. Everyone had gone home for some rest, yet Victoria realized that the time had come and demanded to stay. When I walked into the room and looked at Peter and how far he had now degenerated, I also knew the end was here. No longer could he make anyone or anything out, his bodily functions were all working via machines and tubes. His breathing was extremely labored, the black lung disease taking vicious punches. His weight had deteriorated to skeletal proportions. I immediately called home and informed James how critical Peter was. He must have been expecting the call and informed me he would call everyone in.

As I watched Peter lying there gasping for his last breath, a myriad of thoughts began racing through my head. Victoria was talking aloud to Peter while holding his hand, yet I barely heard anything. I repeatedly asked myself, "Why?" I really couldn't understand why God was doing this to my father, yet I knew it was my duty to accept it. I was sad, and questioned why Peter lived such a hard life for many other people's benefit yet had nothing to show for it.

Most of all, I wondered why I was feeling sad and lonely when I didn't even know the man lying in front of me. I knew what I called him and what he stood for, yet I never had a conversation with him in which we would express our feelings to each other. That element, the lack of emotion within me, would haunt me for many, many years. It is only recently, after many years of being told the opposite, I have realized that it's O.K. to cry, to show emotion and feelings about someone, be they male or female, friend or family. I thought I was realizing what it took to be a man at that moment because I was able to block out everything that makes men vulnerable at all times, expressing their feelings.

Victoria's conversation with Peter was becoming more intense and she began to pray aloud to God to take this man from his misery. James and the family still hadn't arrived and time was quickly running out. I really didn't know what to do, other than stand there and wish for things that would never be. If only God would do me this one last favor. Suddenly, Peter's breathing came in much longer intervals and I knew this was the end. Victoria sensed it and squeezed Peter's hand one last living time while she repeated over and over aloud, "It's O.K. to die now, it's O.K. to go."

Finally, in one last fight for life, Peter succumbed. He had soaked every last breath out of his worn body long after many anticipated he would. Moreover, he went to his grave with a secret that would haunt both of us for many years, yet I would eventually unveil this secret and free his mind forever. His pride and integrity had held fast through many difficult situations, and he would go to his resting place with both of these intact.

There was no Christmas that year. We took the tree down on Christmas Eve and prepared for the viewing and funeral on the 26th and 27th. The only facet of the situation which I was truly able to comprehend was that my father was dead. He would no longer be a part of my life.

The viewing would be the first time I was to experience death so close to me. It would bother me for many years that I was not able to cry at the viewing or funeral. True tears are the ones which not only fall from sadness but are also the result of an absence within the heart. I have come to realize that death creates a void within oneself. Unless we can see past this void, toward the fond memories of the person who has passed on, we will never be able to truly bury them. This was the situation with Peter. Although he now was gone, I would not be able to get over the void left by his departure for many years.

****

I took to drinking hard that summer. I was mad at the world and drinking was an easy escape, at least for the moment. I had virtually no home life. I stayed at friend's houses most of the time. The only time I seemed to stop by the house would be for fresh clothes and to check on Victoria's condition. Unfortunately, she would never get over Peter passing on and only realized how much he meant to her after he was gone. By then it would be too late.

Victoria, too, saw alcohol as a quick fix to the problems which she deemed insurmountable due to Peter's passing. For, with his death came a decrease in income, something she was not prepared for. Once again, James would be the sole bread winner. It would now be up to him to feed, clothe, and maintain Victoria, Jocelyn, Adrian and me.

With the death of my father, I would develop a coldness toward people's feelings. It's not that I couldn't understand the feelings of others and what they were experiencing, I did. I just didn't care. This attitude, combined with alcohol, would not make for a nice me. However, I didn't care. For some reason, in my mind, God didn't care about me, so why should I be concerned about others? Pain being felt by others would become a moral victory for me since they had to experience what I had experienced. I would carry this attitude with me for many years, although it would decrease in its severity once I began college. It would not be until I finally discovered the truth about myself that I was able to put to rest these deplorable feelings. For the truth would bring about a cleansing. I would realize that I am not a negative person, just a victim of circumstances. My circumstances happen to be unique, but they are real, and only the truth would help me understand why I was feeling the way I was.

****

I carried Peter's death on my shoulders through the remainder of that school year and well into the next. In just a year's time, I had gone from a happy-go-lucky seminarian to someone with a very bad attitude and a drinking problem. Unfortunately, in this area of the country, drinking problems become the norm within many families, especially the youth. Every night I would drink heavily beer, liquor, it didn't matter, as long as it did the job. The job was to take me away from the heartaches I had been through and maintain anger within me at a fever level. When one night's anger had been satisfied, I wanted to do it all over again.

I didn't care about sports any longer. The dreams I aspired to there had already begun crumbling around me. Besides, the last thing I needed the beginning of my junior year was a football coach screaming in my face. I was now on a mission to destroy myself both mentally and physically and, in a short period of time, was managing to do a fantastic job. Alcohol would only serve to increase the pace at which I was able to do this.

****

Fortunately, God really does provide guardian angels to watch over us. At a time when I hit rock bottom, at such a tender age, He sent mine. Her name was Patty Stock, the younger sister of one of my classmates. Patty and I began dating by accident. (I was supposed to have gone out with her sister but ended up with her.) She immediately realized the animosity within my mind and heart. With help from her parents, I gradually began to see daylight at the end of the tunnel. I realized life was not a conspiracy against me, that there were good people in the world who cared about me. Most of all, I learned with their help to accept what I could not change, that hurting myself and others was not the answer. Although a year younger, she understood me better than any of my family or friends ever could. She would become a pillar of stability for me through the remainder of my high school days, the worst of which were still to come. Also, in a few short months, she instilled in me once again a feeling of pride, a pride that I had all but forgotten through the shadow of a liquor bottle or beer label. She convinced me that sports were a necessary release for me, and I should play basketball again that year. Regardless of the bad shape I was in, I would work my way back and gain the respect of my peers and most of all, of myself. It would not be easy, and the availability of alcohol would make it all the more difficult. But I was once again made to believe in myself.

****

Several important things happened to me during that basketball season, and they would have an impact on me for the remainder of my life. Two of these incidents occurred when we played my hometown public school, Saint Clair. The rivalry between the two schools was extremely intense and tensions were running high. Once again, we were perceived by the people of Saint Clair as aristocrats, although many of the town's people knew my background, and that I was definitely one of them.

The first time we played Saint Clair that year was at home, and our gym was filled to capacity due to the nature of the rivalry and circumstances. This was the second year we were allowed to compete against the public schools, and the animosity had not decreased one iota. During many people's lives, they seem to feel as though they are experiencing *deja vu*, and this would be one of those for me. In between the J.V. and Varsity game, while we were waiting to go out on the court for pregame warm-ups, it happened. Since this was to be a huge game of pride for Mark Ryscavage and myself, we were both "talking it up" to each other, trying to get ourselves psyched. After all, we were shortly going to be playing against our bitter rivals, all of whom we had grown up with. This is what we had been practicing for and dreaming of for many years and we needed no interference from extraneous sources. Suddenly, from the locker room below, ran the team manager up the stairs, visibly shaken. Unfortunately for Mark and me, we were the first two people he met so he unloaded on us.

Manager:

> "Fellaz, Fellaz, yooz ain't gonna believe it! Fodder Badner jest asked me if I wanted a blow-job in da locker room! What should I do?"

Mark and I (in unison):

> "Get outta here, we gotta game ta play."

Unfortunately for the Catholic religion, school, and student involved, Mark nor I were willing to listen and react. If we had listened and addressed the situation immediately, we would have been able to save the high school and Catholic religion an awful lot of embarrassment and monetary loss in the future. For, ten years later as I was sitting in my living room preparing to watch "60 Minutes" air a segment on pedophiles, Father Badner would re-enter my life and take me back to a time before a basketball game years earlier. There, for all the world to see, was Father Badner on national television, the focal point of a highly publicized pedophile incident in Schuylkill County. Although I should have believed the student, I chose to ignore it, understanding all the while that it was probably true. In the meantime, young boys were being molested, many times on film, by Father Badner, and he would not be caught for eight more years, until one young man finally had enough courage to come forward.

Upon our visit to Saint Clair's home court, another event would happen which would help mold the path my adult life would take. For, much like the pride Mark and I felt playing against them on our home court, it was doubly intensified when playing in front of virtually our entire town, except we were now the enemy, playing for the other team. I was having an exceptional game. Right before halftime, they stole the ball and we were all racing down court at full speed. Suddenly, without advance warning, the record playing inside my mind changed speeds. Their guard was going to attempt the lay up and I knew in my heart, I was destined to block the shot. I did, cleanly. Unfortunately, the antiquated Saint Clair gym had a wall three feet behind the basket. As I came down, my left foot became wedged against the wall. Physical pain, like I had never felt before, surged through my body. I was lying there, writhing, and nothing was done because no one realized the severity of the injury until later, when x-rays were taken. Even our team doctor thought I would be able to play the second half, but it was to no avail. I was like a horse who was hobbled beyond repair. The x-rays would show that I had shattered virtually every bone in my big toe area, and immediate surgery was necessary with the first of three prostheses (artificial implants), being inserted. In one split second, the first of many of my childhood dreams would be shattered. I would never be the athlete my family envisioned.

****

Shortly after my first surgery, with no initial warning, Victoria became extremely ill and had to be placed in intensive care. I was used to this by now with Peter. Patty and her family were instrumental in helping me understand this, but still within my mental framework was the hard surface I had created to ward off any feelings toward others. This was, after all, something which would quickly pass. It was difficult enough having to navigate myself with a cast up to my knee from the surgery and all the mental handicaps that ensued from this. I had become quite adept at not wanting to acknowledge pain and suffering within others due to all I had endured over the past several years.

The many years of worrying, chain-smoking, and drinking had now totally enveloped Victoria's health. She was a woman who was now beaten both emotionally and physically. She had witnessed a deterioration within her family structure which she could never have planned for. Worst of all, many of her children did not follow the religious path to righteousness which she so desperately tried to enforce. All that she felt was good and right had backfired on her in ways only she could not or would not see or acknowledge. Everything she had strived for with her family had now turned out exactly the opposite.

****

Victoria and I never became close, as a mother and child should be. Over time I became afraid of her and never would trust her. This was due to those early memories of how she tried to dominate and control the lives of her children who were adults, the tirades she threw, the beatings she gave me for no apparent reason other than alcohol, and her perception of me and what I truly stood for in her life—the downfall of her family. She never once told me she loved me, never once sought me out to comfort her. Unlike Peter, there were absolutely no similarities between us. This is why it was much easier for me to block out any type of feelings when she became radically ill. Whatever feelings I had for Peter developed over the time of his lengthy illness and my respect for his desire to live. There was no way I could develop this respect for Victoria. I knew her simply as an entity, not someone I appreciated and loved.

It was a cold November evening. I was out with a friend who lived directly across the street from the Good Samaritan Hospital. We had been out cruising and decided to call it a night and go back to his house. As fate would have it, Hugh spotted me getting out of the car and called to me. This was a one-in-a-million coincidence, him spotting me while he was walking toward the hospital. I was still trying to recover from the surgery I had a year earlier, my left big toe was now a half inch smaller than it had been. Sports was out of the question, but with Patty and her family's aid, I was coping mentally. Hugh informed me that he had been driving around trying to find me for over two hours. The hospital had called home and advised James that it would be best to call the immediate family in. When I heard this, denial instantly came into my mind. I was still having a hard time accepting the fact that eleven months earlier my father had died. I was not acknowledging the fact that this time would be the last; Victoria was going to give up her fight to the numerous illnesses. Only when I turned the corner at the nurses' station going toward her room and saw all my brothers and sisters crying was I forced to accept the situation. Hugh and I were too late; she had already breathed her last breath. James ushered Hugh and me into her room for a last chance to pay respect to the person we knew as our mother. There she lay, her belly blown up from all the drugs as though she were pregnant, her eyes closed, and not breathing.

Just as I failed to show her love when she was alive, I was now doing the same in her death. Hugh was crying profusely and all I could do was stare, swallow hard, and accept it. Tears rolled out of my eyes down my cheeks, but once again I was not able to cry those tears which are necessary when a void is created, the tears which come when you truly love someone who has left your life. I would not feel that emotion then for Victoria, nor would I ever for the remainder of my life. Now, after the truth has surfaced, I feel an even deeper animosity toward her. I could never show her any "true" feelings of love because she insisted on the truth never being a part of my life. Writing this gives me a certain sense of cleansing, however, it is from my perspective only.

I have learned to forgive a lot of people, but the absence of love from Victoria is unforgivable. Had she been alive when I discovered the truth about myself, I might have gained a better insight as to why she chose to keep my life a secret. Maybe I could have accepted her reasoning and forgiven her.

****

Throughout the viewing and funeral I maintained that tough-guy facade I was taught at an early age. I never once cried tears that meant anything. The tears I did cry were directed more toward myself and how lonely I suddenly felt. Both my parents were now gone from my life without me ever getting a chance to know who they really were. Without ever being able to look them directly in the eyes and say "I love you Mom, Dad," and they reciprocate to me. I never felt the pride from my parents that I saw directed toward Frank, and for this I was angry. It was the anger I had built up in me after Peter's death, now compounded to the power of ten. Even with Patty and her family's care and understanding, I was once again a very bitter person. I felt robbed and cheated, and I did not know or understand why. Both my parents were dead, less than a year apart. These should have been the best moments, days, and years of our lives together. Now all the questions and moments together, enjoying each other, all boiled down to one cold, cruel fact: I was going to have to face the remainder of my life alone, with no one to ever tell how much I loved them, nor they me.

****

There comes a time in a person's life when they finally cross the line from adolescence into maturity. What the Miller family failed to realize is that I crossed that line when Peter died in front of me. Apparently, my true mother never crossed that line. It is at the point of Victoria's death that I believe the truth should have finally been told to me. From this point forward, for seven more years, not one of my brothers and sisters, bruncles, smants, and smother, had the guts to come forward and break tradition. Instead, they would hide behind the shield of their religion, lying and concealing the truth.

****

Christmas time was once again upon us. This Christmas was like the last for me, a tragedy. Through all of the past twelve months, I never let my emotional defenses down, I kept my machismo strong. That is, until Christmas Eve 1972.

I was once again a very angry man. Even though I was still dating Patty, alcohol again became a convenient release for me since it was the happening thing to do. Everyone was doing it, including Patty and her family, so it just seemed a natural way of escaping. Patty picked me up for midnight Mass and I was already shitfaced. We went to Saint Mary's in Saint Clair. During Mass, for some unknown reason, I began to experience flashbacks of my life. From the dishes breaking as a child, to the fight with Hugh many years earlier, right up through the deaths of my parents. Various emotions, happiness, sadness, hatred, loneliness, but never love. I stood there at that Mass and realized that I had never been shown love by my parents like so many of my friends' parents showed toward them. Not only that, I never loved my parents like so many of my friends did theirs.

I left the church in a fog, Patty not realizing what was going on inside my mind. All the emotions were still rattling through me. I was a volcano ready to blow, for the first time. She drove me the few short blocks to my house, neither of us speaking. I was thinking how I would like to be able to regurgitate my life, in one ferocious hurl.

By the time we got to my house, Patty realized it was time. She stopped the car in front, with snow falling all around us and said two simple words, ''Go ahead.'' I did! I cried like I never thought possible. I had finally let all my defenses down, I was vulnerable to God and man. I cried for everything and everyone, but mostly for me. For I realized I was truly on my own now, all alone in a world full of uncertainties.

****

I cried for an hour straight, not knowing the real reason why. Unfortunately, it was only for the moment, for I soon regained what I thought were my senses. The remainder of that school year would be spent alternating between reality and fiction, between the real me and an inebriated me. I found solace when I was drunk and able to ignore the events in my recent past. It was beginning to create an enormous strain on Patty and me, since she decided that I would prefer to carry on a relationship with my friends and a beer than with her. I simply could not show her any sign of love, since I had never been shown any, and this is what she was expecting from me. What I did not understand at this point is that, due to the dysfunctional nature of my family, I would never be able to truly love anyone, ever, in my life. I simply did not know or understand what that emotion would feel like. To this day, it is much easier for me to say to someone, "I love you," than to truly mean it.

****

By my senior year, I had already undergone two surgeries and had completely withdrawn from the mainstream that should have been my adolescence. Shortly after the second surgery on my foot, I came down with an acute case of tonsillitis and had to undergo yet another surgery to remove my tonsils. This further compounded the depression I was experiencing. The worst part of these hospital stays was that only my friends would be there to visit and console me, there was no family, no parents. Patty and her family had become my pseudo-family, but this would be short lived since our relationship would soon be doomed due to my attitude and personality.

I was going through life as a very bitter person. I had no family, no money, no one there to help me understand what was transpiring in my short but crazy life. Once again, alcohol and its escape would be where I would turn to help me forget, if only for the moment. By this time, I had also experienced the new wave escape that was becoming popular with the counter culture—marijuana. The combination of the two helped take me even further away from what I perceived to be my problems. Although I did not necessarily like smoking, and still don't today, I did it mainly as a statement of rebellion, to show that I was cool, whatever that meant. What I truly hated worse than anything, what really affected me the worst, was going home to a house without anyone in it. It was depressing, no doubt. The loneliness! The reality that no one would be there for me if I became sick. No one to talk to within my family if I needed someone. Most of all, no parents to emulate. The only family members at home were James, who I rarely saw, and Jo, who was busy raising Adrian. Strange, Adrian was two years old and already parentless. There was simply no logic in this equation. For some uncanny reason, I felt really bad for him, realizing that he would never know who his real parents were, since it was obvious he was adopted, and also that he would never get to know the parents of the family which adopted him. How could I have realized that I was a victim of the same circumstances?

****

Patty eventually abandoned me, principally because I was too busy feeling sorry for myself and not paying any attention to her feelings and needs. Although our departure from each others lives was abrupt, it is only now as I write this that I have come to realize how vital a part of my life she was through a very critical time. She was always there for me, at my lowest points, and I was too wrapped up in myself and my problems to take the time to say thanks, both to her and her family. Through all the setbacks I had endured, from the sports that I cherished so much to the death of my parents, I had contemplated suicide many times. Although she never directly discussed it with me, as I reflect now on situations, I am sure Patty was aware and did everything within her power to be sure nothing happened to me. Thank you. Hopefully you realize now that I will never forget what you did for me.

The word suicide, and the connotations thereof, are simply another means of escape from reality. Those people who contemplate it, or do it, are experiencing a vulnerability in their lives, coupled with extreme depression. For me, the act of suicide would be the ultimate escape, my swan song to the world, or so was my twisted thinking at the time. I had no one to turn to and no reason to live. The only person who seemed to care for me had just walked out of my life. Alcohol was no longer an escape because of the immunity I had built up to it. Marijuana only heightened my depression, and I decided to stop that since I didn't need to be cool or accepted anymore. I didn't need anything! What I did want was out. Out of this fucked-up town and life I was living. My whole childhood and adolescence seemed to be a nightmare that I could not wake from. Most of my family had long abandoned ship, and those who remained were caught up in their own world of survival. The people I should have been able to turn to at a time like this were dead, and I never got to know or love them. I felt that I had nothing left to live for.

The desire to win, to succeed at all costs that was ingrained in me at an early age had left me. Graduation would soon be upon me and I had no interest whatsoever in going to college. I had wanted to play football and basketball my senior year, chasing that elusive scholarship, but because of the surgeries, this was now impossible. Foremost on my mind, entering the last few months of my high school education, was what method would be best to leave this world. I wanted to prove to everyone, friends and family, that the events of my life had driven me to the lowest depths possible, my own death.

Fortunately for me, God once again provided a guardian angel, this time his name was fear. Although I truly wanted to put an end to everything, the ultimate fear of doing this is what is enabling me to write about it today. For all that I had been through, and how tough I thought I was, the one thing I could not accept as a challenge was how to take my own life with dignity. My choices in this matter as I saw them were limited. Drugs, alcohol poisoning, swallow cold steel, or slicing with a blade. In all instances, as I contemplated these choices many times, fear inevitably won out. Eventually, after I realized I could never do this to myself, the fear that had kept me from doing it began to turn to something else, although I would not realize it for several months to come.

****

As graduation day approached, reality set in very hard. To this point, I had not applied to any college, nor were they beating my door down to offer me the scholarship I had dreamed of. Several small colleges were interested in me for my basketball skills, however, once they realized the extent of my surgeries, their interest diminished. Suddenly, the reality of becoming part of the regeneration process, which I vowed I would never do, awakened me to the fact that I had better act quickly unless I was willing to accept the inevitable. Much to my surprise, shortly after my graduation, James sat me down for what was to be the only formal conversation we would ever have. As I look back on it, it would be the only time James would formally accept responsibility for me and my future. It would be the only time he would intercede and act like my parent, and to this day I am thankful he did. The conversation lasted only five minutes, at best, but the outcome would dictate my future as being a viable member of society, not someone who would go to their grave a nobody:

James:

> "So, what da ya tink yer gonna do wit yerself now dat yer graduated from high school?"

Patrick:

> "Don't know. I haven't really taught about it. Why da you ask, what da ya care, anyway?"

James:

> "Well, are ya tinking about goin' ta college, or what?"

Patrick:

> "All my dreams about goin' ta college were erased da first time da doctor sliced open my foot. I wanted ta go on a sports scholarship, so mom and dad would a' been proud a' me. Dere ain't no colleges want me now because I'm too slow, what wit my foot all screwed up, or what?"

James:

> "Well, in dat case, I took da liberty to enroll you at Bloomsburg State. Mudder and fadder were able to put enough money away fer ya ta do dis."

Patrick:

> "How can dis be? I never filled any paperwork out ta apply ta go da school. Dere's no way I can get in now witout doin' dat, or what?"

James:

> "Like I say, I took da liberty ta do dat fer ya also. Ya were accepted and ya begin next month."

That was it, my informal scholarship into college. What I would not realize for many years is the reason James had filled out all the paperwork: *a copy of my birth certificate was a prerequisite to being accepted.* James handled the acceptance process from "womb to tomb," even dictating which school I would go to. However, I didn't care. Suddenly, I had a new lease on life. Because of James and what I believed was his attempt to care for me, I would now be attending college anyway, although it was not the way I had always dreamed about going. Moreover, something was beginning to come over me which I hadn't felt in several years, pride. Because of the revelation that I would be attending college, with a chance to break away from the regeneration process, a new feeling of pride enveloped me. I was scared, because this would be yet another time I would be away from home on my own. But it would definitely not be like the seminary life I had gone through just three short years earlier.

****

To say the least, I was riding an emotional roller coaster my last two years of high school. I had been through a lot, mentally and physically, and was now going to be given an opportunity to better myself through our collegiate educational system. What had transpired recently could now be put behind me by moving to a new place with new challenges. I still maintained a degree of bitterness, but the thought of a new start in a college town helped block out those negative memories I was harboring. Besides, it was time to move on. The old house and what I had seen there were a reminder of the goals I had set earlier in life, go to college and break away. I would arrive at college not knowing really what to expect, yet ready to accept the challenge. For there is one thing that was certain in my mind at this point; I would never return to live in the town of Saint Clair, with all its guarded secrets, for the remainder of my life.

FOOLING YOURSELF

(THE ANGRY YOUNG MAN)

You see the world through
your cynical eyes
You're a troubled young man
I can tell
You've got it all in the palm
of your hand
But your hand's wet with
sweat
And your head needs a rest
And you're fooling yourself if
you don't believe it
You're kidding yourself if you don't believe it.

Why must you be such an angry young man
When your future looks
quite brite to me
And how can there be such a sinister plan
That could hide such a lamb
such a caring young man
And you're fooling yourself
if you don't believe it
You're killing yourself if you
don't believe it.

Get up Get back on your feet
You're the one they can't beat
and you know it
Come on let's see what
you've got
Just take your best shot and
don't blow it.

Written by Tommy Shaw
©1977 Alamo Music Corp.
Stygian Songs (ASCAP)
International Copyright Secured

CHAPTER SIX

REBOUND

Emotionally and physically, I was spent. Mentally, I had been given a new lease on life when Brother James took the liberty of enrolling me in college. Bloomsburg State College is located in the hills of North Central Pennsylvania. In earlier times, it was called Bloomsburg State Teachers' College with the curriculum limited to future teachers. Recently, it became Bloomsburg University, encompassing a wide variety of degrees since it has experienced tremendous growth over the years. Ideally located for me, it was just an hour's drive from Saint Clair, all of it through mountain roads, going through many of the dilapidated coal towns that had at one time been very prosperous and powerful.

The beauty of the college, besides its location in the mountains, was the weather and people. When I attended, it had barely four thousand students. Over the course of my tenure, I got to know many of them personally. Located where it is, people living or attending school there live through four distinct seasons, with fall being by far the prettiest. The myriad leaf colors throughout the area make for a postcard type atmosphere. We were close to the Pocono Mountains and two hours from Philadelphia, New York City, or Pittsburgh, in any direction.

James dropped me off at my dormitory for orientation week and I was on my own. I had two suitcases full of clothes as my only material possessions. I knew no one and liked it like that. I was starting anew with the constant knowledge that I didn't have anyone at home I had to care for, or for that matter, who would take an intense interest in my well-being. The people I would meet and who accepted me as their friend would never know what I had been through in high school. Nor would they ever find out anything about me unless I chose to tell them. Of course, with my departure for college, those Miller family members who had knowledge of my situation were believing that I was now safely away from Saint Clair and I would never find out about the real me. They also were banking on my never returning to that town after college. In other words, everyone believed they could now breathe easier, the shadow of the truth would no longer be hanging over their heads.

I learned from James that the funding for my school was not done by Peter and Victoria putting money aside. They didn't have any extra to do this. Fortunately, both Adrian and I would still receive the disability benefits from Peter and the dreaded Black Lung disease until we were twenty-one. Therefore, it was imperative that I graduate in four years. There was no room for mistakes or misfortune. If all went well, my benefits would cease right at the point of my graduation. I would be cutting it real close, and this would be a needed inducement for me to perform.

****

What I was not ready for was the amount of partying that goes on in college. Every night, a sorority, fraternity or apartment complex found a reason to party. Be it Monday night football, Tuesday being grateful for Monday being over, Wednesday being hump day and two days before the weekend, Thursday preparing for Friday, and Friday welcoming the weekend, I never was lacking for something to do or people to do it with. Unfortunately, colleges do not offer degrees in partying. If they did, during my first two years there I would have achieved a perfect 4.0. Never having learned how to study properly, I was in constant danger of falling below the 2.0 area, which is barely making the grade. For some reason, I found it much more fun meeting new people (especially women), than getting serious about what I was there for. The first two years in college I was relying solely on my basic intelligence and the help of those women I befriended to maintain a passing grade.

I developed an incessant need for everyone (again, especially women) to like and accept me. I was not conscious of this, but with my happy-go-lucky personality, it was easy for those people who met me to do. I was unconsciously trying to be loved by women, yet I would never be able, or want to, reciprocate. Unfortunately, I would do whatever it took to gain their friendship and love, including lie, yet always be unwilling to divulge any part of my real self or my real feelings to those who were trying to unmask me. For lying would come easy to me in all of the relationships I would become involved in during my college days. In most instances with women, although not all, sex was my ulterior motive. Even if I was not sexually involved, I constantly strived for their acknowledgment that I was their friend. It was strange, as I look back. I was looking for everyone's acceptance and love simply because it was something never shown me but which I needed desperately.

****

During the summer of my sophomore year, I got a job working in the records section of the Schuylkill County Courthouse, located in Pottsville. In cabinets where I was working were all the adoption records handled by the court. Since I was never told whose child Adrian was, there were times when my curiosity was too intense to handle. On the other hand, I knew that James would come totally unglued if he were to find out the way I found out the truth. Therefore, just to test the water one evening, I informed him that I had an opportunity to see Adrian's record (although I never did look). Needless to say, the water I was testing was boiling hot. James became delirious with anger, admonishing me never to go near there.

How was I to know the reason he was so upset was because right behind Adrian Miller's file would be one belonging to a certain Patrick Miller? This was yet another one of those times I should have realized something was wrong by the way James reacted to my statement about seeing Adrian's records. Even after I informed him I was only kidding, he never backed off the anger that he displayed. Needless to say, I never went near Adrian's records for fear of a replay of the tirade which James exhibited.

****

As if I really needed another reason to party during the first semester of my junior year, I decided to pledge a fraternity. Zeta Psi is a national fraternity and very well-known among many of our major colleges. It has many distinguished people among its alumni. It also has never had a wilder bunch of "brothers" than we did at Bloomsburg during my tenure. Back then "hazing" was still very popular among the fraternities and sororities. The sheer embarrassment of having to go through pledging is unfathomable unless you've been there. Today, most colleges have banned hazing due to the legal liabilities that are attached. Many of the rituals were degrading physically, emotionally, and mentally. Despite tradition, I agree with the decision of the colleges to outlaw hazing since it has a propensity to dehumanize people. As you are already aware, I'm not into degradation at other peoples expense. Therefore, it should come as no surprise that I was not a prized "pledge," and almost told them to shove their brotherhood several times during the process. In the end, I'm glad I didn't since the upside is that it does create a feeling of family and friendship. It is also a team concept in a whole different vein. Many of these people would take the place of the true family element that was lacking in my life.

As I stated, one of my fraternity's major accomplishments during my years is the type of parties we would hold. Our fraternity house was always packed when we opened the parties up to the general student population and it was a very good way to meet new people, always trying to put women at the top of my priority list. Our fraternity was unique in that we were one of the few to enlist "little sisters" to join in our brotherhood. Although they were never officially indoctrinated with the fraternal rituals, our little sisters were an asset in various areas. They helped in all our major social functions, fund-raisers for charities, and helping us to make passing grades through all of the partying we were doing.

It was during one of our charity events, while both brothers and little sisters were working on a float for a parade, that I met Jan. A year ahead of me and definitely much more mature, Jan and I had very little in common. Therefore, we rarely spoke during my first semester with the fraternity except to exchange passing pleasantries. Part of the reason we rarely communicated is because Jan was one of the few women who could intimidate me. She did it through her striking beauty and exceptional intelligence. She had long, beautiful red hair which intrigued me from the start. She was very personable, although one had to know her before she would open up. She had a wonderful sense of humor but rarely showed that side of herself since her intelligence far overshadowed it. Her intelligence was also a deterrent for me since she often-times knew when I was lying to her or bullshitting her about something. It would be hard to put anything over on her without careful planning and the act of lying which, by now, I was becoming a master of.

During my second semester junior year, I was voted vice-president of the fraternity. My relationship with Jan also increased in its intensity. With my new position I was directly responsible for many of our major functions and diverted much time and attention to this. I was floundering with my classes and was still flirting dangerously close to the dreaded 2.0 grade point average.

Jan must have been sent from God as another guardian angel since she became acutely aware of my situation and took great pains to give me a sense of direction. To begin, she informed me there was absolutely no sense in being a political science major (which is what I was), unless I intended to go to law school (which I didn't). She analyzed all the credits I had amassed and informed me I was perfectly suited to become a teacher without having to take any additional credits. I changed my major to secondary education with political science as my minor. Actually, I hate politics but it was the easiest avenue I could envision to graduate from college.

Next, Jan did something none of my teachers were able to accomplish. She taught me how to study. She taught me how to decipher relevant information from bullshit in the textbooks and how to transfer the facts to the tests I took. She did such a good job, that my final semester of college I achieved a perfect 4.0 GPA which would raise my final grades to 3.0, or a B student. In short, she is the reason I made it out of college and got to where I am today.

Once we started dating, Jan also worked diligently on other areas in which I was grossly lacking; etiquette, manners, and class. She realized it would not happen overnight and that there would be no possible way I could go home with her to meet her family until she made some adjustments and fine-tuned me considerably in several areas. After I took her to Saint Clair to see what life had been like for me so far, Jan also resigned herself to the fact that what she was about to undertake would be a monumental task. She would have to do this gradually and discreetly since there was the distinct possibility I would become offended if I were to realize what she was attempting to do.

If we were to try and create any type of concrete relationship, it would be important that I pass the litmus test of her family. It certainly would not be easy for me to gain acceptance from her family since I was basically just a backward kid from the coal mining region who spoke terrible English and who cursed more often than he used basic vocabulary. Also, it was unknown to me during the first several months of our relationship that Jan's father was a Harvard graduate in chemistry, *magna cum laude,* and a senior chemist for Colgate-Palmolive based out of its New York City headquarters. Needless to say, when she finally revealed this information to me, all I could utter were two words, "Holy Shit!"

You can understand the paranoia that must have been going through her mind when she even thought about taking me to meet them. A four-month crash course in class certainly would never be enough time to smooth out all the rough edges. Jan also failed to inform me, although I should have grasped it the first time she told me about her father, that her family was well to do, living in an upper class area of New Jersey. However, the reality of the situation was soon to hit me smack in the face.

Without James's knowledge, I purchased a 1964 Ford LTD from a fraternity brother whose father was part owner of the dealership. He sold it to me for 200 dollars, and it would be my first purchase on credit since I agreed to pay installments of 10 dollars a month, no interest. I was very proud of that vehicle since it was the first material thing I ever owned that was worth something. It had low mileage, was very clean inside, and had lots of room which, due to my height, is what I look for in a car. Also, lots of room in a car came in handy during those early years for various and sundry other activities. Due to the car size, we nicknamed it "the boat," and would have many fine times in it. I also put in two huge speakers which took up the entire back seat for my stereo system. With this knowledge of my new-found transportation, you can already imagine how we must have looked the day we finally set out for New Jersey to meet Jan's family.

****

Jack and Katie Schurman had, for all intents and purposes, a real life Brady Bunch family. Their three children, all girls and all redheads, were born with extreme intelligence. In fact, all three are considered genius by my standard. Of course, my standards of brilliance are unique.

Sandy, the eldest daughter, was already married and living in Biloxi, Mississippi. Next was Janet, in her senior year of college, a year ahead of me. Third was Vicki, perhaps the most intelligent of the three, very analytical. Vicki was in high school the day I walked into the Schurman household and entered their lives. The house was the finest I'd been in during the course of my life. I had not yet equated that with a degree in chemistry from Harvard came jobs in which you are called "sir" by everyone.

Jack was not yet home during my initial entrance where I met Katie and Vicki. I really don't know what Katie was expecting her daughter to bring home, but I must have totally blown her mind. A tall, lanky kid from the coal region who had never been outside a three-hundred-mile radius of his home. To her, I'm sure I seemed as naive as I acted when, in reality, I had already seen so much. I believe my happy-go-lucky personality combined with my backward naivete immediately put her at ease. The place was immaculate and big, with large rooms in each area of the house. This was so different from the confined houses I had become so accustomed to.

When the door of Jack's car finally closed in the driveway an immediate apprehension came over me. I realized I had never met anyone with this man's intelligence before. I also realized I faced a situation of "acceptance" which I had never had to deal with before. Upon his entrance into the kitchen where we were all standing, he immediately acknowledged and kissed his wife (a tip off of the Brady Bunch syndrome). After that he acknowledged each of his two daughters with a hug. In what seemed like an eternity, he finally turned to address me. After performing an image scan on me, his first words ever directed at me would be, "Janet is right, you do remind me of a big dummy." From that first sentence forward, Jack Schurman and I went through a 1970's, premature for its time, male bonding process.

Other than my first true role model—my brother Frank—Jack Schurman turned into my first adult hero. He was of extreme intelligence, with a quick wit and often would be drumming up reasons to have a party at the house on weekends. Until I got to know him, his daughters said he rarely cursed, and even then, nothing major. I knew we were meant for bonding when he took me on a tour of the house, including the basement where I would be staying. After going through the large, three-story structure, it was time to go downstairs into what, in the homes I was accustomed, would be called "the cellar." When he and I stepped down the eight carpeted stairs, I fell in immediate lust "with the room." Big floppy couch, color TV on a swivel, air conditioned (very important), and a HUGE BAR. The liquor collection awed me. However, when Jack opened that huge refrigerator and displayed all those different bottles of imported and domestic beer, all I could mutter were two brief words, "Holy Shit." Jack responded to me with two simple yet understandable words, "No Shit!" At that point, we both grinned, and the bonding process began.

Saturday of my first weekend with Jan's family we were to attend the wedding of a friend of the family's daughter. For this trip I had to pack the one and only sport coat I had, a blue-pattern polyester that I believed I looked simply dashing in. Even during the dinner, at a time the open bar closed, Jack had me out at the cash bar in the lobby of the hotel. He introduced me to drinks and liqueurs that, until that time, were most definitely obscure to me. Both of us became crocked during the course of the reception. In fact, I decided during that first day's festivities that I liked and respected Jack, Katie, and their family so much, that I was going to add to his collection of bar glasses. For there, sitting at a very fancy wedding reception by my standards, was a drunk coal miner's son putting empty cocktail glasses in his suit-coat pocket. Jack thought it was a riot and couldn't stop laughing. Judging by Jack's reaction, I thought I was doing something good. Katie, Jan and Vicki shook their heads as if to say, "Lord, help us." I was doing good. I got past the security in the lobby on the way out to the car after the reception. I made it, we were at the car. Jack was unsteady also, therefore Katie would drive. However, he insisted on opening the door for everyone, like the true gentleman he was. As he was opening the rear door of the side I was sitting on, I lost my balance. The car door and my jacket pocket collided simultaneously. I could only say, "uh-oh," knowing I now had a pocketful of cubic-zircon. Jack and I laughed all the way home. I couldn't even feel the shards of glass in my leg.

I threw up that night, but made strides into acceptance by the perfect family by simply being myself. As I look back, Jack would often speak to me and treat me like the son he never had. Over a short period of time and visits to the house, we gained respect for each other, in very different ways. He already had my respect for his extreme intelligence. However, he was also able to let his guard down around me—the corporate guard. When he was with me, he could be himself, and yes, he did a lot of cussing to me about situations as he perceived them in the world. When you took the 8-6, Monday thru Friday suit coat off of Jack, he was able to shed his stress and be a down-to-earth man, someone I could relate to and talk to easily.

He gained respect for me in that, once he taught me something about life in general and the maturation process, I never forgot it. From shaking hands while making direct eye contact with a person, to proper etiquette while eating, I always retained his knowledge and would use it to my fullest benefit in the years to come. As a result of Jack's respect and confidence in me, I began to gain Katie's acceptance. Vicki still viewed me as a seemingly unintelligent, backward kid, but then she still does today. One thing I can comfortably say is that the Schurman family did everything possible to make me comfortable during my visits when, upon first impressions, they had every reason to show me to the door at gunpoint.

****

During my junior year, with Janet's help, I started getting my priorities in order. I had a great semester gradewise, under Jan's tutelage. I was not trying to land every attractive woman I met. I had now met someone I became accountable to in an off sort of way. We slept together frequently, ate together, did our laundry together (actually she did mine and I followed for the "oral" support), and studied together. I was having to adapt my lifestyle to something I had, until this point, never had, but would have for the remainder of my life—accountability. Odd as it would appear, I was liking it and gradually conforming to an unwritten code, as written by Jan. We were traveling to Jan's home in New Jersey once a month, and would visit Saint Clair sporadically. She realized when I was back with the locals, the bonding process would begin and I would ignore her while becoming extremely drunk. She didn't like that, nor those people who could have that type of control over me.

During the second semester, my life had taken a dramatic turn for the better. I was well on my way to graduating from college, had met a mature woman with a great family. That summer I attended school and worked in the bowling alley for additional income. By this time, I had completely moved in with Jan and was forced to learn another area of accountability, sharing expenses. I had never, ever, dreamed of one day having a checking account and the responsibilities thereof.

I looked forward to our visits to New Jersey. I also believe they looked forward to me, what with the way I talked and how naive I was about life in general. No matter what the occasion, I always felt comfortable—secure is another term—in the presence of Jack and Katie Schurman. I was jealous of Jan because it appeared to me the perfect upbringing in relation to mine. I guess I was most astounded because I felt that people who were "well-to-do" carried attitudes about them.

Visits to the college and, more specifically, Jan's apartment, were totally different situations when Jack and Katie came to Bloomsburg. Although I believed they knew we were living together, we had to take every precaution to prove we weren't. I would have to haul all my clothes to the frat house, along with toiletries, books, anything which could prove my habitation of an extended period. Jan was about to graduate with her elementary education degree, while I was preparing for my senior year. Over the course of my junior year, I managed to raise my GPA to 2.7, no easy feat when one has to reverse the snowball up the mountain. Jack and Katie were taking an extended vacation through the South and were planning to stop in Bloomsburg for an evening on their return to New Jersey. Jan was planning to inform her Mom and Dad she had decided, with their blessing, to pursue her masters degree in reading. Therefore, when I graduated with my B.S., she would receive her M.Ed., and everything was well on its way to becoming "O.K."

When I saw their car pulling into the apartment driveway, I immediately knew something was wrong. I intended to be waiting at the door with a cold one for Jack, and a hug for Katie, after their long drive. Katie was driving, and Katie never drove when Jack was present unless he had been partaking of inebriating substances. Jack was lying down in the back seat, and had been for several hours while Katie drove. While in Oklahoma, Katie's home state, Jack informed her he wasn't feeling well. He told her he could not pinpoint any area directly, yet, his body felt clammy and sore all the time. Jack tried to drive on the return trip but was too weak. He also realized it was severe, because he refused to see a doctor until they got home, in the confines of their friends and local environment.

I lifted him out of the back seat and, for a quick, fleeting moment, he looked like Peter the day he had taken sick in front of me. Instead of spending the evening at a local hotel, Katie took us aside and said she didn't like the looks of Jack, his lack of energy and wit, and was going to go on to New Jersey, an additional two hours drive to compound her exhaustion.

Jack could do nothing but lie down on the bed and rest. He was clammy, experiencing chills, and had a defeated look about him, something he would never allow to happen. Although I could not pinpoint the reason for my respect toward him at the time, I now realize it was his attitude I appreciated the most. He had an attitude much like the one Coach Wolfe instilled in Da Boyz. He simply never accepted no, or anything negative as a solution, only another problem. No matter what he attempted to undertake, be it building a state-of-the-art stereo system by himself, to analyzing a complicated chemical theory, he was always positive. Fortunately, I had a chance to experience this personality firsthand and would be able to emulate him and those beliefs he stood for in life. However, this new twist with the Jack Schurman I came to know took a Nolan Ryan curveball when I saw and was aware of the look in his face, much like the faces of the people I believed were my parents during their last moments on earth. I was able to feel what was going through Jack's mind as being inevitable, even with the never-say-die attitude he had. He knew that what had taken control of his body was bigger than anything he ever attempted to conquer. He realized that this was bigger than any equation or challenge he had ever battled. This was going precisely at Jack's strongest trait, his physical and mental strength.

****

It didn't take long for the doctors to discover what had taken control of Jack's body. It was thoroughly riddled with cancer! It had taken him down so quickly, with no warning, everyone was taken by surprise. Except me! The look of death is obvious, regardless of the denial that people experience. Recognizing the obvious makes it easier to accept the jolt that your body experiences the first time you hear the prognosis. For those who have never experienced that look, the shock intensifies itself drastically.

The next three months were spent traveling between college and New Jersey, with Jan having to endure an excruciating school schedule. She was going to get her master's, including thesis, in one year. The complication of the cancer intensified the stress that she was trying to deal with. On top of this, she was constantly trying to keep me on the right path. She was devastated by the news of her father. I was devastated and I only had eighteen months with him. I can't imagine what she was enduring with the kind of closeness they experienced as a family. I only knew how painful it was from the perspective of someone who wasn't close to his parents, never had a heart-to-heart with them or told them he loved them. Jan's parents told their children and showed their children how much they loved them every opportunity they got.

The cancer was too far advanced to believe chemotherapy could combat it, although it was tried. On a Friday evening we drove from Bloomsburg to New Jersey, realizing all the while that this time could be the last. Upon seeing Jack on late Friday evening, both of us knew the end was very near. He was relying totally on life support apparatus and heavy dosages of pain medication. Although heavily sedated and in intense pain, he was still very lucid, to the point of reading a novel, even at this stage. I wish I could remember the name of the book that would accompany him into the next life. On Saturday, we proceeded to the hospital again. Once again, Jack was lucid, although intermittently. Once again, we retreated home believing he was going to buy one more week, and we would stop by the hospital on the way back to college the next day.

****

Katie was already at Jack's side, having accepted the look of death and determined to be there for his last dying breath. She was pale and weak, looking much older than when I first met her. The past several months had drained her emotionally, mentally, and physically. Suddenly she was having to assume the responsibilities that Jack had done for so many years. Checking account, savings account, auto insurance, all those things that an unsuspecting wife is left to deal with while at the same time preparing to undergo the death process.

When we walked into the room, I knew the end was very near. He was coming in and out of consciousness and I stood in the background while Jan, Vicki and Sandy stood close by. During a spell of consciousness, Jack recognized me trying to blend in with the wall in the corner of his room. A smile came over his face and he immediately said, ''Come here, you BIG DUMMY.'' I was hoping this scenario wouldn't happen because I didn't know if I could handle it. In a short period of time, I had become closer to this man than in a lifetime of my family structure. This was the father I was looking for by proxy, and he was gone just as quickly as he had entered my life. I walked up to the bed, with Katie relinquishing her spot at his side so he could speak to me. He took me by the hand and said something to this affect: "Never stop chasing your dreams, dreams are good, they give you something to strive for. Remember, you're only as good as your dreams, and dreams are limitless, they have no end, only a beginning. Go for your dreams and never look back. Help take care of Katie and Vicki, take care of Janet and accept the fact I love you, even though I won't be around to prove it. Be happy for the times we had together, not those we'll never have. Most of all, believe in yourself as I believe in you."

I excused myself from the room and found a place to cry. I didn't know what he was going to say to Katie and the girls, but if it was like his words to me, they experienced the final chapter of unconditional love between a father, his children, and spouse. Even in his last days, Jack did it with class. He hung in there long enough to tie up all loose ends. My crying was from the heart, and I was already able to see through the void to all that Jack represented that was good. At all that he would transpose to my personality. From helping me take the step from adolescent immaturity to full-blown man. I had no secrets with Jack, and I realize this now. In less than two years of a relationship that, for all intents and purposes should never have been, we had come a long way toward respecting each other. Even his goodbye words to me would be of relevance, since they would stay with me, even as I write this.

We debated not returning to campus, however, upon the insistence of Katie, we returned to attend classes the following day. The ride back was long, few words were spoken yet we acknowledged silently to each other that the end was near. We arrived back in our apartment in the late afternoon and within hours the phone rang. It was Don Schurman, Jack's brother, advising us that Jack had expired. Nothing unexpected, yet shattering all the same. We packed in the middle of the night and Jan wept as I drove. What she failed to see as she sat there mourning was that I was crying, too. I was letting my guard down. At first I tried to reconcile myself that I was crying for Jan in her suffering. What I didn't realize, with those silent tears running down my cheeks obliterating sight, was the quality of the potential friend I had recently made. Once again, repeating through the back of my mind, began racing the simple question, "Why?" "Why the fuck is this happening

to me again?" I thought I was through caring about feelings—people.
"Why are you taking these people from me, God?" In essence, I had
become closer to Jack than I had to Jan. The reason, simple. Male
bonding is much easier than trying to express oneself to a woman. Men
understand each other and their feelings much more so than they
understand women, be they spouse, acquaintance, friend, or unknown.

****

Just when my life was rebounding from all the setbacks I had
experienced, I was faced with another sorrow. It seemed as though
having to accept death was becoming the norm for me, not the
exception. With each death I encountered, I became more and more
immune to the feelings that should be associated with it. With the
passing of Jack Schurman, I had only fond memories and no
unanswered questions, no secrets being withheld into the next life.
Therefore, the void of death was much easier to see through and I was
able to put him to rest in my mind with those pleasant memories.

The funeral was very sad. Aside from the respect he earned in his
job, Jack was also very respected within their community. There was an
extremely large turnout at the church and I was surprised at how well
Jan kept her emotions in check. Katie and all the children had
responded extremely well to the shock and heartbreak they had been
through recently. They were all mature enough to realize the pain their
father was in and that, due to the severity of the illness, death, although
difficult to accept, was the only possible solution. Katie and Vicki
would now be sole occupants of the large house, with Jan and me
visiting whenever we could. Although never admitting to us she was
aware, Katie certainly knew Jan and I had taken up full-time residence.
I vowed that as long as I was a part of this family, no harm would
come to that woman. She, too, had accepted me at face value, never
asking me to change my personality and be someone I couldn't. Over
time, she and I would adopt a mother-son relationship, much to the
surprise of those people who knew us both. Some things can never be
explained in words, only actions. I will always love Jack Schurman and
will always live with the fond memories of how he molded my life in a
positive fashion. God will always be with him.

****

I had now begun my senior year, well on my way toward becoming a Secondary Education graduate. My second semester would be spent student teaching and that summer, taking some additional courses required for my graduation. If all went well, I would have my diploma by the middle of August, 1977, and Jan would have successfully achieved her master's degree. We even had an opportunity to take a couple of courses together. This turned out to be a humbling experience for me.

My student teaching was done at Shikellamy High School in Sunbury, Pennsylvania, fifteen miles from our campus. I would be teaching seniors various social studies courses. From the first time I stepped in front of my first class, I felt comfortable speaking and was never at a loss for words. In fact, I really enjoyed the challenge and became a strict but fair teacher. I demanded the students work also, a prerequisite for becoming involved in my classes. Each week we would have an open forum discussion on any current event they chose. Some of the subjects they decided on became the focus of intense debate. Give many of today's students credit: if they're given a challenge, in most cases they respond.

That was my last full semester in college. I received a perfect 4.0 for my student teaching efforts and felt good about the impression I had left on those students whom I taught. When teachers are successful in getting their students to retain what they are taught combined with leaving a positive impression, then they have truly accomplished something. I had definitely grown up during that period. I was feeling a sense of pride for what I had achieved. With the completion of our courses, an avenue for a crucial decision had arisen:

Jan:

> "So, what do you suppose is going to happen with us after we graduate?"

Pat:

> "I dunno. Really haven't thought about it much."
> (I was gradually breaking away from my coal miner slang).

Jan:

> "Well, when do you think would be a good time to

start? When we're both done school with no income!''

Pat:

"Well, what do you think? What do you want to do?''

Jan:

"If you ask me, we either get married or get to our destination and get on with our lives. I don't have time for guessing games here, are we going to get married, or what?''

Pat:

"I guess so. What do we do next?''

The very next Saturday we rode with James to Philadelphia where there is a street that is called "Diamond Row," with jewelry store after jewelry store competing against each other. We spent the entire day with Jan looking for the perfect ring, finally drawing one for a vendor who made it to her specifications. James picked up the tab from what I had left in my savings account. Just like that, I was engaged to be married.

Katie, Vicki, and Sandy were already expecting the news. In a short time, I had gone from totally noncommittal in my life to the biggest commitment I would ever undertake. There was only one problem: I couldn't understand why I decided to do this. Was it that I felt sorry for Jan because of her father's recent passing? Was it just that I was scared because I had never been alone before and marriage seemed like the most convenient thing to do? Whatever the underlying reason, one thing was for certain, it wasn't because I was head over heels in love. I had never loved anything or anyone in my life. Not with the unconditional love that is supposed to go with the vow of marriage. I was already questioning how a marriage based on convenience and the need for companionship would work out.

****

On May 29, 1977, two weeks after my student teaching ended, I formally took the vow of marriage with Jan. We were married in a

Caldwell, New Jersey, Methodist church with a Catholic priest present for the service to satisfy my family members. I was so nervous, I forgot to shave before the ceremony. If one looks real close at our wedding album, they can see the stubbles on my face. Fortunately, I am not heavily bearded. I also had a real dark tan after having gone to Fort Lauderdale with my best man, Jim Kane, a week before the wedding. Jimmy was the person who loaned me the money on my first car and we are still very close today.

The wedding reception was hilarious if one could have seen the two factions represented. On one hand was Jan's family and friends. Very formal, very refined. Then there was the contingent from Pennsylvania, always ready to party at a wedding, especially one that had an open bar. All our derelict friends from college were there to add even more spice to the event. As one can imagine, when strangers get together at an event such as this, with much alcohol involved, the bonding process comes quick. Everyone was drawing together at the end, having a great time. Bruncle Frank gave us a Mexican vacation as a wedding present with a week-long tour of Mexico City, Puerto Vallarta, and Acapulco. He also slipped a hundred-dollar bill in my hand before we started to our honeymoon suite, where I invited all our college friends in for drinks. I guess I was still nervous, even after it was all over and still needed some male bonding. Jan never forgave me when they all trooped into our wedding love nest and sat around drinking.

After the wedding, we still had the remainder of the summer to think about our options. With Jan's master's, a teaching job would be much easier for her to acquire. In 1977, teachers were not in demand, although I could have gotten a job easy enough. The problem with me was the pay. The starting salary for a first-year teacher was $1,050 a month, merely $12,600 a year. It didn't seem right to me after the education process we had recently undergone. One thing we knew for certain, once we both graduated, it was shit or get off the pot regarding supporting ourselves. Katie nor James would any longer be responsible for our financial well-being. On our wedding day, James gave me the remainder of my savings account, $450. Jan's last semester of education was taken care of, but that was it. So, with my $450, and whatever possessions we had, we were going to be set free to face the world as a young, married couple. No immediate plans, no immediate future.

****

Right before Jan and I were married, James finally tied the knot at age forty-four. Therefore, he moved out of the house in Saint Clair. He sold it to Jocelyn and her husband, Ducky. She still had the responsibility of raising Adrian, as well as her own children, which she was now in the process of having. I rarely went there any longer, only on family get-together occasions. The Miller family all accepted Jan and believed her to be too good a catch for me. I reserved opinion, realizing many of them were intimidated by her intelligence and upbringing. Whatever, the general consensus among them was that I was in better hands with her than she with me. Actually, I felt the same way but dared not admit that to anyone.

****

During our honeymoon in Mexico, Jan and I would have much to discuss relating to our future. Shortly after our wedding, Jan's sister Sandy, and her husband, Ron, who was in the Air Force, were reassigned to Lackland Air Force Base in San Antonio, Texas. Sandy informed Jan that jobs were plentiful there, especially for those with college degrees and asked her to consider moving down. When Jan hit me with this in Mexico, my first thought was, "no way." I informed Jan that moving south would leave no one close by to help Katie and Vicki, should they need any. Besides, I had never envisioned myself living in the South. "People were backward there, weren't they?" I was beginning to sound like the pot calling the kettle black. Imagine, someone who had roots like mine thinking people in the South were backward when I'd never been there. In any event, the thought of even considering that was already out of the question to me.

It was during our Mexican honeymoon that Jan and I had our first misunderstanding as husband and wife. It happened on our first day in Acapulco. Jan, having red hair and fair skin, burns quickly from the sun. She decided to go against that intense sun, insisting to me as I watched her swimming and sunbathing that she wasn't getting burned. This only after my observation and insistence that she was, in fact, turning bright red. However, she persisted in insisting that she was not getting burned, it was simply the intense glare from the sun reflecting off her.

"O.K., I'll go get us a couple more drinks." Two and a half hours later, when the heat was far too intense for me, and I don't burn, I insisted we go up to our room. When we got there and finally adjusted to the normal lighting, Jan looked like a bright red Christmas light. Her skin was literally on fire. She felt it immediately and was beginning the initial stages of sun poisoning. She tried to shower, but her skin had already tightened up and the sting of the shower stream hurt all the more. All she could do was lie in bed, crying from the intense pain. I don't guess now was the proper time for me to do this, but I really had to make an observation, since Jan had never been wrong. "Ya know, Jan, I don't wanna say that I told you so, but I did. Look at you, ya can't even move. What am I supposed ta do now while you're laying there like a lobster ready to be served with butter? This is our honeymoon, ya know!"

O.K., I may have overdone it a little and should have had some compassion under the circumstances. However, I felt like I had to make my point since I felt I was now being screwed on my honeymoon. Not by my wife but by the sun.

Needless to say, my statement to her went over very well by her rebuttal: "You prick. How many times have I helped you and been there for you when you needed it? Who's been there for you through all the horseshit that you've pulled on me. I never asked you for anything, and now that I really need you, you pull this shit. Just get out of here, I'll get through this on my own."

I left the room extremely upset, and hoped this wasn't going to be an omen of things to come. Of course, as a man, it never dawned on me that she had a point. I felt bad for her, and mad at the way she reacted to my statement, not realizing at the time I had her at a distinct disadvantage. I did realize that she needed medical attention and found my way to a pharmacy with help from a chicklet vendor. If you've ever wondered what happened to all those little boxes of chicklets you used to see, they've been shipped to Mexico where kids ten and under peddle them to the turistas. The conversation with the pharmacist was also very interesting, especially when it came time for me to pay. I didn't have a clue about the Mexican currency. He had me at a disadvantage and realized it. I had no idea if he took advantage of me, nor did I care.

The medicine helped and we were next headed to Mexico City. There, she got a case of Montezuma's revenge and became violently ill. Oh, she also hurled on a bus ride from Puerto Vallarta to Acapulco. All in all, I think we'd both pass on a return to Mexico, what with all the fun we had on our initial visit. Those times Jan wasn't under the weather or fried to a crisp, we had a great time and met a lot of fun people. I'll never forget it as long as I live!

****

Since I would be graduating at the end of the summer, the college would not have an extravagant ceremony like they held at the end of each semester. Jan had successfully obtained her master's, including her thesis, in one year. No easy feat. I was impressed since I had watched how hard she worked.

I, on the other hand, chose to party hard that summer, shortly after we returned from our wedding. I only had two basic courses to complete, my perfect 4.0 tucked neatly into my ego. Since Jack was gone and Katie was recovering from his death, I really had no one to care about coming to my graduation. Therefore, I had requested they mail my diploma to Saint Clair. I would have Jo forward it, or I would pick it up, depending upon where we chose to take up residence. I knew that within ninety days, Jan and I would have to come to an agreement about where we wanted to live and work.

We had tossed around going back home to live with Katie since Vicki was soon to start college and she would be all alone in that large house. In the end, we both decided against confronting Katie with this, since she seemed to be doing fine on her own, working with charities to keep her mind off her recent sorrow.

Another thing both of us agreed upon wholeheartedly was that we did not want to return to my hometown area either. The total exit of coal as a viable commodity had left the area depleted of its energy. Businesses were failing and downtown buildings were being boarded up in the major hub of the county, Pottsville. The area had definitely lost its lifeline when coal lost its appeal, yet the regeneration process is still ongoing today. I think about Saint Clair occasionally, when I am trying to put situations in perspective in my life.

Since I had to come to some major league decisions soon, the thought of moving to Texas intrigued me. There is always that stigma applied to Texans that they all ride horses to work and everybody wears a ten-gallon hat. Images of cactus and cowshit would often flash through my mind when thinking about this possibility. "Jobs are really easy to find here, especially with a college degree." I didn't know Jan's sister Sandy well, but I was beginning not to like her. Actually she and Ron were a fun couple, but his Air Force mentality and my nonchalant personality could never coexist. To all of us who were raised in Saint

Clair, Texas was a foreign land you read about or see in the movies.

****

When I finally made up my mind and realized what I would like to do, I knew it would meet with Jan's approval. Unlike Jan's initial reaction to the southern sun, I loved it. Having lived through 22 years of snow, the absence of it on a year-round basis appealed to me all the more. Our decision to move would also open the door for me to what would eventually be the employment avenue I would pursue. A business that to this day never ceases to amaze me.

I had sold "the boat" to a fraternity brother and we sold everything else that could not be packed into Jan's car. We said goodbye to Katie and family and headed to Saint Clair for a going-away party. With my departure from home for good, all those who had held the secret for so long would finally be able to breathe easier. The distance between myself and the truth now would always be in their favor. Everybody could finally relax, or so they thought.

The party was your basic "two kegs in da back yard" routine, and I said goodbye to many of my family and friends. With our car loaded with the necessities of life, I couldn't help but smile. Many things had worked in my favor, in a very awkward way, and I was able to achieve the college degree I had always dreamed of except I had to come in the back door from the way I had anticipated. It took awhile for me to understand, but learning and working on my own gave me a much greater sense of satisfaction.

I had many things going in my favor; a great wife, a college education, a car loaded with clothes, escape from Saint Clair which I had always desperately wanted, and $450 to our name. The way I saw it, we were rich. I had been through a lot and believed I had finally made it to the mountain.

As we drove down through Maryland, West Virginia, Virginia, and all those cities and states on the route we were taking, I was awed by the beauty of our country. I hoped that someday I would have an opportunity to see all of our states, to understand the entire picture. I was constantly deep in thought as we drove on, extremely apprehensive about what we were about to undertake. We decided to start our married life together where it would take some time to overcome the culture shock. Once that happened, the rest would be history.

CHAPTER SEVEN

GO SOUTH, YOUNG MAN

"Welcome to Texas, The Lone Star State." Make no doubt about it, you don't need a sign to tell that you have entered Texas in early September. The combination of heat and humidity spells it out plainly. Especially if you are in a '72 Nova, yellow with a black top and no air conditioning. With the windows rolled down and sweat dripping off us, we could easily have passed for a large bumble bee searching out pollen.

The Texas heat can do funny things if you're not used to it. A mirage effect is created by the radiation off the roadways and one can see the reflection of the heat as it bounces off, or so it seems. Also, as I would find out in my first week there, too much of this intense heat without proper precautions will make one experience vertigo and heat prostration.

Another surefire way to know you're in Texas happened on the first night we arrived in San Antonio. As we were nearing the exit toward our final destination, exhausted from three straight days of un-airconditioned driving, a large football field appeared on our left. The stadium lights were on and a game was obviously being played. The parking lot was huge and cars were parked everywhere, including outside the fence on the road. Jan was driving and I distinctly remember saying, "Holy Shit, dare must be a pre-season game goin' on dare, Cowboys-Oilers maybe!'' As we viewed the entire far sideline, I was in awe. The stands were packed with people. There was no other explanation in my mind other than a professional, pre-season game. Within ten minutes, we were at Sandy and Ron's house and I was informed that what I saw was, in fact, Northside High School stadium and the game being played was between Holmes and Jay, two bitter high school rivals. The only time I had seen that many people together at a sporting event was at Veteran's Stadium in Philadelphia. To be informed that this was a high school game with eighteen thousand people in attendance was mind-boggling to me. Especially after what I was accustomed to in both high school and college. A big game for Bloomsburg might draw five to seven thousand people. Make no mistake about it, they take their football very seriously in Texas!

****

Although the '77-'78 school year was already underway, Jan was hired to teach first grade on her first day of interviewing. I, on the other hand, did not wish to commit my signature to a teaching contract since I wasn't sure if this was my true ''calling'' for employment. Therefore, to test the water, I was hired to teach on a full-time substitute basis at a local Catholic school. The teacher I was substituting for was out on an extended medical absence. Consequently, the position was full-time substitute. What a coincidence that Jan and I would both be teaching first grade at the same time. Although my degree was not in elementary education, my credentials from Bloomsburg were adequate to hold the position if I chose to go back to school and pursue my certification in that field. Not hardly! That initial semester, trying to instill our educational system in six- and seven-year-olds reaffirmed my belief that this was definitely not my chosen field. Constantly needing attention, these young children would have me totally frazzled by the end of the day. ''I have to go to the bathroom (all day long),'' ''Johnnie's pulling my hair,'' ''Billy's picking his nose and eating it.'' All these distractions left very little room for teaching. On the other hand, Jan would come home bursting with joy at her achievements of the day in molding her children. We were literally at opposite ends of the spectrum when evaluating our successes or failures in our classrooms. Therefore, it came as no surprise to Jan when I informed her I was advising the school that I would not be returning for the spring semester. It just wasn't me, trying to teach children of this age.

****

With both of us receiving an income for what we were doing, we had taken up residence in an apartment off Bronco Lane (appropriate for Texas), within walking distance of Jan's school. I was prepared to hit the streets shortly after Christmas to test the water and see what "really" was out there in 1978 for a young whipper snapper like myself.

After my initial interviews that week, I received three offers of employment, all from companies I had never heard of. All three provided an income which would far surpass that of a teacher, plus a benefits package, something neither Jan nor I had paid much attention to up till this point. However, at Borg-Warner Acceptance Corporation, when the branch manager mentioned the words "car and gas," I was all ears. We still only had one car and knew a second was imminent after I had found gainful employment. When I formally received and accepted their offer, both Jan and I were ecstatic. There was, however, something I was still hazy on—exactly what my job description would be. I had no idea that Borg-Warner was a finance institution which offered loans to retail customers on "any" household items. From air conditioners to furniture, we financed it and consequently, had to collect it.

By the way, the automobile came at a price. I would also be a field collector going into some of the nicer areas of town to ask for money or call a truck to take the refrigerator out of the kitchen. Or, the air conditioner out of the wall, whatever. It all boiled down to the essence of the job, "loaning money out and collecting the money back, with interest, in return."

When I started work and realized exactly what the job entailed, I began to learn about the world. I was so naive at the time, I never realized that borrowing was done to acquire. To my knowledge, I had never been privy to a collector calling ours, nor anyone else's house I knew, to ask for money owed. I did not become aware until then that credit is what our country and, for that matter, all the countries of the world, depend upon to survive. There is a certain percentage of people or countries who are unable to live up to their contractual obligations. That is when I would enter the picture.

Upon beginning my employment, certain contingencies had to be met. Successful physical examination and urinalysis, copy of valid driver's license, copy of social security card, copy of birth certificate to verify citizenship, to name a few. Most of these I was easily able to supply, however, when it came to a "certified copy" of my birth certificate, I realized I had never seen mine. I had to call Jo in Saint Clair and advise her of the necessity for this document. She had never seen my certificate either, but she would look through a stack of paperwork James had left her after the official sale of the house. Once again, I informed her of the urgency and left it at that, expecting to receive the document. It was not a top priority at the time because I was allowed to start my new job with the understanding the certificate would be forthcoming. With that, both my employer and I seemed to forget about it until someone from the corporate office realized the absence of the document in my employee file.

Toward the end of June, I was called into my branch manager's office, concerned I had done something wrong. He reminded me of the company's contingencies of employment and advised I had two weeks to provide the document. In all honesty, I had totally forgotten and I believed Jo had done the same. After the meeting with my boss, I immediately phoned to inform her of the predicament I was in and to ask for immediate help with the situation. I still don't know whether Jo had purposely stalled, hoping that everyone involved would forget about it, or whether she honestly forgot to look. I can never get a straight answer on this since she has always refused to discuss the issue with me. However, she asked me to hold on while she obtained the papers James had transferred to her. With me holding, concerned by the severity of the situation, she began flipping through the pages. After what seemed an eternity, she finally came back on the phone to inform me she had found it. I asked her to immediately place it in the mail. As I look back now, I remember her seeming reluctance to do this. I will always be apprehensive about her total knowledge, or ignorance of me, toward unveiling the secret. My guess is that Jo, in consultation with James, would try to second-guess my naive, unexploring nature, and hope I did not peruse the document after receiving it.

If that was the case, congratulations, you were right. I would simply have opened the envelope to see that it was in fact, my certificate. Next, I would put it in my briefcase, take it to work and shoot a copy for my files, then file it somewhere with other important paperwork that is rarely, if ever, consulted. What they would underestimate was the intelligence of my new spouse. They had no idea she would be the one to go out and retrieve the mail on this day, July 11, 1978, my twenty-fourth birthday.

****

I've replayed the scene many times. Each time it seems like it happened yesterday. Each time I seem to remember another trivial detail or something that was said.

It was Saturday. Both of us were off, although I had worked until eleven knocking on doors. After that, I would begin the obligatory drinking ritual that had been instilled in all of us at a young age. To a coal miner, the birthday of anyone was a festive occasion and definitely a drinking holiday. I'm sure that for many still living in the region, the same ritual applies today. Jan and I were discussing, as I was tossing beers, how odd it was that every Christmas and every one of my birthdays, Rose Mary always sent a present. In most instances, she would send a pair of jeans with a card and cash, the only one of my family members to do this. I was saying how nice it was of her to do this since we had just yesterday received the package and card.

It was very hot outside as can be imagined on a July day in San Antonio. I was swimming at the pool most of the afternoon and at the same time swilling suds. With the hot Texas sun dehydrating my body, combined with my desire for liquid, in this case beer, I was well on my way to full-blown bombed when Jan announced she was going to check the mail.

By this time, I was back at the apartment to continue the festivities and the opening of presents. I was feeling good, having evaluated the recent accomplishments of both Jan and myself while trying to look into our bright future.

It was then that Jan walked through the door with the mail. She had gone through most of the mail when she came upon writing on an envelope which was unmistakably Jo's. I already knew what it was, so it was no big thing. However, as is her nature, Jan took the document from the envelope and immediately began to scrutinize it. Eventually she stopped thinking about what she was reading and looked at me. I couldn't pinpoint her look but it was more of a question in itself.

Jan:

> "I'm going to tell you something, Pat. It's something I've suspected for a long time but could never prove nor say anything to you about. You were adopted at birth, Victoria is not your real

mother, Rose Mary is. It states this plainly on your birth certificate!''

Pat:

"Come on, Janet. It must jest be a typo or somethin'. Dare's no way dat's right. How could dat possibly be?''

I was already in acute denial, realizing what was told me could very well be possible. All sorts of thoughts immediately began to swirl through my head. This information, combined with the alcohol, certainly had thrown an interesting curveball into my birthday party. Jan rarely drinks, even to this day, and was perfectly lucid while she held that document in her hand. The document which contained the truth. The document which would inform me that my entire life, to this point, had been a lie. Just then, as if meant by fate, the phone rang. As was her nature every Christmas and birthday, Rose Mary was making what was to me her semi-yearly, obligatory call:

Rose Mary:

"Happy Birthday, Patrick. Twenty-four today, huh!'' (Rose Mary does not maintain a heavy accent.)

Pat:

"Yeah, tanks, tanks." (I always reverted to my slang whenever one of my own called).

Rose Mary:

"So how's the job comin'?''

Pat:

"Good, good, tanks. Say, do ya mind if I ask ya a question, Rose Mary? We jest got my birth certificate here in da mail and it says here dat your my mudder. Are you my mudder, Rose Mary?''

Rose Mary:

"We'll have ta talk about it sometime!" Slam!

The moment she hung up the phone, reality set in. Hard, heavy reality, the truth! My first reaction was to laugh. As I was laughing, I realized I was laughing at the truth I had uncovered. I was laughing and uncovering truths in my mind which suddenly began to sting with pain at the reality of all the falsehoods told. I was having extreme difficulty keeping my tears intact with the myriad of emotions going through me at that point, because the emotions had now turned to anger.

It was only six years since Peter's death and I was still bearing the scars. Suddenly, it dawned on me that all those beatings I had taken was Peter sending me a message, only I didn't understand it. He was trying to tell me I was different, I really didn't belong to him yet he had to live with the lie everywhere he took me, every time he talked about me, or to me, or thought about me on his own.

And Victoria. Surely she had been behind all the lies, with James at her right hand. "Adrian! If I'm not me, then who is he?"

During the few minutes after my conversation with Rose Mary, Jan stood by accepting the emotions which were going through me. She did not attempt to rationalize it for me at that point. Within a half hour my whole life changed. It never dawned on me to think about who my father might be. At this point, I was still in a state of shock, literally. The thoughts and emotions coming together all at once with the mixture of alcohol made it a very difficult situation to deal with. I was thinking by this time how I wished I could vomit my entire life and start over. Only this time, everyone tell the truth. That way, I wouldn't have to believe I had witnessed my parents' deaths and undergone all that internal agony. I would be able to realize that both my parents were alive, not past nightmares which I was trying to erase.

Two hours after the initial shock, I realized it was time to start ascertaining the truth, to see what really happened. I would also demand that the identity of Adrian's parents be made known to me. Of all people, I would be the one to tell him the truth about himself. He would not have to find out the way I did, on my own. After twenty-four years, finding out this way delivers severe scars, many that will never go away, they will always be there as a constant reminder. With the anger that was brooding within me, I began to make the calls. I wanted to be told the truth, and intended to get this information from my family, starting with the oldest and wisest, James.

James:

"Hello." (Still maintains a distinct accent).

Pat:

"Jimmie, dis is Pat."

James:

"Yeah, happy birthday, I been meanin' ta call ya. Twenty-four taday, huh?"

Pat:

"Yeah. Look, I got sometin' ta ask ya. Am I adopted?"

James:

"What? Don't be askin' such stupid tings! Who told ya dat?"

Pat:

"It says so on my birth certificate which I got taday an Rose Mary jest admitted it ta me on da phone."

James:

"Don't be ridiculous. Besides, how would I know if you were adopted, I was out ta sea at da time in da Navy. Dare's no way you were adopted, dough. Peter an' Victoria are your parents."

Pat:

"Cut da bullshit an' shoot straight wit me, Jimmie. I know da truth. Why can't ya tell it to me?"

James:

"Because da truth is dat yer Peter an' Victoria's son. Dat's all I know. Like I tol' ya a minute ago, I was on a ship in da Navy."

Pat:

> "Whoze kid is Adrian, Jim? I know ya know whoze he is. Cough it up, I wanna know, NOW!''

James:

> "Dat's none a yer business. Jest let it be dat he'z a friend a da family's who needed help, dat's all. Drop it!''

Pat:

> "No, I'm not gonna drop it. I'm gonna find out da truth an' if I find out yer lyin' ta me, I'm gonna tear ya apart! DO YA UNDERSTAN' ME?!!!!!''

James:

> "Who da ya tink yer talkin' to like dat, huh? Anyting dat was done fer you is because we taught it was best fer ya at da time!''

Was this an admission? Was James telling me that what I was saying was correct yet he refused to admit it? I didn't know, but I caught this when he said it and definitely intended to pursue.

Pat:

> "Jimmie, ya jest admitted ta me dat ya know I wuz adopted. Why don't ya tell me what'z zup? Why can't ya tell me da truth?''

James:

> "All I know is dat I was out ta sea at da time. When I came home on leave, you were dare an I didn' ask any questions. I jest accepted it, like you should now.''

Pat:

> "Accept it! Accept it! You can't even admit it, much less tell me da truth. Whatz a matter, whaddya afraid of? Fuck you, Jimmie. I'll find out da truth and den I'm gonna get back ta ya!'' Slam!

"Dis is unbelievable, Jan. Jimmie wouldn't admit ta anyting udder dan what dey told me is da truth. I'm gonna call Susan. If anybody, she'll tell me da truth." I was infuriated all the more at the end of my conversation with James. I knew inside of me that if he was present at the time, I would have dished out physical abuse to his body.

It was now imperative that I get some questions answered, and Susan was the best person I could think of in my family to indeed tell me what the fuck was going on. What I didn't realize was already going on was that the phone lines between all members of the Miller family were buzzing with activity. The secret they had all tried so desperately to keep in my presence had suddenly been revealed in my absence. They never planned on the suddenness or the circumstances. They were now deep in conversation with each other about which course of action to take. However, most of the conversation was going on between the older bruncles and smants; James, Rose Mary, and Clarice. They did not have a chance to warn Susan before I got to her.

Susan:

"Hello." (She has not retained much of her accent since moving away at an early age).

Pat:

"Puffer, what'z zup?"

Susan:

"Not much. Happy birthday. Twenty-four, or what?"

Pat:

"Yeah. Let me ask ya sometin'. Did ya know dat I'm adopted?"

Silence. It was obvious that I had her at a distinct disadvantage. If I were to ask that question out of nowhere, surely I was aware of the true circumstances. On the other hand, if she were the one to spill the beans, and I wasn't on to something, only shooting in the dark, then she would be in deep shit with James. Forget about Rose Mary, James would be the one to worry about. By far, he wielded the most power in the family.

Susan:

"I found out at Hugh's wedding. Clarice made a statement ta me about it as if I knew, but it was the first time I ever heard about it. It really took me by surprise, Paddy."

Pat:

"Took you by surprise?! How 'bout me? How come ya never tol' me?"

Susan:

"Paddy. Think about it. How could I be the one ta tell you about it when it's been kept a secret for so long? But, does it make any difference Paddy? You were loved, regardless."

Pat:

"I was loved!? How can ya possibly say dat? You were gone from da house ever since I was little. You weren't around. You have no idea what I went tru in dat house."

Susan:

"It's not gonna change anything, Paddy. What's been done has been done. There's nothing anyone can do ta change this. You're just gonna have ta learn ta deal with it."

Pat:

"Do ya know who my fodder is, Susan?"

Susan:

"You have to understand, I was very young. All I remember is that he was very tall and handsome. I think his name was Bill, but I'm not sure. It happened so long ago, I never equated you ta him, I was only a little kid."

Pat:

> "How come he never tried ta make contact wit me?
> Does he even know I'm alive an' who I am?"

Susan:

> "I don't know anymore than that. You'll have ta
> talk ta Rose Mary or Jimmie about it. Oh, Cookie
> (Clarice's husband) went ta school with him. They
> graduated from Saint Clair High School together."

Talk to Jimmie! He did know, or she would never have made that
statement. What amazed me even more was that Uncle Cookie and my
father had gone to high school together and yet Cookie never once
mentioned anything, ever, about this man in my presence.

Pat:

> "How come I was never tol' 'bout dis by anybody
> Susan? Specially after Peter an' Victoria had died?
> Do ya know what I had ta go tru in dat whole
> ordeal, huh?"

Susan:

> "I'm sorry, Paddy. I really am sorry about how all
> this has turned out. I told them they shoulda told
> you long ago. There was nothin' I could do about
> it. Accept that and accept the fact I am truly sorry."

Pat:

> "Who can I talk wit who will know anyting more
> an' be willin' ta tell me?"

Susan:

> "Clarice knows somethin' about your Dad, but I
> don't know how much. Jimmie knows everything,
> how much he'll tell ya, I don't know. Frankie was
> thirteen at the time, he might know somethin'.
> Other than that, I dunno."

Pat:

"Well, I guess I'll call Frankie an' Clarice. Den, I may try James again dependin' on how much I find out. If I find anyting more out, do ya want me ta keep ya in touch?"

Susan:

"Yeah, I'm curious to know but don't let them know we're talkin', O.K? I don't know how much they're gonna want you ta know, Paddy."

Pat:

"O.K. Susan."

Susan:

"I love you. I want you ta know that regardless of what ya find out."

Pat:

"If ya really love me, Susan, den answer one question fer me dat I definitely believe ya know da answer to. Whoze kid is Adrian?"

Susan:

"Oh Paddy, you're askin' me ta tell one of those secrets that no one knows. Please find out from someone else like Frankie or Rose Mary. But, please don't ask me ta answer that, Paddy."

Pat:

"Dat's da point, Susan. If someone doesn't draw a line in da sand an' start tellin' me da truth about anyting, I'll never find out about anyting, ever. Please tell me, Susan, it'z very important ta me."

Susan:

"Well, you're bound ta find out but please, don't say I was the one who told ya."

Pat:

"O.K."

Susan:

> "He's Jocelyn's. She got pregnant by a guy from
> Minersville when you were in the seminary. They
> sent her away to have him when she began to
> show."

How could I have been so blind? All of a sudden, numerous thoughts were once again swirling through my mind. The tirade James threw when I was working at the courthouse, all the times people refused to discuss him with me. And there he was, living with his mother. Those who he thought were his parents were dead when he was two and three. Yet, his mother was still intimidated. Certainly not by Peter, but the presence of Victoria through James intimidated her into keeping the truth from her own son, and he had lived under the same roof as she since he was a child. It was a real shame, I thought, because he was calling her "Jo" and referring to her as his sister, rather than "mom" which she truly was. I was having difficulty coping with my own situation. Adrian's was hard to understand, also.

It was at this point I realized how naive I had been all my life with all these lies being told around me. How I should have realized the obvious truth about situations, especially Adrian, but was too ignorant to notice. With this new information to digest, I finally regained my senses enough to conclude the conversation.

Suddenly, a whole new wave of emotions swarmed through my body when I began to think of how blind I had been to the truth. Within three hours, my mind and body were forced to deal with all this. It never dawned on me to get a good cry out, because I still thought sissies cried. No, I was mad, very mad, and wanted some answers. I decided my next call would be to Frank, although I knew he would say very little, as he always was wont to do:

Pat:

> "Frank, I guess ya heard by now, huh?"

Frank:

> "Yeah, I heard. What can ya do? Nuttin' can
> change anyting now." (Frank still retains a heavy
> accent).

Pat:

"How long did ya know for, Frankie?"

Frank:

"Since I wuz a kid. I wuz told never ta say anyting about it an' I respected dare wishes. Whatdaya want, me ta be da one ta tell ya, or what? No way, I was told never ta say anyting, an' I never did. Dat's all I can tell ya. Ya wanna know anymore about it, I suggest ya talk wit Jimmie."

Once again, someone had made reference to James' total knowledge without realizing James' denial of involvement to me. I decided to see how much James had talked with Frank about my recent discovery:

Pat:

"Dat's jest it, Frank. Jimmie said he never knew anyting about it cuz he was out at sea on a boat wit da Navy. How can he tell me anyting more?"

Frank:

"What? Get outta here. Jimmie wuz never on a ship. Closest he ever wuz to a ship, he got his picture taken on one. If anyone can tell ya about all dis, it'z Jimmie or Rose Mary. Udder dan dat, dat's all I know. You'll always be my brudder ta me."

Pat:

"Tanks, Frank. I appreciate dat. I'll see ya."

I now realized that James and Rose Mary were holding all the cards on the truth. I still had to speak with Clarice, Hugh, and especially, Jo. However, I now had information that James was lying about everything he told me and I wanted him to know that I was aware of this. Therefore, I decided to ring him up again for another go 'round.

Pat:

"Jimmie, I found out some more information an' I

know you've been lyin' ta me, 'bout everything. Ya know much more dan yer tellin' me.''

James:

"Who tol' ya dat? What da ya know?''

Pat:

"I know dat the closest ya've ever been ta a ship was ta wave at a lens. When are ya gonna stop lyin' an tell me da truth? Why is tellin' da truth so hard for ya to do? ''

James:

"Watch how yer talkin' ta me. All I know is dat I'm jest followin' mother and fodder's wishes. It's what we taught was best fer you at da time.''

Pat:

"It'z what ya taught was best for me at da time, fine. But, why didn' ya tell me after Victoria died? Why did ya insist dat everyone carry da lies forward? It coulda been ended dare an' I coulda handled it. Don't ya understan', it'z much harder findin' out like dis, realizin' everyone knew 'bout me except me. I was da brunt a everyone's whispers an' I never could understan' why. Now dat I tink about it, everyone, includin' all my friends' parents, had to have known. I'm in shock realizin' dat a whole town could keep a secret like dis. What udder lies have ya tol' me, Jimmie?''

James:

"Hey, watch da way yer talkin' ta me. Who do ya tink ya are anyway, talkin' ta me like dat. All I ever tried ta do yer whole life is try ta help ya. An' dis is da way ya talk ta me? You have no 'preciation whatsoever fer what I've done fer ya. If ya wanna talk ta me anymore, call me back when yer not talkin' dis trash!'' Slam.

Now I was really pissed because James was not trying to put himself in my shoes at all. What mattered to him was the proper execution of Victoria's wishes including those regarding Adrian.

Approximately four hours had passed since uncovering this information, and I was becoming drained. Through the whole process, I continued to drink and that was helping to deepen the animosity that was in the pit of my stomach. I had to think, to try and put all this in perspective. I told Jan I had to go out and try to get my head straight before I talked to the remaining members of my family. I headed down Bronco Lane toward Jan's school which was less than a mile away.

The sun had gone down, but it was still extremely hot, well into the upper nineties. As I walked, I was trying desperately to put everything into perspective without getting emotional. It was when I began thinking about Peter and his treatment of me after his first series of strokes, that I lost all control. The abuse I had suffered by his cane began to well up all at once, and the tears began to flow. After a short period they weren't flowing, they were exploding out of my eyes. It is not an easy situation to handle emotionally when you come to the realization that your whole life, and all that you were made to believe about it, was a complete, unadulterated lie.

Anyone passing me on the street had to wonder what was wrong since I had absolutely no control over the tears and the way they were flowing. Suddenly I began to run, as if running would help me forget the events of the day and all that I had learned. I must have run two miles without stopping. When I finally did, I was drenched with a combination of sweat and tears. I was four miles from home and the running finally helped me to stop crying.

As I walked, gasping for breath, I began to make decisions in my mind about what I wanted to do. I decided to call Clarice the next day and find out how much she knew, especially with her husband Cookie having gone to high school with my father.

I also decided to call Jo and inform her of how much hurt I was experiencing. I would inform her that if she didn't tell Adrian the truth about himself I would do it for her. It would be left up to her which way she preferred this to happen, her or me. In any event, I felt it my duty to tell him so all the lies being told could stop.

Then, I would call Rose Mary, my new found smother, and try to get the skinny on what really happened some twenty-four-plus years ago. If anyone should tell me the truth about this whole mess, I guessed it should be her.

Most of all, burning within me was the desire to stop this from happening to anyone else, ever again. Therefore, I would write about it and, if I touched just one person who read it, then I would certainly produce a moral victory. I felt robbed and cheated and was bound and determined to reveal the lies for all to see through my writing.

Shortly before I returned to the apartment, I finally achieved the hurl I hoped would happen since four o'clock that afternoon. It was violent and it was the only time I could remember vomiting feeling good to me. I had cried a combination of alcohol, emotions, and tears, and was finally over the absorption of the recent shock. When I walked back in the door, Jan was waiting patiently. No TV on, she was sitting and, I'm sure, hoping I hadn't gone out and done something stupid. She got up from the couch, came over and gave me the most affectionate, loving hug I can ever remember from her. It was a hug which reassured me that she was with me and would help me work through this. It was a hug which told me that she was my new family now, we have to work together at putting the past behind me. Most of all, the hug signified a relief on her part that I was, in fact, all right, that I had gotten through the most crucial time with no harm to myself or anyone else. That moment with Jan signified her true love for me and the questions I had about that. She put to rest my doubt about her feelings concerning me.

I showered and sat at the kitchen table until five-thirty that morning writing. The result is the Prologue to this book, done solely out of emotion. When I stopped writing at five-thirty in the middle of a thought, it was because I had come to a striking revelation. I could not accurately write the story without both sides. I had to stop because I realized I could go no further than two chapters, at best. I would put the introduction away until I was able to portray the truth as judged by me. For that to happen, I would have to locate my father. At this point, all I knew was that his name was Bill. It would be stored safely away in my briefcase for fourteen years, the time it would take for me to find him without the help of my family. I didn't realize that my emotions were about to turn to bitterness, probably the worst kind to experience next to jealousy. Imagine, finally finding out the truth after all this time and then find out that some people would persist in trying to keep the truth from me.

When I finally went to bed, the sleep was from exhaustion, yet I kept coming in and out of consciousness with thoughts of the truth and something that would enter my mind even as I slept. The next day would be a busy one, spent keeping Ma Bell stock at a premium. The initial onslaught was over but I didn't have a clue that the war was about to begin. The mountain I was about to climb would become, at times, as steep as Mount Everest. Those who knew the entire truth would yield nothing in the effort I was about to undertake to find my father.

****

When I awoke the next morning, I wished beyond hope that the previous days festivities were a bad dream, definitely not celebrated the way someone's twenty-fourth birthday should be. I had a big day ahead of me, intending to talk with Rose Mary again, as well as Clarice, both of whom could give me information on how to find my father. I also planned to call my brother Hugh to see what, if anything, he knew. If Hugh knew about me, I would be crushed since he is the sibling I spent most of my childhood and adolescence with. I had to wait until noon, Texas time, to ensure Rose Mary would be home from church. I was prepared to spend the entire day on the phone, if need be, to gain some sort of perspective on what the bottom line was pertaining to my father.

Rose Mary:

"Hello."

Pat:

"Rose Mary, dis is your son, as I have come ta find out. I need ta talk wit you."

Rose Mary (defensive):

"What do ya want me ta say? It was a mistake, it happened, and dat's all I can say about it."

Pat (even more defensive):

"Is dat all ya plan ta say ta me after I find all dis out? Are ya jest gonna ignore it like it didn' happen? I have some questions I need some real, true answers on. Are ya gonna help me, or what?"

Rose Mary:

"What kinda questions?"

Pat:

"Who is my dad? Where can I find him? Why didn' ya tell me about all dis after we buried Victoria, jest to name a few?? (I would never refer to her as mother or Mom again.)

Rose Mary:

"What does it matter who yer fodder is? He didn' want nuttin' to do wit ya, so dare iz no sense discussin' him. As far as mudder and fodder, to us you were our baby brudder. Don't ya think it was hard on me havin' ta hold dat inside a' me all dis time? Ya have no idea of the hurt I've been through, Patrick."

Pat:

"Dat still doesn' answer any a' my questions. As a madder a' fact, it sounds ta me like yer tryin' ta dodge da issue. Who is my fodder, where is he, and whatz dis all about?"

Rose Mary:

"Patrick, I don't wanna have ta relive dis all again. It happened. Why can't ya jest accept this an' let's put it behind us? Believe me, I feel jest as bad as you do."

Pat:

"How could you? You were part a da big lie! I waz da one everyone wuz talkin' 'bout. I WUZ DA LIE!!!"

Rose Mary:

"Hey you. Stop talkin' ta me like dat. Everything that wuz done fer you is because we love you.

Everything that was done fer you was done wit yer
best interest in mind. As far as why mudder and
fodder took you in, we all thought it was what
would be best fer you.''

There it was again, ''what we thought was best for you.'' It
became apparent to me I was getting nowhere in this discussion, and I
was thinking this is where I would get a lot of answers. A deep, deep
anger was rapidly coming over me. I wanted answers, and it seemed all
I was getting were questions.

Pat:

''Look, jest tell me dis! What is my fodder's name?
Please, at leas' tell me dat.''

Rose Mary:

''His name is Bill Roman. He wuz from Saint Clair
but I haven't seen him since before you were born.
An', it's obvious he don't care 'bout you, because
he left. I have no idea how ta reach him, all of his
family moved away. Dat's all I know, please don't
ask me anymore because I don't like talkin' 'bout
it.''

That was it, I had had enough of this fluff. I cannot recall ever
getting ugly to Rose Mary. However, maybe the hard line approach is
what she needed.

Pat:

''Let me tell ya somethin'. Yesterday, my whole
life changed in front a' me. I found my sister is my
mudder, an my fodder is still alive, a living
unknown. Every time ya look at me, you're
reaffirming a lie you've been living for all deez
years. Ya know what ya are, yer a hypocrite!
Proclaimin' ta be religious, God-fearin', yet every-
day ya wake up, yer involved in a lie. An' now ya
want me ta jest brush it aside, water under da
bridge! Bullshit! Now, I better get some answers
an' I better get em' quick. Ya better look at yerself

in da mirror, put yerself in my shoes an' walk around in 'em. Maybe den you'll realize what it'z like to be the punch line in everybody's joke. Dat's what ya better tink about!"

Rose Mary:

"You listen here, an' listen good. You were loved, buster. There isn't a one a' us who wouldn' give our left arm for ya. I also went through a lot a pain, more than you'll ever know. I can't help you wit dis, I don't know anything more! Goodbye!"

That was all. What was basically the contents of a conversation I anticipated lasting the better portion of a day, done in fifteen minutes. Jan had been watching and listening as I was speaking with Rose Mary and could tell that I was hurt when we hung up. I was already realizing my situation may be futile, and it had just begun.

Compounding matters was the distance. I would have to spend quite a bit of money flying or drive two thousand miles for a face-to-face confrontation with someone. Their game plan was simple, "Don't talk!" I knew no "Roman" family in Saint Clair nor had I ever heard the name. It was not a common name with a "ski," as in Romanowski, at the end.

I would next try Clarice, since I already knew Cookie and he were buddies growing up. Of course, Cookie became a successful contractor and chose to live his life in semi-exile on their farm. The chances of him keeping in touch with my father were probably slim, but at least I could learn something about him, anything.

Cookie:

"Hello." (Hard of hearing with a very heavy regional accent)

Pat:

"Cook, dis is Paddy. How ya doin'?"

Cookie:

"Oh, good, good, Paddy. Do ya wanna talk wit Clarice?"

Pat:

> "Nah, actually you could probably help me, Cook.
> I'm sure ya found out by now dat I found out I was
> adopted."

Cookie:

> "Yeah. I always tol' dem dey shoulda tol' ya a
> long time ago. Victoria Miller was weird ya
> know!"

Pat:

> "Yeah. I'm beginnin' ta figure dat out. But what
> can ya tell me 'bout my dad? I unnerstan' ya went
> ta school wit 'im!"

Cookie:

> "Yeah, but I haven' seen him in a long time, since
> a class reunion. We use da be good pals. Hiz
> nickname was "snail" cuz he did everything slow.
> He wuz good in basketball, real good. He'z tall an'
> we all use ta be amazed at how big his dick wuz. It
> wuz unbelievable, Paddy."

Pat:

> "Yeah, well at leas' dat part makes sense, if ya
> know what I mean, Cook. Do ya know what hez
> doin' or where I can find him? Any direction ya
> can give me would really be appreciated."

Cookie:

> "Last I heard, Paddy, he was principal of a high
> school somewhere aroun' Reading (Pennsylvania). I
> can't say fer sure, dough. He had da couple a
> brudders but dey all moved away. One a dem wuz a
> musician, I tink he played peeanna or sumtin'."

Pat:

> "Cook, it'z real important ta me dat I find my

fodder. I jest wanna figure out what da fuck is goin' on aroun' here. Nobody wantz ta help me, ya know like it'z some kinda sin or sometin."

Cookie:

"Dat's jest it, Paddy. It wuz a sin ta dem. I had hell ta pay when I knocked Clarice up an hadda go in front a' Victoria. Ya ask me, she wasn't playin' wit a full deck. She wazn't gonna get anywhere wit me, dough. Ya know me."

Well, I had at least found out three interesting revelations from Cookie that no one could tell me. First, my father and I had nicknames based on our pace when we were young, "snail" and "putt putt." Secondly, we both received our degrees in secondary education. Now, I know some of you reading this are thinking I'm going to say the third revelation is that we both had the same body attributes.

No, I never knew that Cookie and Clarice had a shotgun wedding! I was beginning to realize that the strong religious beliefs of the Miller family members only went so far. Perhaps they believed in "Divine Intervention" as a means of birth control. I now had knowledge that Rose Mary, Ellen, Clarice, Susan, Frank, and Jo had produced children in unusual circumstances for that time. That was six out of nine, well over sixty per cent, and it was proof profound that Victoria's method of birth control, ignorance, didn't work.

Pat:

"Hello, Clarice. How ya doin'?"

Clarice:

"I'm O.K. How ya doin'? I guess ya been through a lot, huh?" (She has not maintained a heavy accent).

Pat:

"Yeah, ya might say so. Can ya give me any sorta insight in ta what happened back den? Nobody seems ta wanna talk wit me about it."

Clarice:

"Paddy, Rose Mary's really broken up 'bout this. Go easy on her, will ya. She' been through an awful lot over this situation goin' back many years. Mudder put her through hell and what was done has been done. I haven't seen your father in over five years and we had nothing to say to each other back then. Your family is us. We all care for you and love you. Why can't you just accept that and get on with your life?"

Pat:

"Why is it dat everyone is more concerned about Rose Mary's feelings? I'm the one whoze been fucked here. I'm sorry Clarice, but dat's jest da way I feel."

Clarice:

"Hey, Pat. Ya gotta filthy mout an' I don't appreciate it. I told ya', you were loved. We all loved ya jest like you were one a' us."

Pat:

"Geez, dat's great. Since I find dis out, we're beginnin' ta talk about me in a different tense, tings really change quick, or what?"

Clarice:

"I didn't mean dat like dat, an' ya know it. I suggest ya take some time an' let this shock wear off. Maybe ya will come ta realize that we really were doin' what we thought was best for ya at the time."

Pat:

"Is dat it? Is dat all dare is ta say Clarice?"

Clarice:

''I don't have anything more ta say, what ya see is
what ya get.''

And that was it—my two best sources of information about who I
really am and they closed all possible avenues. I was bewildered,
befuddled, but mainly, hurt.

It was bad enough for them to keep the secret and gamble on the
odds. To continue to conceal the truth compounded my frustrations.

Overnight I had learned never to trust anyone again. This has put
an enormous strain on my marriage over the years. There's nothing I
wouldn't do for some people. But I can't discuss myself and my
feelings, especially with my wife. There are so many things I wish I
could talk about, yet I'm afraid of getting burned. This is because of the
cruel lie I discovered in 1978.

Jan was doing her best to help me through this, but her family life
and mine were totally different. I didn't know if she was grasping the
situation as I perceived it. She couldn't possibly understand the
enormity of keeping this secret so well for so long.

I guessed the phone call to Hugh would be a formality, because I
knew that if he knew anything about my dad, he had probably been
forewarned not to volunteer any information. Strange, Hugh and I had
shared a bedroom for fifteen years and we never once hugged each
other or talked openly about our feelings as brothers. Yet, it goes
without saying that we would go to the wall for each other, no matter
what.

Hugh:

''Hello.'' (Heavy, heavy accent).

Pat:

''Hughie. (Pronounced U-E, coal slang), whatz
zup?''

Hugh:

''Nuttin. I heard. It blew my mind, Paddy. I had no
idea, I want ya ta know dat. Dare's only six years
'tween us, how wuz I ta know? I never knew, I
swear ta God. I wanna tell ya, when Susan called
an' tol' me, it blew my fuckin' mind. Man, I'm
sorry.''

Pat:

"It hurts, man. All dat time I, no we, shoulda known. All da signs were dare, we jest didn' read 'em. Ya know U-E, I never could figure out why Peter usda whack me wit his cane, now I tink I know. He was tryin' ta tell me sometin' da only way a man whoze hadda stroke can. He wuz tryin' ta tell me I'm not one a yooz guyz. It'z a weird way a tellin' me, I know, but maybe dat's why. Anyway ya look at it, it stinks. An ya know whatz da saddest ting about it? Everybody knew but me......"

Hugh:

"Me needer, I swear."

Pat:

"Everybody, U-E. Da whole fuckin' town, everybody but me!"

Hugh:

"Paddy, I jest wanna say sometin' one time, an' only one time! I know ya been tru hell deez past two days and I feel sorry 'bout dat. I jest wanna tell ya I never knew, an' ta me you'll always be my baby brudder. I never tol' ya dis before, but I tink ya know it, I love ya, man. No madder what happent, you an me are brudders an' always remember dat. Do ya hear me?"

Silence.

Hugh:

"Do ya hear me, or what?"

Pat:

"It'z hard, U-E. Ya gotta unnerstan'!! It all happent so sudden, ya know. I mean, it makes sense an' all but nobody wants ta talk 'bout it! Kinda like it'z jest sumtin' I should jest shrug off an' accept.''

Hugh:

"Ya know how Peter an' Victoria wer Paddy. Life was....different den, ya know? We jest did tings 'cause we were tole to an' never questioned it. I don't know man, I never knew 'bout it, but I'll do what I can ta help ya, ya know dat! Man, we're brudders, I tole ya dat!''

Pat:

"I know, man. I may need ta call on ya on dat someday. I'm gonna do whatever it takes ta find my dad, but I guess ya know dat already.''

Hugh:

"Yeah, I figured dat out. I was tinkin bout it last night. An Paddy, I don' blame ya. Go for it. But, be careful. After all dis time, he may not be so eager ta see you!''

Pat:

"I never even taught about dat. Tanks, man. Take care.''

That was the only time I can remember Hugh expressing his fraternal feelings toward me. It wasn't an overwhelming "I love you," with all the fluff, it was him speaking from the heart. I truly believe Hugh did not know until I found out.

****

I spent two days trying to sort things out, listening while Jan tried to put the entire situation in perspective.

I was also adamant about resolving the situation with Adrian. Jo knew I felt it was ludicrous that she was raising her son as her brother. I called her the next day to let her know that if she did not inform Adrian of the truth, then I would. She tried to tell me it was none of my business, but his situation was just like mine. He was old enough to accept the truth, especially since he never knew Peter and Victoria, and he should be told immediately.

****

I realized that in order to locate my father I would have to find
some way to crack the shell, to find someone who would talk with me
and help. All that I had been able to establish was his name and that, at
one time, he and his family lived in Saint Clair. I knew that he was tall,
and according to Susan and Clarice, very handsome.

Further conversation with James and Rose Mary would prove futile
although I found out from James that my father was not willing to
accept responsibility for the situation and simply walked away from it.
It seemed that the best source of information about my father's family
would be from the townspeople themselves although most of them
would still be reluctant to talk.

One of the first people I spoke with from town was Pretzel
Bender's mom, Catherine. As I expected, she reluctantly confessed to
knowing of my adoption. However, she was emphatic about not
knowing who my mother or father were. When I informed her it was
my oldest sister, she stated it made perfect sense to her, all the pieces of
the puzzle were coming together.

When I asked her about my father and his family, she did
remember them but stated the entire family had long ago left the region.
My grandfather owned a bar (how surprising) two houses down from
Saint Clair High School. He also was one of three morticians doing
business in town. Both my grandfather and grandmother had passed
away while living there and the remainder of the family left. Both the
bar and mortician's practice were sold. She remembered that all the
children were tall. Other than that, there was little she could tell me.

A sense of total futility had set in after my conversation with Mrs.
Bender. I realized that those people who knew anything about the truth
weren't talking and those who might possibly talk openly with me
didn't have enough knowledge. I was soon to embark on a mission that
would lead me down many different paths in search of one thing, truth.

****

Over the course of the next several months, I would undergo a
dramatic change in my personality, although I wasn't aware of it. Jan
would become aware because she was closest to me, witnessing the

transformation firsthand. I began my initial period of not trusting anyone, including Jan. I wasn't aware of it, but it was planted firmly inside my soul. Subconsciously I was thinking that if my own family would deceive me then anyone, or everyone, would do this to me.

The sad part is that I would also become a master of deception and lies and it would take a long time until self-realization of this set in. It would not be until I was in my third year of business that I would meet someone who would make sense to me about life in general. A person whom I continue to emulate today as a true role model in my life. Someone who would help me to understand about life and people, what makes them tick. I was gradually able to unleash some of the venom inside of me.

****

Due to the way I immersed myself in my work, twelve-hour workdays and weekends would become second nature. Those early days collecting delinquent accounts by phone and in person taught me a lot. I began to understand the world of credit and how many people's lives revolve around it. My attitude of distrust would sometimes come in handy while collecting. However, I would never place anyone in a situation of losing their dignity. Done properly, even the difficult task of collecting money can be rewarding. I learned that by treating all people humanely, they would be much more responsive to my requests.

SECTION III
THE TRUTH

Peace of Mind

Now if you're feelin' kinda low
'Bout the dues you've been payin'
Things just comin' much too slow.

And you wanna run but somehow
You just keep on stayin'
Can't decide on which way to go.

I understand about indecision
But I don't care if I get behind
People livin' in competition
All I want is to have my Peace of Mind.

Now you're climbin' to the top of the company ladder
Hope it doesn't take too long
Can't you see there'll come a day when it won't matter
Come a day when you'll be gone.

I understand about indecision
But I don't care if I get behind
People livin' in competition
All I want is to have my Peace of Mind.

Take a look ahead
Take a look ahead
Look ahead.

Now everybody's got advice they just keep on givin'
Doesn't mean too much to me
Lot's a people out to make a legal livin'
Can't decide who they should be.

I understand about indecision
But I don't care if I get behind
People livin' in competition
All I want is to have my Peace of Mind.

Take a look ahead
Take a look ahead
Look ahead.

CHAPTER EIGHT

CLIMBING THE CORPORATE LADDER
(WHILE TRYING TO FIND DAD)

Sunday, July 11, 1993. It seems appropriate that I would begin winding this book down to its conclusion fifteen years to the day since I discovered the truth. Unbelievably, on the Oprah Winfrey Show this past Friday, there were twin sisters who found out late in life that they were raised by their grandmother, and their older sister was actually their mother. There was also a psychologist on the show whose advice to them was to put the situations of the past behind them. They must learn to deal with the events of their situation and go forward. That remedy is much easier said than done. To make the simple statement of putting the events of the past behind us is folly, since this can never be done. It is only when all parties who are involved in the injustice come together that any sort of understanding can be reached.

****

It took just six short months until I received my first promotion at Borg-Warner. My boss resigned his position with us to work for Ford

Motor Credit, the financing arm of the Ford Motor Company. When the new opening arose, I was given the promotion because of the desire I had already shown at the first position I held. The challenge of managing other people as well as myself was received with great enthusiasm, since I had never been given this type of responsibility before.

Many times during my lunch break, or after work on my own time, I attempted to locate my father. I checked information for every town and city around the Reading, Pa., area. I called every middle and high school in the area, based on Uncle Cookie's information, all to no avail. I also spoke with many of the neighbors I lived near in Saint Clair. Some would admit knowing of my situation, others would adamantly deny any knowledge. In either case, no one could or would render any information.

Doing my job and trying to find my father paralleled each other because, in both instances, I was trying to locate people. When collecting delinquent accounts, many times I would have to trace people down through investigative research. In my job, however, I had much more information at my disposal. With my father, all I had was a name and a few insignificant pieces of information. My success ratio on my job far surpassed any luck I was having in locating my father. Over time, I would gradually lose the intense desire I originally had to accomplish this, and was beginning to accept the futility of the situation.

Borg-Warner Acceptance was located on the first floor in the Koger Executive Center in San Antonio. On the third floor, a small office housed the employees of Chrysler Credit Corporation, the financing arm of the Chrysler Corporation whose purpose is to aid the dealer body in financing retail customers on new Chrysler products. Over time, I got to know the young man who was the lone collector for this branch of Chrysler Credit. He had a company car and was the designated runner in all "gofer" situations. Over time this young man, Ron Barth, and I spoke frequently, since we were both involved in the same line of work—skip-tracing people to collect delinquent debts. I realized after speaking with him that there was much more money involved in automobiles, since they far outpriced air conditioners, refrigerators, TV's, etc. Ron gave me many tips on finding people. Although I was the Collection Manager, managing my own department, I was still relatively ignorant in many areas of the finance business.

As Ron and I got to know each other better and he became comfortable with my satirical/comic personality, I also became increasingly more intrigued by his work. I asked him for an employment application in the event they should ever have an opening. With Ron being the sole collector in the office, chances of this seemed slim unless he moved up. He took the application and promised to let me know immediately if anything should become available. He also informed me that his boss, Loren Blevins, and I would bond well since we had a lot in common. Not having met the man, I had no idea what he was talking about and let it go at that.

A mere two days after I filled out the application with Chrysler, my old boss with Borg-Warner called from Ford Motor Credit to inform me that Ford was in need of good collectors because they were growing rapidly. It was late 1978, and Ford, General Motors, and Chrysler were becoming extremely aggressive in the loaning of money as a means of getting new vehicles on the street. Consequently, more collectors, preferably with experience, were needed to handle the inundation of delinquent accounts. The combination of my experience, work ethics, and college degree, made me all the more appealing as a future employee. Because I was already intrigued by what Chrysler Credit did, I immediately made an appointment for an interview, thanking my ex-boss for the lead. The money and benefits would be much better, and I already thought I was rich.

By this time, Jan and I had saved enough to purchase our first new vehicle, a Honda, and our very first house. We assumed the mortgage of an Air Force Captain who was being transferred. Jan's sister and brother-in-law would be our next-door neighbors. The house was all brick with three bedrooms, two baths, and a large front and back yard. Before we made the big move on this huge investment, Jan sat me down to ask if I had enough maturity to accept the responsibility of the upkeep on the house. Over time, Jan would adopt a philosophy of treating me like one of her first-grade students, something she knows pisses me off. I readily accepted the responsibilities that would be given me, because I never thought I would have another opportunity at a beautiful house such as this to live in and call my own. With the additional income I would be receiving from Ford, if they chose to employ me, we could easily meet all obligations with our combined incomes. The move made sense.

The interview went smoothly, my credentials were well-accepted, and I was hired as an Assistant Customer Accounts Representative (ACAR) for the Ford Motor Credit Corporation. I had to resign from Borg-Warner. Unbeknownst to me, I was about to enter the "big-leagues" of the finance industry—automobiles, with all the inherent risk they represent.

Ford was already well-advanced in their understanding of employee training and relations. Duties were very regimented and we were constantly being graded by a stopwatch on how many calls could be realistically made during a certain period of time. This philosophy would work well when grading workload, however, it would work against the company from a customer service point of view. There is no way a company can put a stopwatch to their customers' needs, and Ford would eventually realize this.

My new job duties would include telephone and field collections, the latter being done at night when our customers were most likely home. I would now begin collecting on a commodity that would be visible, something I could latch onto if need be. Much different than having to request someone to allow me access to their house to take the refrigerator or television, I would now become a master thief, and it was legal. Never once did I realize how dangerous what I was doing could be, especially in some of the neighborhoods I went into at night. High crime and drug areas. I attacked my job with much enthusiasm and no fear.

During this time, I basically forgot about trying to find my father because I was too busy with my career. Besides, the futility of the situation depressed me. I chose not to think about it. James's game plan was working at that point.

****

We planned our first trip back to the East Coast about this time. Jan's mother, Katie, and her sister Vicki were still there, although Vicki would soon be moving to Austin, to attend the University of Texas. We would be visiting many people in a short period of time with much ground to cover. At a family get-together being held at Frank's (by now Frank had achieved much success and wealth), I planned to address the situation with Adrian, since Jo still refused to tell him. He was now a senior in high school and still referring to her as his sister. I also had intentions of grilling members of my family for any new information which could help me find my father. I hadn't thought about it much lately, but this would be the first time I would see the members of my family since I found out the truth.

Jan's mother had visited us frequently in Texas and, since all three of her daughters would be living there, we would talk with her about selling the house and moving. Jack had left her with more than enough money to ensure a good life, and we thought it best to have her move south. While we were visiting her, she informed Jan of some lumps which had appeared on her head recently and wouldn't go away. Jan suggested she go to the family doctor about them. Katie appeared apprehensive since she knew what the future might hold for her. She had no outward signs of illness, nor did she feel ill at the time, so I first suspected the lumps could be a reaction to a bee sting, insect bite, or something along those lines. She agreed to see the doctor after we left, and also gave us a tentative agreement to put the house up for sale for her future move to Texas.

The party, which was held in our honor, had virtually everyone we knew in attendance including friends of ours from college. I took pride in the strides I had already made in my employment moves, comparing myself to many of my friends and fellow graduates. When I finally got around to a one-on-one with Adrian, he informed me that he was made aware of the truth about his situation two weeks earlier, but not by his mother. Frank's daughter, Alice, had told him at school one day, perhaps in anticipation of me telling him. Jo insists that she had informed Adrian, but he states she still has not sat him down to tell him the truth. He told me that at first he was hurt. He also went through an initial stage of denial. However, he was accepting the situation and dealing with it.

****

Upon returning home to Texas, we received a call from Katie telling us she had gone to their family doctor who, in turn, sent her for a battery of tests. She had received a call from the doctor explaining that the lumps which were appearing were cancerous. It was the first time I had ever heard of "cancer of the lymph nodes." The news absolutely floored me.

Jan spent much time that summer in New Jersey tending to her mother's needs. The cancer spread like a fire burning out of control and soon had consumed her entire body. Chemotherapy was of no use, although it was tried. All the plans which we had for Katie's future were for naught since she would expire within a few short months.

Jan's parents had both become parent figures to me and both were taken from me through extremely painful deaths. Katie's passing really affected me. She was a woman who never had a bad word for anyone. She accentuated the positive at all times, even in her final months, never letting the seriousness of her illness affect those who were close to her. At her funeral, as I was saying my final goodbyes, I realized how much the lives of Jack and Katie Schurman had influenced me, all for the better. Through them, I believed that anything is possible if I wanted it bad enough. They taught me that whatever the human mind can conceive it can achieve. To a large degree, I owe a debt of thanks to Jack and Katie for helping me write this book. Without their guidance, I would never have learned about ''desire,'' and the true essence of the word.

****

I had lived all of my life in a part of the country with few blacks and no Mexican-Americans. The dark beauty of the Spanish women struck me as soon as I arrived in San Antonio. Not knowing what true, unconditional love was, nor if I could really love someone, I was open to temptation.

Maria was already working with Ford when I began. Of Mexican-American ancestry, she was the most beautiful woman I had ever met in my life. She had it all, slim, attractive body, beautiful long black hair, and an even more beautiful face. She was so beautiful that I was intimidated by her and rarely spoke to her for fear of being rejected. After awhile I noticed her paying attention to me. She would arrange her workload to be at lunch the same time as I was, although I usually brown-bagged it in the lunchroom. Gradually we began to speak about our lives and families, my background and hers. She was single, still living at home with her parents, and had many things going for her—new car, money in her pocket at all times, and beauty. I asked her early on why she was still single. I made no bones about the fact I was married. Someone could have blown me over with a feather the night she asked when I was going to invite her out for a drink.

****

I was not prepared for how fast the relationship escalated. I was working late, repossessing cars with her by my side. Being a young, immature man, I never gave a thought to the possible ramifications of Jan finding out, since I had no intention of that happening. I was in it for the fun. Maria, on the other hand, fell in love. I told her that I was a wild card who had no problem in saying the word "love," but had absolutely no idea what it was, or how to show it, even in my marriage.

I didn't realize how deep Maria had fallen, but she had gone way overboard. In time, she began talking about me leaving Jan, calling me at home, or having friends call me at home to see if I could get away. I became scared of the situation and began yielding to Maria's demands, with the hopes of avoiding a showdown.

There's something about lying. From the moment the first one is told, everything spoken after that further compounds the lies. When Jan inadvertently found out about the affair and confronted me, I was actually relieved that I could stop lying, although it probably would mean the end of our marriage. There was no doubt I was sorry, more for Jan than for myself, but I acknowledged the truth. She knew when we became engaged that it was the biggest gamble of her life. Jan had never done anything to hurt me. Now, I had given her a reason never to trust me again.

After much crying, Jan informed me that it would either be Maria or her, I would have to choose. She let me know that she was willing to keep the marriage going, but she would have a very hard time ever trusting me again. If I chose to continue our marriage, I would have to resign my position with Ford immediately, regardless of any monetary bind it may put us in.

She should have dumped me and started over. Perhaps it was one of God's guardian angels who prevented that from happening and intervened on my behalf. On the day I walked into Ford to resign my position, Ron Barth contacted me, a year and a half after I filled out the employment application with Chrysler Credit, to inform me they had an opening.

****

My interview with Loren Blevins, the branch manager, would last for two hours. During this time, I probably spoke for three minutes. Little did I realize that I was not only interviewing for a position with this man, but that he would one day become the father figure I had been envisioning since I discovered the truth. I would come to emulate his knowledge and work ethics, plus the honest standards of living which he set for himself and his family.

Loren Blevins easily could have been a successful minister, for he was blessed with the gift of gab. People that know him on a business or cursory level would never suspect that behind every story he told, there was a moral. I was extremely fortunate in learning under Loren, since he is, in my estimation, the quintessential automobile man, knowing the business inside out, backwards and forwards.

During my initial interview, Loren told me a story that I would come to realize the value of in the future, during my climb up the corporate ladder. Loren, who is originally from Oklahoma, likes to tell stories about football, especially the Dallas Cowboys. He equated much of the finance business to positions on the football field, and asked me to follow through on his thinking: *The quarterback* (branch manager), *sometimes has to hand the ball off to one of his halfbacks* (sales representatives), *they in turn may have to* (spoken with a very heavy Southern accent and very, very slowly) *hand the ball off to one of the linemen* (me), *so that we can take that fuckin' ball down the field and score.* He eventually got around to the subject matter, which was teamwork, and how the success of every team, including the Cowboys, depends upon it. I often look back upon my initial interview and realize the accuracy of what he was telling me.

****

I should have realized the job with Chrysler would be different when, within the first month I began, Chrysler Corporation announced that it was on the verge of filing bankruptcy. Things were looking very bleak back then. However, our branch of Chrysler Credit maintained a very positive attitude because we were beginning to grow. My responsibilities as the only collector varied from getting the mail in the morning, opening the mail, sorting the payments for delinquents, telephoning every delinquent account every day, making a lunch-run around noon, to telephoning accounts while trying to handle situations that could arise from a base of five thousand retail customers. After work, a quick bite before I hit the streets in my company car to go out knocking on doors, looking for delinquent automobiles.

Through hard work and patience, I was awarded the position of Collection Supervisor with two collectors and a clerical employee under my supervision. I was beginning to understand Loren's lectures, and how they related to life and people and how accurate his theories generally were.

Jan's and my relationship was still tenuous at best, and I felt very bad whenever I thought about what I had done. She would frequently bring up the subject of my infidelity during this period as a reminder that all had not been forgotten.

After Katie's death, each of the three daughters would receive a substantial amount of money from the estate's assets. We decided to sell our house and move up in both size and amenities. Our new house was huge, bigger than any I'd been in to this point, including Jan's parents'!

Shortly after moving into our dream house, Jan began wanting a child. We had agreed that our three dogs would be our children. I was hesitant to change this, as our marriage was on shaky ground, however, we began to build a real relationship together. The result would be our only child, a girl, Linsey Kae Miller, born April 7, 1983, Methodist Hospital, San Antonio, Texas.

The first night we brought Linsey home, I sat in her room and stared at her sleeping. I kept thinking about how I was going to make things different for her than they had been for me as a child. Materially, we had already achieved this. However, I was thinking about this from a parent-child perspective, how I would change things from what I remember about my childhood. I would be sure to tell her how much I loved her every chance I got, although I still could not perform this simple task in my relationship with Jan.

****

Although I had slowed the pace down for finding my father, I never lost my desire to do this. I was constantly trying to get Rose Mary to tell me something new. She continued to stick to her basic story of name, rank, and serial number. The college she maintained he attended still remained the same and incessant phone calls to this institution would prove futile.

In my new position as Collection Manager, I would come in contact with many people whose job it was to find people; private investigators and repo agents. One day, I got on the phone with a private investigator out of Austin who made the statement that "there is no human being alive I can't find. All I need is a name." We entered into a personal contract for him to locate my father. All I could give him was what I thought I had: his name and supposed field of employment, and that I felt he was living in Pennsylvania, provided he was alive.

Before I go into the remainder of this story, I must inform you that my first roommate in college was a behemoth of a man named Mark Roman. He stood 6'4'' and weighed well over three hundred pounds. He was strong, very strong, the kind of guy you wanted on your side if a brawl broke out in a bar. Over time, I got to know Mark's family, who lived in Wilkes Barre, Pennsylvania. I would go there for holidays and the Roman family always made me feel welcome when I arrived. Mark's father, Frank, was a principal at one of the local schools and had been so for many years. They went out of their way to make me comfortable upon my visits.

Within twenty-four hours of procuring the services of the P.I., he called to state he had found my father. I took down the information about my father, the fee for his services, and became very, very nervous. Without thinking to consult Jan, I decided to make the call. The area code was 717, the same as that for Saint Clair and Reading, therefore, it made sense. It never crossed my mind when I was given the name of Frank Roman and his phone number.

Frank Roman:

> "Hello."

Pat:

> "Mr. Roman, my name is Pat Miller an' I'm callin' you from San Antonio, Texas. I was wonderin' if you could give me a few moments a your time. It's very important." (By this time I had gradually dropped my miner's slang and began adopting more of a Southern accent and pattern of speech).

Frank:

> "Well, alright, I guess. What's this about?"

Pat:

> "Well, ya see sir, I came across some information several years ago which induced me to look for you. I hope you're sittin' down because I don't

think there's an easy way I can say this. I think
you're my father!''

Silence. I thought perhaps the silence was his form of admission to
me. After he had time to gain his composure and some sense of control
over this conversation, he came back on:

Frank:

"Pat, did you say your last name was Miller?''

Pat:

"Yessir, I did!''

Frank:

"Pat, did you ever attend Bloomsburg College in
Pennsylvania?''

Pat:

"Well, yessir, I did. How'd you know?''

Frank:

"Pat, this is Frank Roman, Mark's father, your old
roommate from college. I think someone is playing
a terrible joke on you!''

Needless to say, I didn't pay the investigator his fee. But, what's
the odds in that whole scenario happening, calling someone two
thousand miles away to tell them you think they're your father, and
having them know who you are?

****

Having become successful at my current position by running a
tight ship, Loren promoted me up the ladder to my next managerial
position, Credit Supervisor. Ron had accepted a position in the auditing
department, allowing for this internal movement. I would now be
entering into the real nuts and bolts of the automobile finance industry,
the extension of credit to potential Chrysler buyers. With Loren's
expertise and wisdom, I would learn how to read people on paper
without ever meeting them, based on the information supplied on their

credit application and a copy of their credit report. Little did I know that I was stepping into the job which would become the most rewarding, yet demanding, position which I have held.

At the very same time I was offered this position, Lee Iacocca, as our new President and C.E.O., was introducing the K-Car and soon-to-be Caravan to the American public. This would also coincide with rebates being introduced into the public mainstream. An exciting new line of vehicles for Chrysler, the proper management team, and marketing of our product—combined with low interest rates and rebates—all made the key ingredients of a buyers' market. A dormant Chrysler, as I had known it during my first few years with the company, was getting ready to blow its doors off, with the influx of business we were receiving.

I was accepting a position which would demand most of my time, seven days a week. I would spend a lot of time meeting and getting to know dealers, letting them know we wanted to be their number one source for financing. Since many of these meetings occurred after business hours, or on weekends, in a bar or restaurant, they would place another enormous strain on our marriage. Although Linsey was occupying much of her time and attention, Jan still wasn't over the pain and would often remind me of it. What I was trying to accomplish in my life now was twofold: success for Chrysler, and a stable, comfortable environment in which to take care of my family. I was taking a chance that I could face the challenge and keep my marriage intact.

****

The gamble and the long hours would pay off. In five years we would go from one of the smallest branches in the country to one of the most powerful, in both numbers and stature. It was a direct result of our office coming together as a team. Loren had made us realize that without our dealers we were nonexistent and wouldn't have jobs.

However, after five years of credit and the successes I had gained there, I was getting antsy to move up the ladder. It was the first time that I felt enough confidence in myself to talk with Loren about my future in the company. I'll never forget that conversation.

Pat:

"'Scuse me Blev, gotta minute?"

Loren:

>"Yeah, yeah, sure Pat, come in. What's on your mind?"

Pat:

>"Well, Blev, I don't exactly know where to begin, so I'll spell it out for ya as best I can. I put in five long, hard years in da credit department for ya an' I was just wonderin' what I gotta do to get promoted up da ladder. I'll be honest with ya, I think there's people out in the office in higher positions than myself, that I'm puttin' in twice the hours they are, both in and out of the office. Tell me what I gotta do, please."

His answer, as most of his are, would be prophetic and would set the stage for what is one of my favorite and well-used lessons learned from Loren.

Loren:

>"Pat, lemme first be sure an' tell ya' that I appreciate the job you're doin' for me out there. I know we never hear that in this job enough, the simple word 'thanks.' I think it's no secret that I've taken a likin' to ya over these years, an' I hope you've learned a lot from me. I know there's been times you've got upset with me out there, as well as me towards you with some a' the decisions you've made. But, you made them. And I'm proud a' the fact you at least took a stab at them, although they were wrong. But now ya hit me with a question that's very hard to answer, or, should I say for anyone to understan' the answer to. Pat, for as long as ya live, in whatever line a work you may endeavor to undertake, lemme be sure ta tell ya somethin'! Don't worry about those above you who you may deem incompetent, or who are having a difficult time performing their jobs. These people will wash through the system on their own by way

of their own inadequacies. No, Pat, worry about
those below you not performing at their job
functions, thus holding you back. For, until ya get
all those people who work for ya capable a' takin'
your job, you're stuck!''

How true his words would be. In essence, he said that those people
we know that are in positions of power are there because they have
earned it and are respected for it.

The real strength of his statement lies in the training of those who
work for us. Employees become a mirror image of those leadership
abilities which their supervisors display. If the manager is one who
leads by example, it will reflect in the hunger of the employee. A
hungry employee is one who is never satisfied with where they are.
They are always learning, with the goal in mind of moving up the
ladder. Those people come to work because they want to, not because
they have to.

****

As the Credit Supervisor, I now had avenues available to me to
help locate my father. At my disposal were credit bureaus covering all
areas of the country. Although it is illegal to try and run a credit report
without a person's written consent, I considered the consent tacit, since
he was, after all, my father. It would once again prove futile without the
correct spelling of his name and his Social Security number as an added
identifier. In each area of the country, every bureau I would run on a
William Roman would come up empty. Therefore, I never broke the
law.

****

I also kept trying to elicit information pertaining to my father from
every member of my family over the years. One link I possibly had was
through Clarice and her husband, Cookie, who had gone to school with
him. Any doubts I had ever developed about my family not wishing to
help me find my father were erased one lonely night when I had
decided to telephone Clarice, since I hadn't talked with her in awhile.

Clarice:

''Hello.''

Pat:

"How ya doin' Clarice, it's been awhile!"

Clarice:

"It sure has Paddy. How ya been doin'?"

Pat:

"O.K. Linsey and Jan are doin' great an' my job couldn' be goin' any better. I'm even beginnin' ta talk like a Texan. Listen, "ya'll wanna come ta our house for some Bob E Q?"

Clarice:

"That's really good. You do that real good for a misplaced coal miner."

Pat:

"Yeah, tanks. Say, uh, have ya'll run across any more information on how I might locate my daddy?" (Now if that doesn't sound Texan, I don't know what does.)

Clarice:

"Well, uh, ya know, it's funny you should ask. Cook an' I jest went to his thirty-fifth class reunion recently and I saw him there. He never even said hello or paid any attention ta me, so I never did talk to him. I just never got a chance to take him aside."

Pat:

"You what!???? Clarice, you know I've been tryin' to locate my dad all these years. You know I can't stop thinkin' 'bout it an' that I've been tryin' to do it. Why? Why wouldn't you talk to him for me an' tell him I've been tryin' ta locate him?"

Clarice:

> "Paddy, I swear, I never got the chance. If you'da
> been there, you'da understood. I swear ta God!"

So there it was! My father was still alive and residing somewhere in the U.S.A. I had tried everything I could think of. I couldn't get the adoption records; the high school and college records gave me nothing that would help. I couldn't bluff any information out of my mother or James. At least I knew he was still alive somewhere!

****

Finally, after much lobbying on my behalf, Loren was able to get me promoted to the position of "Sales Representative," although he still asked me to maintain close supervision of the credit department until the new supervisor would feel comfortable. By this time, both Chrysler and our branch of Chrysler Credit were in full bloom, growing by leaps and bounds. Along with the success achieved by both the company and our branch, I had established myself as a force with our dealer body. The team attitude that was displayed by all employees in the branch also had much to do with our success.

My new job requirements would be geared toward sales efforts and learning the financial end of dealer credit, something that up to this point I had not done. I had put in many hard years and long hours on the credit desk, and the results were the great strides we had made as a branch, as a team. After only four short months in my new job, Loren called me into his office one morning.

Loren:

> "Pat, lemme be sure an' tell ya, our company an'
> especially me have noticed the hard work you've
> put into your job. You have proven yourself on the
> direct firin' line for many years runnin', and have
> also proven yourself a leader to your people. I
> always tol' ya to be patient and the results of your
> hard work would take care of itself. I got a call
> from my boss this mornin' and he wanted to know
> if I thought you were ready for an assignment that
> would entail you runnin' the internal operations of
> a large branch that is showing the results of too

much growth too quickly. The branch is in Houston, Pat, an' it's one a the largest, most powerful branches we have in the country. I tol' them, 'Hell, yes, he's ready ta handle that,' 'cause I believe you can do it. They want you to report on Monday an' I already tol' them you'd accept 'cause I knew you would. You'll receive great exposure in the Houston automobile market. Do a job like you've done for me here an' the sky's the limit. I hate ta lose ya, but I'll never hold a good man back from betterin' himself. Just take those work habits with you that you learned here, an' you'll do just fine. You're a young man an' the company is putting a great deal of stock in your future by offerin' you this move. Just do me proud, which I know you will, an' you'll enjoy the same success as you have here with us!''

And that was it—the result of my hard work and dedication and the "thank you" shown by my company and immediate supervisors, a chance to supervise the internal operations of one of Chrysler Credit's most powerful branches, with a staff of over fifty people.

Once again, one of Loren's principles would come true since those people who worked directly for me all became hungry and were ready, willing, and able to do my job. Those people I had seen as roadblocks ahead of me were taken care of when I leaped over them in grade and authority level.

Although the Credit Supervisor job was the most demanding I had done from a stressful, time-consuming aspect, my new position as Operations Manager of the Houston Branch would demand every ounce of energy I had, from both a mental and internal point of view. I would have to muster every organizational skill I had acquired, and teach those people who would learn under my tutelage the same. Having received this information on a Friday and being asked to report Monday, I was in a joyous state of shock. Jan and Linsey were excited, because we had lived in San Antonio for eleven years and were ready for a change.

I was sad over the weekend, as I reflected on the dealers and employees I had worked with who helped make me the success I was becoming. I would miss all those people, and I felt sure they would feel the same about me.

However, the one person I would miss the most would obviously be the one who, to date, had made the biggest impression on my life. Jack Schurman, Jan's father, had gained my admiration and respect for his intelligence and ethics, however, I only got to know Jack for a short period of time. Loren taught me about the real world through his parables. About people, and how to read them. How to know when someone is lying to you or being straight up. He taught me how to meet, greet, and make conversation with people I didn't know, making them comfortable with me and the personality I project. He taught me how to inject humor into my conversations and how to be dead-solid serious during business. Much like Jack, he taught me to go after whatever goal I had set for myself in life. Over the years, we had become very close to Loren, his wife Fran, and their two sons. As I began to develop images of how I wished my father would be, Loren was always at the top of my list.

****

By this time, it had been ten years since I found out I was adopted. I still knew as little about my father as the day I found out. I would continue to grill Rose Mary with any phone call I placed to her. Still, her story would not waiver. It was ridiculous to even try and talk with James about it.

I had bid farewell to all my friends and headed for Houston, monstrous in size in relation to San Antonio. I only thought I had seen traffic on the freeways of San Antonio. Houston would be awesome, a bumper-car-lover's paradise. As Loren would come to say to me whenever he was in town on business, "Pat, lemme be sure an' tell ya that I have been in most a' the largest cities in our country an' I wanna tell you what! Houston has the craziest drivers I have ever seen in my life." (At this point, he would wave his arm through the air when describing the situation). "School buses passin' me in the right-hand lane an' little kids throwin' me the finger out the back window 'cause I'm only doin' 65! Lemme be sure an' tell ya that this is sure-fire craziness right here in America!"

****

The first day I reported to my new branch, I was caught off guard by its size. It was huge. The collection department alone looked to be the size of a football field. The automobile business was booming for Chrysler, with all their successful new product designs, and branch offices were growing faster than anyone could possibly anticipate. Morale within the entire corporation was at an all-time high, due to the influx of market share we were beginning to experience. By now, the domestic automakers had finally regained the toehold they once held against the imports, because we were actually building a better product than the Japanese, at a cheaper price!

I was extremely fortunate during my five-year tenure in the Houston Branch. I was promoted from Operations Manager to Assistant Branch Manager after three years. I had gone from knowing nothing about finance to second-in-charge in one of the most powerful branches of our company, in only fourteen years. This was done with extreme hard work and patience, the latter having been difficult for me to acquire. I also had an opportunity to work under the auspices of Snowden Nantz and Bob Edenfield. Both of these men display an acute knowledge of money and finance as it relates to the automobile business.

Snowden Nantz is perhaps the best numbers man I have ever met, being able to analyze and store unbelievable calculations in his memory bank. What's even more amazing is his "recall" of these numbers on a moment's notice. His ability to do this is intimidating to people like me who are shit-for-brains without a calculator.

Under Bob Edenfield's tutelage I would learn about discipline and courage. He fears no one when it comes to his job and performing it properly. Under his supervision, I learned how to speak confidently to some of the wealthiest, most powerful automobile moguls in the country. I learned how to take risks and stand by the decisions I made, right or wrong. Even when my decisions would turn out to be wrong, Bob made them into a learning experience for me.

****

Perhaps the most impressive employee who has ever worked for me is one of the front-line people who make a successful corporation what it is. When I arrived in Houston, one of the first persons I met was the senior clerk for our branch, and also the secretary for Snowden, Bob, and me. From the beginning I noticed her antiquated dress habits, her shy demeanor, and also, with twenty-plus years of service under her belt, her vast experience. I latched onto that experience and virtually learned what my job entailed from her. Marilyn was shy and unassuming. However, the wealth of knowledge which is contained in her mind from all those years with the company has been a key factor in further solidifying my learning experience.

I watched, listened, and learned from my bosses above me, but the knowledge I learned from her has gone a long way toward the success I am now, and further hope to become. I also owe Marilyn credit because, over the years, we would become very close friends. She was someone who, over time, I would learn to trust. She also was the person who would discover where my father was, and how I could find him. Marilyn is one of the few people whom I came to trust enough to tell the truth about myself, and who would patiently sit and listen to me talk about the day I would eventually find my father, and what I would say to him. She was a part of the times I would spend trying to locate him, always coming up empty.

Every year since I can remember, Chrysler has sent me a questionnaire updating pertinent information about myself and my family. One of the questions asked is, "What goals do you wish to achieve while working for us?" Each year I would have the same response to this question, "I hope one day to utilize my degree in education in a training/teaching capacity." Little did I realize that I would one day have an opportunity to fulfill this goal.

In April of '93, I was honored to become one of twelve Regional Marketing Managers within my company's infrastructure. It is a position which is appointed by the highest offices, with many acknowledgments and confirmations throughout the approval process. The job entails much analyzation and recommendation, and the promotion can only be granted by those people above me who believe in me, and those below me who have, through proper reinforcement, worked their tail off to get me where I am.

My job requires much air travel and many hotels. A good portion of the last half of this book has been written in an airport, on an airplane, or in a hotel room. I am receiving great satisfaction in my current position in many ways. I'm getting a chance to see some of the beautiful cities in this great country of ours. In these cities I have met many fine people. I also have the chance to teach others in my company how to become more effective and efficient automobile finance experts. From where I began my career in the corporate ladder with Chrysler, right up until today, I owe many thanks to a great many people, far too numerous to mention. It is truly an honor to work for an upwardly mobile, successful corporation like Chrysler. Being able to view the entire picture from an executive position truly makes me appreciate the work ethic we have instituted within all our employees.

****

It was a hot October afternoon in Texas, the temperature well into the nineties. Work was winding down. Snowden, Marilyn (our secretary) and I were sitting in my office rehashing the day's events. Somehow we became sidetracked and began bullshitting about one thing or another. A few days earlier, Marilyn and I were discussing the last time I had spoken with any members of my family about helping to locate my father. I asked Snowden, "If someone showed up on your doorstep and claimed potential ownership thirty-eight years after birth, what would you do?" He answered that after the initial shock and heart resuscitation, it would certainly be an interesting discussion with the new-found offspring. I began to talk about how it sure would be neat to find my father if he was still alive, just to blow his mind. By this time, I pretty much resigned myself to the fact I might never meet him.

I had been searching fourteen years, off and on. However, on this particular day, after bringing up the subject, a wild hair once again began growing inside me.

Cookie:

"Hello!" (Extremely loud because of undeniable deafness).

Patrick:

"Hello, Cook!" (Texas drawl and screaming into the phone because of his impediment). "How ya'll been doin?"

Cookie:

"Paddy, ya talk like ya got a corn cob stuck in yer ass. How yooz guyz been doin?"

Patrick:

"Sorry, Cook. Good, good, thanks." (Hallelujah, I finally had lost the slang, although I could turn it on for yooz guyz anytime yooz like). "Say Cook, have you heard or found out anything about my father? It's been a long time since we last talked."

Cookie:

"Funny ting ya should ask, Paddy. Jest da udder day I wuz lookin' trew one a' my desk drawers in da den an' I found one a' my old yearbooks. I wuz gonna call ya when I got a chance. I foun' out yer fodder's name has an "s" on da end a it. His name is Bill Romans. I never knew dat, all da years we pal'd aroun' together. I hadda laugh at da picture. Yooz two guyz look identical now dat yer grown up!"

Patrick:

"No shit. Isn't that something? Rose Mary was romantically involved with him and didn't even know how to spell his name. I'll bet Victoria's rolling over in her grave."

The oddity of the situation floored me. While I was on a roll, I decided to try Rose Mary. At least, rub a little salt in the wound.

Patrick:

"Hello, Rose Mary. How have you been?"

Rose Mary:

"Hi. It's been awhile."

Patrick:

"Say, I just got off the phone with Cookie. Believe it or not, no one, including you, knew how to spell my father's name correctly. His last name is Romans, with an "s" on the end. I just thought you might want to know that. Look, it's been fourteen years since I found out I'm adopted and that you're my mother. I really want to find my father, it's important to me. I want you to think. Is there anything else you might be able to tell me, now that we know his real name?''

Rose Mary:

"Oh, Patrick, there you go again. Why can't we ever have a decent conversation without bringing that up? When are ya goin' ta give up the ghost, huh?''

Patrick:

"I'm never going to let this die! Not until I find him, dead or alive. I think you know that by now.''

Rose Mary:

"Look, all I know is what I've already told you many times. It was a mistake. He didn't want anything to do wit it, so he went off to ''Millersville'' for college. I never saw him again after that. That's all I can tell ya!''

Patrick:

"Ya know, you slay me! This isn't a conspiracy. If I find him, I'm not going to reunite the two of you in a ballistic love tryst. Why can't you understand that I want to find and talk with my biological father? I just gotta know some things.''

Once again, I was upset after my conversation with her. It was the same old story that I had been hearing for fourteen years. "It happened, he went off to 'Millersville,' and that's the last time I saw him." I replayed that line twice in my mind shortly after my conversation until the light in my simpleton mind finally went on like a nuclear bomb. "Hey, that's the first time I ever heard her say 'Millersville College.'" Up until that point, it had always been East Stroudsburg. I had never contacted Millersville before, not to my knowledge, and not with my father's correct name!

****

All the while, Snowden and Marilyn had been listening to my conversation with both Cookie and Rose Mary on the speaker phone. After I hung up with Rose Mary, and we were once again involved in small talk, the light went on. This was the most information I had to go on since my quest began! I began getting a weird sensation, as if something was going to break. I began to feel that I was getting close. It was a combination of nervous apprehension and an adrenaline rush. Before we left the office for the night, I told Marilyn to remind me to have her call Millersville College in Pennsylvania the next morning. For some reason, in the back of my mind, I knew I wouldn't need to be reminded, and I knew I was close.

CHAPTER NINE

"GOTCHA!"

It had been fourteen years and a lot of closed doors since I began looking for my biological father. The recent leads I had uncovered were once again piquing my curiosity, but I had learned long ago not to get my hopes too high. Somehow, this time seemed different.

As I had instructed the day before, Marilyn set about the task of inquiring about the attendance of a Bill (William) Romans at Millersville College. I had a clear view of her. When I saw her rise to come toward me after only five minutes, a sinking feeling like I had experienced many times before swept over me. I could only assume it was a dead end.

Marilyn:

> "Remember that time you had a private investigator try and find your father? How much was he going to charge you?"

Pat:

> "Based on the limited information I was able to give him, he told me it would probably cost in the neighborhood of a thousand dollars."

Marilyn (In her Texas country drawl):

> "I'll tell you what! I'll find 'im for you an I'll only charge half as much, how's that sound?"

Pat:

> "O.K., Mom, what'z zup?"

Marilyn:

> "Well, here's his home address and home phone number, here's the school he is at and the phone number there."

I didn't know whether to hug her, or punch her, for fear she was trying to put one over on me. However, I knew she would never do that, since she knew how long I'd been trying to locate him.

Marilyn had contacted the alumni association, and it had given her all the information, including his home address and phone number. After all the inquiring I had done through various institutions, only to be told "no" due to the "Privacy Act," here was someone spilling everything, including home address and phone number. I was shocked to find out that alumni associations are empowered by those graduates who join to release all this information. Alumni associations are not covered under the infamous "Privacy Act."

Suddenly, a dose of undeniable fear arose within my body. After thirty-eight years, if this really was my biological father, would it turn out like U-E had said to me many years before, "Maybe he might not wanna hear from you?" Panic, fear, exuberance, finality—all swept through my body. I began to think back over the years, the struggles, the heartaches, the lies, and I became sad. For if this really was my father and he, in fact, did know I had been born, maybe U-E's philosophy would ring true. Perhaps he simply wanted nothing to do with me since, as Rose Mary had said, "He went back to college and we never heard from him again." Now I was scared to know the truth and whatever it held for me. However, I had come this far and I saw no reason why I shouldn't ascertain that this definitely was my biological father.

Secretary:

> "Good morning. Bla, Bla, bla bla, bla bla, school.

Can I help you please?''

Pat:

"Yes, Ma'am. I was wondering, do ya'll have a
Bill Romans teaching there?''

Secretary:

"Well, yes sir, we do. But he's in class right now.
Is this an emergency, do you need me to interrupt
him? If not, can I take a message and ask what this
is about?''

Pat:

"Yes Ma'am. Please don't interrupt him, but would
you ask him to return a call to Pat Miller at,
bla-bla, bla, bla, bla, bla-bla.''

Secretary:

"Will he know what this is about, sir?''

Pat:

"Proba'ly not, Ma'am. Would ya tell him I'm
calling from Houston, Texas, an' that I'm with the
Chrysler Corporation.''

While talking with the secretary from the school I realized that I
had an important decision to make. *Yes, Ma'am, would you have him
call Pat Miller at this number an' tell him I think he may be my father!*
I believe that might have blown her mind and his, and sent a
Pennsylvania high school into a total frenzy.

Still, the anticipation of a return call and whether he would
recognize the name were all setting off Mount Saint Helens in the pit of
my stomach.

After the phone call, I had to go into a board meeting in
Snowden's office. "They" were meeting and I was bored. I couldn't
get the possibility of the truth out of my mind and the monumental
mountain I had climbed to get there. During the course of the meeting,
realizing what I had been through to get where I was, Marilyn knocked
on the door and stuck her head in long enough to look at me and say,

"It's him!" At that moment, more than ever before, the reality of the hunt coming to an end had set in.

Bill:

> "Mr. Miller, my name is Bill Romans. I had a message here to call you. It states you're calling from Houston, Texas, and that you are with the Chrysler Corporation. Since I don't have a Chrysler product, I have absolutely no idea what this may be about!"

Pat:

> "Bill, I don't exactly know if I've got the right person, either. However, if you don't mind, I'd like to ask you a simple question to see if you are possibly who I've been looking for. Have you ever been in or around the town of Saint Clair, Pennsylvania?"

Bill:

> "Well, yes, I was born and raised there."

Pat:

> "Well, then, I guess I do have the right person."

Bill:

> "The right person for what?"

Pat:

> "Bill, I don't know exactly how to tell you this, so I'm going to hit you right between the eyes. I believe you're my father!"

Once again, as with my college roommate's father many years earlier, silence. It was a silence which probably only lasted five seconds but, for me, seemed like an eternity. For I realized I had already played my trump card.

Now, after thirty-eight years, he had the opportunity to deny it or, simply hang up the phone on me. After a lifetime of anticipation and apprehension, he came back on the line, "I believe you may be right!"

After all these years and dead ends, I finally realized the success of my quest. However, I always believed that if I ever found him, there would be a million questions I would have which I needed answers to. At the point when he admitted my true parentage, my mind virtually went blank. Thank God, he was the one who broke the ice.

Dad:

> "How did you find me?"

Pat:

> "It's a long story that covers many years, but in the end it was luck. I have a question. Did you know that I was born and that you had another child somewhere in this country, provided you have other children?"

Dad:

> "Yes, I knew you were born, but that's all. It is a long story, one that can't be told quickly over the phone. Here's my home phone number, why don't you call me tonight."

Pat:

> "What about your wife or family, won't they mind?"

Dad:

> "I've been divorced for over five years and none of my children live at home any longer. We'll talk about all that later, O.K.?"

I knew he was on the level with me about calling him later, since I already had his home phone number, and it matched the one he had given me. My stomach was literally in knots when I got off the phone, since I had just realized the culmination of a fourteen-year odyssey. Always in the back of my mind during the conversation was the fear of rejection. After all this time and searching, would he simply tell me to "go to hell and stay away from him?" After hanging up the phone, when I realized that he was not going to deny me the privilege of getting to know him, I went out into the office and high-fived everyone in sight. Most were not aware of the search I had been through over the last several years, but they knew something extraordinary had happened in my life.

That night, I telephoned my father at home. We talked for a long time. I found out about my grandparents, their lives and deaths. I found out about why my father's marriage failed after twenty-five years. Many of the reasons seemed to parallel shortcomings that I was experiencing in my marital situation. We discussed my father's family, my two half-brothers and half-sister who were not aware of my existence. My father told me how difficult it was for him to live daily with the apprehension that I would show up on his doorstep, thus ruining the family atmosphere that he had established over the years. I asked him many questions relating to me; health questions, personal questions regarding my conception and his relationship with my mother. However, many of the questions I wanted answers to would have to wait for an eventual face-to-face confrontation, should our relationship ever progress to that level.

One aspect of our first conversation which impressed me was the candor with which my father spoke to me, almost as if he was glad the shadow he had been living under for the past thirty-eight years was now behind him. It was as if he was expecting my call or knock on the door through the years, and now that it came, he was relieved. I still didn't know what he looked like nor if I would ever have a chance to meet him, but I certainly came to like the person I spoke with over the phone. Unlike my mother, he held no pretensions about what happened many years before. In fact, I was under the impression he wished to bury the untruths which were my life, and that we could begin a relationship, although late in both our lives. In short, he came across as a genuinely nice guy, and I was already feeling robbed after only two phone conversations. Because of the way I felt after I hung up with him that night, I decided to write him a letter explaining my feelings, the lies I had to deal with in my life, and the ensuing struggle to find him. I decided to write, since I found it much easier to express myself that way. I also enclosed pictures of myself, Jan, and Linsey, in the event he wished to pursue a relationship. I wished this more than anything else in my life, but I would definitely leave it up to him as to the path we would take.

****

It had been two weeks since I had located, spoken, and written to my biological father. The reality of finding him had not fully enveloped me until the day of my third and, hopefully, final back surgery. (These were due to injuries sustained from bodybuilding). As I was lying in my room, still heavily sedated from the anesthesia and morphine which were flowing through my body, the phone rang. Due to my obvious incapacities, Jan had to answer. I was expecting it to be any one of a myriad of well-wishers, and was totally taken off guard when she said, "It's your father, would you like to speak to him?" Until then, he hadn't really given me any indication of how he wished to progress in our new-found relationship, but this one phone call in my time of need signified his desire to go forward, regardless of the ramifications it may have between him and his family. When I hung up the phone after our brief conversation, I turned my head to where no one could see me, and tears of victory, not pain, streamed from my eyes.

****

While convalescing from my recent surgery, one of the highlights of my day would come when the mail arrived. Having been used to the extreme fast pace of my job, recovering from these surgeries was more excrutiating from a mental point of view than the pain. I had no idea until then, how much bullshit mail and propaganda arrives in our lives on a daily basis.

On one of my daily mail runs, as I was flipping through the day's advertisements, including correspondence to my wife from Ed McMahon telling her, once again, we were still in the running for millions of dollars, I came across a letter which seemed as if I had mailed it, and it was being returned for some reason or another. Between thinking about the money Jan had invested in stamps with the Publishers Clearinghouse Sweepstakes, and looking at my own writing, I finally noticed the return address. It was from my father and obviously contained pictures, due to its weight and proportion. In previous conversations he told me that he would try to find some pictures to send, and obviously he had. This would be my first real look at the man who had conceived me, helping to mold who I am today.

The pictures enclosed were of his sons, daughter, ex-wife and, of course, himself. Most of the pictures were of him well into his fifties, a relief for me to see that I wouldn't be bald, just receding. However, he also had a graduation picture from college, age twenty-four, which proved how strong the sperm-factor really is. For, at that age, we were identical and, as I age, I see a lot of myself in him. Jan had found a similar picture of me at age twenty-four and the comparison was uncanny. Dimpled chin and cheeks, high hair line, exact eyes and nose. As Jan and I looked them over, of all his children, especially his sons, I seemed to resemble him the most in looks.

It's very weird, sitting and staring at a family that doesn't realize a piece of the puzzle is missing. Numerous situations and feelings flashed through me as I began to realize the implications of my father's family finding out the truth. I certainly didn't want to ruin any family structure he had created, and informed him early on that I had no intention of doing this. If anything, he would be the one who needed to inform them. He did tell me that he would probably inform his daughter, who was the oldest, since she would be the one most likely to understand the situation and deal with it, although she would not accept it under the circumstances. I left that entire situation up to him, since he would have to deal with it if he chose to tell his family the truth. One thing was certain: he seemed much "straighter" than I during our early conversations, much more proper in his demeanor than I had ever been. Therefore, the decision on whether to tell his other children must have weighed heavily on his mind.

I also wondered whether or not we would ever meet. If so, how would we respond to one another? Now that I found him, I was in a quandary because I didn't know how he wanted me to proceed. I believe we were both curious about the other, especially since we had seen pictures of each other and the obvious similarities.

That night, after going through the pictures over and over again, a great void presented itself. Due to the similarities in appearance, writing, and size, I suddenly began to feel the necessity of meeting my biological father in the event something should happen to him. I felt like only half the movie had been shown, only half of the book written. Up until then, I had been passive in the way I approached my new-found parent. Now, I knew I must meet him, if only just once.

****

One thing I never gave much thought to during the years of trying to find my father was how his family would react toward me, in the event he chose to come clean with them. They certainly would need to understand that I was not trying to take away their father. There was no way I could have an actual parental relationship with this man, not with so many years in each of our lives having expired. What they would need to know is that all I was looking for in this whole sordid mess was a friend, someone who would not be afraid to speak the truth about the situation. Bill was this type of person. He had not denied the situation, nor tried to avoid it, and answered any questions I posed to him to the best of his ability.

Perhaps since the truth had finally been released for him also, he chose to inform his daughter. I don't know if, by doing this, an enormous weight was taken off his shoulders or an even bigger one added. I definitely was not expecting how quickly he would choose to do this. I don't believe I should be held guilty because I am the result of a mistake made many years before. However, it's not fair to hold my father as less of a person, either.

I remember the call well. It was on a Sunday afternoon, the Oilers had won (it wasn't a playoff game), and I was feeling great. My back was healing nicely, I'd be returning to work soon, and I had found my father. I was definitely on one of those rare positive rolls we find ourselves in every once in awhile, where everything seemed to be going right.

The phone rang and I was thinking it was one of my fellow "Luv ya Blue" Oiler fans calling to talk about the game. I wasn't prepared for a female voice on the other end, one I definitely didn't recognize. On top of that, I was on the portable phone and we had a bad connection. I didn't catch her last name, but I understood her first name as Kathi, and then experienced a short, unexpected silence. I couldn't remember meeting anyone recently with this name to whom I'd have given my phone number, especially since I had been convalescing the past month. After what seemed an eternity, she finally stated that she was Bill Romans' daughter, that he had just left her house. I really wasn't expecting this phone call—not so soon anyway. I am rarely at a loss for words, but in this scenario I was stumped. I really didn't know what to say.

Fortunately, during this first conversation, she would do most of the speaking. It certainly would have been a lot easier for me if I had had a chance to speak with Bill first, so I would be aware of how he approached it. I was still in a semi-state of shock because he chose to disclose this to any member of his family so soon. Apparently Bill had taken the letter I had written him, trying to express my feelings about finding him, along with the pictures I had enclosed of myself, Jan, and Linsey, and asked her to read it in its entirety before asking questions. She explained that her first reaction was that he was asking her to read a chain letter, since it was obviously lengthy. After reading several paragraphs, it became obvious to her that it was about someone being thankful for the opportunity to find his biological father and having a chance to speak with him.

It talked about my childhood and how the whole situation in Saint Clair turned out, and that I was glad it was all a lie, that I was given a second chance. She realized soon enough that the person who was writing this letter was, in fact, writing it to her father. The person who had written this letter was calling her father . . . his father, also.

Kathi was very cordial during our conversation and thankfully, she was trying very hard to deal with it. She informed me that her main concern was for me and that everything had worked out under the circumstances. I found that very admirable of her and was touched by her concern. She did tell me that it was hard to deal with inasmuch as she had always prided herself in being the first-born, who had the first grandchild, and suddenly this had been stripped away from her. She, too, was having to deal with the fact that her father, whom she loves very much, had misled her family, also. It never dawned on me that I would bring hurt into people's lives simply by being alive. I still hadn't put this conversation in the perspective that I was also talking to my half-sister. To this day, I wonder if she has put the situation into that same perspective.

Our initial conversation concluded on a positive note, as positive as it could possibly have been under the circumstances. She was not going to tell her brothers about me unless actually confronted with the situation, in which case she would not mislead anyone. She did tell me that she was going to tell her mother, Bill's ex-wife. As an ex-wife, I can't imagine how she felt when informed, especially since she had already remarried. Perhaps I was the answer to a curse she had secretly put on Bill since their marriage disbanded. I simply don't know. In any event, that would leave only his two sons, my half-brothers, who would not be aware of the situation as it currently stood. When and how they would find out would not be up to me.

After my conversation with Kathi, I was feeling kind of upbeat. I mean, she didn't exactly welcome me with open arms and say, "My long lost brother, how have you been?" On the other hand, she had left the door open to further communication and possibly meeting one day, since she also travels frequently with her job. With her understanding, not necessarily acceptance, it would also make it much easier for my father and me to someday meet, since they are very close and it was obvious he was going to mislead her no longer.

****

After several conversations, it became apparent that my mission would not be completely fulfilled until I met my maker face-to-face. With frequent trips to Detroit, it would always be easy enough to have a stopover in Philadelphia. Therefore, I posed this to him and, to my surprise, he was more than receptive to the idea. However, he would prefer to come South, so that he could also meet Jan and his new-found granddaughter. He would try to arrange it to come in for a weekend during his spring break. Of course, I was elated since this would also help to place another piece of the puzzle together. A puzzle which somehow turned out to be my life.

Meeting my father for the first time certainly sent many questions and emotions coursing through my mind. Just the anticipation of finally seeing to fruition a journey I had begun many years earlier was making me very apprehensive. "Do I shake his hand, do I give him a hug, do I call him Dad?" One can only imagine the myriad of questions which I would ask myself each day. I also wondered what was going through his mind about finally meeting the best-kept secret of his life. It had been six months since we were first introduced, with many phone conversations in between, but this was the ultimate.

For my part, I was very proud of what I could display to my father. A respectable job, beautiful home, and a family who hung in there with me through thick and thin. I have come to know some very wealthy, influential people, who all respect me on a personal or business level, or both. I have lived to fulfill a dream I had set earlier in my life. Finding my father and writing this book—the truth, as I see it—is the culmination of that dream envisioned many years earlier.

CHAPTER TEN

PARALLELS
(THE DAY OF RECKONING)

Once again, unbelievable. Today when I got home from work, Linsey told me to sit down and listen to the Oprah Winfrey Show. Bucky Dent, the ex-Yankee phenom, was relating the story of how he found out late in life that his aunt was his mother and the struggle he went through to find his father. His family would not help him to locate his biological father, either. In his situation and mine, we spent many years trying to locate someone who, with the help of our families, we could have easily found. In both instances, we were robbed of the truth!

It had been six months since I had found Bill. His initial appearance in our lives was almost like a dream come true for me, and I am sure Jan and Linsey as well. Linsey, for her part, was extremely excited since she now would have a chance to meet her second living, true grandparent. For Jan, who had traveled this odyssey with me, it was the end of a long, arduous journey.

Waiting at the airport terminal, it seemed like an eternity until he finally made his way up the ramp. It wasn't hard to recognize him since I was looking at myself twenty-four years in the future. To my surprise, he was the one who embraced me in a hug, his eldest son, the one he had never met. Through all the sports I have ever played in my life, all the high level business meetings I have been involved in, and all the people I have crossed paths with, this single moment in my life was the one in which I encountered the most stomach butterflies, the most nervousness ever. He would be with us for three days this first trip, a trip which he informed his daughter Kathi he would be making. I'll sure say this for the man, he has moxie. Since the truth had been uncovered, he was no longer going to hide anything.

****

A father and son who have never met each other go through an awfully quick bonding process. Our looks are uncannily alike, considering the age disparity. Although an inch taller than I, his ideal weight, as is mine, is centered around the 235- 245-pound area. Fortunately for me, my ears are somewhat smaller than his, since he inherited a serious set of wing tips. That, perhaps, is the only area of appearance in which there is any variance whatsoever.

I find it incredible that both of us obtained our college degrees in secondary education. I can see through him that, had I stayed in education, I would also have achieved many successes.

We also have some "weird" idiosyncrasies which parallel each other closely. We both have an innate fear of the sight of blood. So many times, when I had to have blood taken, or give my own blood for my numerous surgeries, I would get very squeamish, to the point of passing out if I watched. Many a nurse, when given the task of drawing blood from me, would be awed at how big a pansy I became considering my size and obvious strength.

Neither one of us has ever taken a liking to fighting, either physically or verbally, although I am not slow to protect myself or my family. Neither one of us likes guns, nor has a gun for protection. We both believe the same about guns, that their ultimate purpose is destruction and killing. Nothing good has ever come from a gun. Hopefully, neither of us will ever see the day when we are forced to own one.

Both of us have lost faith in our church, although we believe firmly in the existence of a supreme being who dictates our future. I, of course, have reasons why I have fallen from grace with my baptized religion. His fall has happened over the course of time. We both still pray, but our prayers usually cover the wants and needs of our family and others, rarely ourselves. Because of this, our prayers are derived from a certain degree of loneliness within ourselves, always thinking about those in need and those who have less than we. This is perhaps the trait I deem most admirable in myself—the concern I have for all people, especially those whom I have a personal interest in.

As much as we both are concerned about others, both of us maintain the same view of friends: "They are few and hard to find." Both of us have built a shield around us about friends, one in which the philosophy seems to be, "Avoid friendships, because they are the ones which cause the most pain." When I was very young, Peter Miller, with his lack of education once told me, "If you can count your true friends on one hand, then you are blessed!" I'll be damned if Peter wasn't right. I, like my father, have amassed many acquaintances through the years, but few we could deem "friend." To both of us, a friend is someone who will go to the wall for you, through thick or thin, with nary a question asked. These type of people we rarely encounter in our lives but they are the true friends, the ones who will never question, only be there to help pick up the pieces.

****

Through all my life, I never thought I would see the day when a personality paralleled mine until I met my father. Both of us have an uncanny ability to meet and greet people we have never met before, yet make them feel totally at ease, perhaps because we have had to interact with so many different individuals during the course of our professional careers. We have a distinct, satirical humor which sheds light on many people and subjects, yet which makes the people we care to share our humor with sit back and evaluate their situations.

There is a unique parallel which has to be genetic, there can be no other logical explanation. Like my father before me who was divorced after twenty-five years of marriage, who was raised in an extremely dysfunctional setting, we both have an extremely difficult time expressing love, either verbally or physically, to those we truly do love. Both of us, through personal experiences, have fallen way short of what was expected of us during the course of our marriages. In his situation, it was a direct descendent of how he viewed his parents' relationship. His father often abused his mother, either verbally or physically.

With me, it wasn't so much the distinct lack of affection shown to me by those whom I perceived to be my parents, as the realization that my whole life has been an untruth. Since uncovering the lie, I chose to view the remainder of mankind, sometimes including my wife, as an intruder into my world. Why, I don't know; I wish I did. If I could find a psychologist or a psychoanalyst I could trust, perhaps they could enlighten me as to why this is so. Regardless, the relationship between Jan and me has not evolved, as it should have, to one of trust and friendship. It really makes me sad to say and write this, but it is true. Due to no fault of Jan's, I have never experienced the true, unconditional love that is created amongst spouses. God only knows, I wish I could find myself in this matter. Jan has shown me unconditional love, and I still have not realized how to accept it or acknowledge it. This has caused an enormous strain in our marriage, much like my father before me, and could end up being our ultimate demise. However it turns out, the bond between Linsey, Jan, and myself will always be strong, and I will never leave them shortchanged, as I feel I have been in my life.

****

Perhaps the trait which I have come to admire most in my father is his complete and total honesty toward our situation. As I stated earlier, never, since confronted with the truth by me, has he sought to hide himself, as the Miller family has. Regardless of the incessant questions I have thrown at him, he has never wavered from telling the truth. Perhaps this is why I lend so much credibility to what he tells me in relation to all the lies I have already heard. For my dad has nothing to lose, only a son to gain. In retrospect, my mother, who had everything to gain by telling the truth, has lost all my respect through her repeated, ongoing lies.

****

On his third day here, my father and I finally had a chance for a one-on-one, with no one around to disturb us. I asked him to relay the comedy of errors that occurred, enabling me to be brought up a Miller and he to be non-existent as my parent. Before he began his side of the story, he already had a general idea about what life was like for me growing up, since I had been sending him each chapter of this book once I started writing it again. This was the one moment in time which my mother and brother James hoped would never happen. From this point forward, I would form an opinion of the truth based on both sides of the story. Until this day, it had always been one-sided—theirs.

To begin, it appears both my father and mother held deep feelings for each other, up until the point of conception. I was led to believe that I was truly "a mistake" that never should have happened, a one-time deal, "conception upon the loss of virginity." Apparently, my mother and father had known each other and had feelings for each other enough to have made love on several occasions. She would even go visit him while he was going to college at Millersville. On top of this, my father had thought it prudent, even back then, to utilize some form of birth control. However, my mother's staunch religious beliefs would not allow this. Hence, I was created.

I am sure that from the moment my mother discovered her *faux pas*, she was undergoing serious stress. Remember, this was 1954, in a town where secrets were very difficult to keep. She was about to become involved in a lie which would be the gamble of her life, and she would ultimately lose. From the time she informed Victoria, the church would also become involved. Both she and my father would have to undergo thorough degradation from Father McHenry, who was interceding on "behalf of God." Whatever he dictated as the best course of action to take, Victoria was sure to be a willing participant. Also, he would be sure that they would both undergo extensive counseling due to the nature of their sins, should marriage become an acceptable alternative.

Bill, for his part, was also in a quandary. He was about to enter his last year of college when suddenly the unexpected reality of marriage became a course he wasn't prepared to study for. Eventually, after all the dishes had finished flying, he would go before the tribunal of Victoria, James, and Peter to express his intentions about the situation he had gotten Rose Mary into. For some unknown reason, Victoria had always failed to realize that "it takes two to tango" in these situations. It always seemed to be the other person's fault; they took full advantage of the situation with her offspring. Never did she accept the blame for not making her children fully aware of the consequences of pre-marital sex.

From the time that Rose Mary announced her pregnancy, there was very little dialogue between her and my father. Other than mandatory visits to St. Mary's and Father McHenry, all communication had ceased until a decision was reached on my future parentage. The decision would be made at a meeting to be held by Victoria, at her house. The only attendee from Bill's family would be Bill, himself, since he was the one solely responsible for inflicting this pain on "the family." Also, Victoria had much more power in her own element, with James at her side. Bill went to the meeting with every intention of asking for Rose Mary's hand in marriage. Present, besides Bill, would be Victoria, James, and Peter. The latter would have virtually no say in the outcome of the meeting. Unbeknownst to Bill, the decision on what to do had been made far before his attendance at this meeting.

Victoria controlled the meeting from the start, well-versed in what she was about to say. She first asked Bill what his intentions were with her daughter. Bill, already anticipating he would have to step up to the pump since he, also, was raised with staunch Catholic beliefs, volunteered marriage as his duty. However, he did have one stipulation to the proposed marriage that would be essential to the lifestyle he had envisioned. He was in his last semester of college and wanted to wait until graduation before the wedding be held. In this way, he would have school out of the way and, hopefully, already have found gainful employment for his new family to subsist on. Victoria would hear none of this. It would either be now or never with Rose Mary, since a wedding five months down the road would virtually ensure that her pregnancy would show.

Victoria was adamant on the immediacy issue, while Bill was equally demanding in his one request. In this one moment, religious pride would rob me not only of my future, but more importantly, a real father. For this I can forgive neither Victoria nor Bill, and I informed him of this during this initial heart-to-heart. He said he could understand my feelings, but he will never understand how I feel on this issue. Rose Mary really didn't have a say back then, much as she refuses to discuss and have a say in her situation with me now. This whole mess was over silly religious pride and stubbornness.

If only Peter had had a say, I believe both sides would have gone back to the drawing board to work it out. Bill told me that he and Peter were good buddies up until that point, that they had worked together at the dairy, with Bill maintaining a summer job there. Therefore, I was truly the epitome of "the milkman did it." But, he would not have a say. Not then, not ever. He would go to his grave carrying a great secret that weighed heavily upon him. That would become obvious in the way he perceived me after his strokes. He did not die a happy man with this great lie stuck deep inside his mind. He would never truly achieve peace of mind to carry him into the next life, whatever that may be.

****

James. Yes, James. Today, I refuse to speak with him because I can never trust him, due to the way he chose to handle the truth with me. Since the time James sat at that meeting, right up until the last time we spoke, he was continuing the lie. Without his mandate to the other family members once I found out the truth, I would have had fourteen extra years to try and establish a parental relationship. Yet, he still insists upon ignorance of this situation anytime I have attempted to discuss it with him.

As for Rose Mary, I can't really blame her for what happened, but I don't respect her, either. One of the biggest scars I carry from this is having to witness the awful deaths I had to endure, those who I thought were my parents. Then, to realize they continued to enforce the lies after their deaths. This is where I lost respect for Rose Mary, for not claiming what was rightfully hers from that point forward. Because that would mean having to reveal the lie to her sons, my five half-brothers, and there was no way she would do that.

****

Bill informed me that since he refused to yield on his request, Victoria revealed her alternative plan. She informed him they were accepting the responsibility for Rose Mary's child. His services were no longer necessary. However, he was absolutely forbidden to make contact with the child, since they would become the parents after the birth. In other words, it was not a request that Bill accept this plan, it was an ultimatum, in no uncertain terms.

On July 4th, 1954, seven days from my birth, Bill Romans was attending an Independence Day picnic. From out of nowhere came James Miller and "Big Bill" Hill, Victoria's brother. Big Bill was six foot, six inches tall and a very intimidating figure. I'm sure James sought out Uncle Bill's help with this task because he didn't have the guts to do it by himself. They threw my father up against a wall in an area they had guided him to, and threatened him with physical harm in the event he ever got a crazy notion and tried to make contact with me. Only after my repeated questioning to James about this actually happening did he finally break down and admit it. This was yet another reason Bill had for avoiding all contact with me.

****

There would be much to do in the Miller family with the impending birth. The church would be needed to aid in the recommendation of an "unwed mother's home," which Rose Mary would be sent to when she began to show. Perhaps it is the same one Jo eventually went to when she became pregnant with Adrian. The church would become a participant in the lie the same as any family member who was aware of the situation and how it was to be remedied.

Attorneys would also need to be consulted for the legal work through the local courthouse. Perhaps a bribe or two was initiated for expediency. Whoever did this would have to be a friend of the family's who could be trusted with his word. The "client confidentiality clause," would be enforced to its fullest during this maneuver. Any documents related to the matter would be retained by Victoria only, and then passed to James upon her death.

There would also be the matter of "getting the word out" to the proper elders so they could help enforce the lies, especially within the confines of the church. This, too, would be done in an expeditious manner.

****

Bill went back to complete his education. Shortly thereafter, his parents passed away. The bar and funeral home were sold, and the remainder of his family moved away from Saint Clair. He would marry and have a family of his own, they would also be deceived in an abstract way. Bill would never have to lie to them about me because they would never know about me. Therefore, there would be no need to ever discuss the issue.

I often wonder what would have happened if both Victoria and Bill had acquiesced, to a degree, to each other's demands. Would I be the oldest of numerous children, all raised under the confines of Bill and Rose Mary's roof? If so, many things would be different, to the extent that none of my life would be like it is. This is yet another area which I have had to work through, as I continuously ponder the "ifs" of the situation. Despite all the bad that I've had to accept and work my way through, I'm happy with who I am and what I've got. I've got my family, who've been through this mess with me, and God knows I have had to let go of a lot of bitterness inside. Writing this book has helped ease a lot of the pain and bitterness.

However, before I was finally able to fully accept myself and the situation I have been forced to deal with, I would endure one final knock-down, drag-out fight with bitterness. In any fight, there are no winners, only losers. However, after this last one, the last blow I was going to endure regarding myself, I felt like a winner because I truly was left with my pride intact. The fight to do this would drain me of every ounce of energy in my body: the following day I would have to say goodbye to the father I had never known. When I realized the consequences of letting him go after so long a struggle to find him, I also realized what a void his absence in my life had been. Moreover, it made me think of how much I truly love my family, regardless of my inability to show outward affection.

****

On the way to the airport, Bill began to speak to me as a parent would his son, continuously aware that we had not really solidified anything on this first visit, other than what we talked about as being the truth regarding each other's lives. He began to speak about his marriage and the reason it had failed after so many years—the fact that he had a difficult time showing affection and love and it cost him in the end. It was difficult for me to follow, because I was trying to erase the knot that was forming in the pit of my stomach due to the finality of the situation. Here he was, an intelligent, educated man, talking about what he perceived to be a parallel in each of our lives, and I could not respond to what he was saying. I was trying to stay cognizant of the conversation, yet there were so many things I was wanting to relay to him other than problems between Jan and me which he perceived. The closer we got to the airport, the more my mind was focusing on one word: "Why?" and bitterness was searing in the pit of my stomach.

When we pulled into the airport parking lot, I still didn't know if Bill had noticed, but I hadn't spoken a word in over ten minutes. All the things I envisioned one day saying to my father were blocked at the back of my throat as bitterness swelled all around me. As we walked from the ticketing booth to the departing ramp, I could only think that I really didn't know what to say. "I love you, dad" definitely would not be appropriate under the circumstances since both of us have a difficult time in that area. Yet, a handshake and an "I'll see you later," also would not be right. It really didn't matter because I was totally speechless, frightened by this last battle with bitterness.

Finally, we arrived at the ramp. The flight was still a half hour from departure but there was nothing I could say. As we stopped and stood, staring at each other, Bill asked me a question which crippled me, making all thought and all sensations in my body go numb. "Well, Pat, have you found what you've been looking for?"

I was ripped! The bitterness inside me toward him made me want to break his face at the realization of how deprived I felt. The other part, the pride I had found in myself and my admiration for Bill, let go from me in a rush of emotion. I could do nothing else but turn and walk away as the tears flew from my eyes. This would be the last time I let these negative emotions get the best of me. However, as I walked back through the airport, naked for all mankind to see in the tears which were uncontrollable, I had to exorcise this one last demon inside of me. All thoughts were negative, piercing in their ramifications. It came to me that Bill was now going home to his real family, a family that will probably never accept me, and I had to go back to my family, which is ready and willing to accept him as one of us. There was no parity to the situation, and the utter futility of it made the tears come all the harder as I realized I was the one who was having to accept the blame for other people's mistakes.

All the way out of Houston Intercontinental Airport, which is quite a distance, I was wiping tears from my eyes. Unfortunately I was alone, because my vision was most definitely impaired as I was trying to drive. It suddenly dawned on me there was no place to go. Jan was in school, as well as Linsey. Besides, it's fifteen miles from the airport to my home. There was no way I could drive that distance in my condition. I finally decided I would dispose of my bitterness toward Bill by writing him a letter. All of the things I had wanted to say at the airport as a goodbye would be put on paper. Therefore, I headed toward my office, which is right across the street from the airport, to achieve what I hoped would bring a "wholeness" to my story, now that I had located and met my biological father.

As I began to write, emotions were running deep and I was sobbing so hard I could barely see the paper. I had originally begun to write the letter with every intention of hurting the feelings of everyone who had been part of the great lie, including my father. With all the crying I had already done and continued to do during the course of the letter, I found myself too emotionally drained to try and hurt anyone. Rather, I directed a letter to my father which stated that I was willing and wanting to go forward, but he would need to be half of the equation.

April 6, 1993

Dad:

There were so many things I wanted to say to you today, however, I couldn't get the words out. This is unusual for me since I am one who has never had a hard time expressing myself. It's almost as though I wish I had never found out about you since, now that I've met you, I feel that I've been robbed. 38 years is a long time to accept being without a father. Your visit has given me even more impetus to finish this crazy book I'm writing. I used to think the moral of the book is that people should tell the truth to others who are in situations like myself. However, I now realize it's much deeper than that. It will also send a message that if something or someone belongs to you, don't ever be afraid to claim what is rightfully yours. I guess the only question I'll ask you 'til either one of us leaves this world is why did you not claim what was rightfully yours, since we have so much in common?

I know that the first 38 years I was robbed and deprived of what was rightfully mine, however, with your consent I want the next 38 to belong to us. I appreciate your having the courage to accept me after I found out the truth. Let's both go forward from here and accept each other for what we truly are, father and son.

Love,

Pat

P.S. I want you to know that as I wrote this letter, I was crying faster than the words could be written.

In essence, it was a plea for a friend. But, it came 120% from the heart, with about as much emotion as I have ever displayed at any one time. When I was done, and emotionally drained, I felt a great relief within me. I had found my father, met my father, and then opened the door for us to start a relationship, if he so chose. If there was ever to be a feeling of wholeness for me in this experience, it was at this moment. For I felt as if I had taken the best punches anyone could possibly have thrown at me, and ended victorious, with my pride intact. At that one moment in my life, I felt as if I had finally won whatever it was I was fighting inside myself.

****

I have done extensive thinking about all I had learned, and how it happened, how it went down. I am continually amazed when I think about how much power Victoria, dead for twenty-three years now, still possesses. She still has Rose Mary and Jo afraid to confront the truth with their children. The strength of the church in regard to birth control has a lot to do with me being here. However, at what point do the staunch beliefs and teachings begin to backfire? I was the victim of a crime by my church which no confession can erase. I was robbed of the truth, something they can never give back to me. I am glad my belief in God remains so strong, because I have definitely been tested through the course of my life. Through thick and thin, I have always held firm my belief in a God that watches over us, as he did when he provided my many guardian angels.

I have had to evaluate my relationships with the people I was brought up to believe were my brothers and sisters. Those who have subscribed to the "you were loved" theory, simply don't grasp what I have endured over these years. It changes a lot of things, having had to evaluate my siblings from varying perspectives, especially how they perceive the situation as it stands today. I can't figure out if it's the threat that I am actually going to go through with this book—but certain barriers to communication have definitely been established. What really floors me is that many of my so-called brothers and sisters steadfastly refuse to acknowledge my father. They don't wish to discuss him or his presence in my life. I know that my insistence on their acknowledgment of the truth toward my situation can only be accomplished by my exposing it to any and all who are willing to try and understand.

One of my smants has told me, on more than one occasion, that I need psychological counseling due to what I have experienced. She wanted me to talk with a priest from their local parish to see if he could shed some objective light. Now, I agree I need counseling, this book being finished is a step in that direction. I'll simply autograph a copy of it for some hot-shot shrink, tell them to read it, and send their analysis through the mail. I will seek advice from many possible avenues. But never could I talk freely with a priest about it. While we're on the subject, maybe some of my siblings could use some counseling. Perhaps a doctor can advise them on how they can come clean with themselves.

If I need a doctor for any reason, it would be to help me understand how to love people and accept those who love me in my life, unconditionally. I must have been extremely hard to live with during the past several years, when my anger spilled over into the lives of those who love me. I had to have been unbearable.

****

One thing I hope this book accomplishes is that Jo and Adrian come together as mother and son, not the sister/brother guise they have been living under. I also believe Adrian ought to try and locate his father. If only to find out about medical information which could help him later in life. Who knows, perhaps they could establish a relationship based on friendship first.

I also hope, with the possible success of this book, to initiate a support group for those people who have had to find out on their own that they have been deceived about their parentage. From hearing those stories of the Bucky Dents and the twin sisters who have appeared on Oprah, to all those stories people have opened up and told me involving their private lives, the best counseling one can get is from their peers. With proper networking, it could work and would help many people relieve themselves of the bitterness that dwells within them. It would be a support group that accepts written and verbal communication, since writing is the best way many of us can express ourselves.

****

The song "Cat's in The Cradle," has always had a special significance for me. It was one of my favorite songs while growing up, even though I did not know the truth at that time. As fate would have it, it came on the radio while I was driving home that day after my father left and I was so emotionally drained. When I analyze the words, it is also somewhat prophetic for me. It tells of all the stages in life that a parent and child are forced to endure together, yet sometimes they never really get to know each other due to priorities which arise in their lives. In the end, when we assume the role of parent and look at the relationships we have established with our children, they seem to parallel the song very closely. The line in the song which particularly affects me is "He'd grown up just like me, my boy was just like me." I see my new-found father now, and can make many analogies to these words, including being very much like my father without ever having met him. I don't know what path in life God has destined for me, but I do know that it was his guidance which allowed me to achieve my dream. Without this guidance and all those "guardian angels" provided me throughout the years, I'd never have made it through!

THE END

Epilogue

Where Do We Go From Here?

The borough of Saint Clair still sits nestled peacefully amongst the enormous mountains of coal whose fruit is no longer the energy choice of our country. Since I left the area, the Pennsylvania Department of Transportation built a bypass around the town. Therefore, very few people purposefully drive through unless they live there. Most of the bars have shut down, but the churches all remain. I have to wonder how many other stories such as mine are buried deep within family and religious history. Not only in a small town such as I grew up in, but throughout our country, our world. I rarely have occasion to go back there. However, when I do, it brings back bad memories. The regeneration process is still going strong with a new generation of families becoming the breadwinners who keep the families intact.

****

Most of the Miller family are still in various areas of Pennsylvania. Jo and Adrian are living under the same roof in that tiny town. She has yet to sit with her son and acknowledge the fact that she is his mother, that a long time ago she made a mistake. It's very sad because she is not going to change her position in the matter, although Adrian freely discusses it with others.

I haven't spoken with James in over two years. To say the least, our relationship has deteriorated due to his insistence of ignorance in relation to me. While I was writing chapter ten, I wrote a letter to "Oprah" about my story. If I could possibly appear on her show I would like to have James on also, so he would be forced to explain to the world why he insists on ignoring this subject with me. Perhaps if he could put some rationale behind it that I could understand, I might be able to release my anger toward him. However, he has never attempted to apologize or accept any of the blame, even after the deaths of Peter and Victoria.

I do owe a debt of gratitude to James for ensuring my college education at a time when I was vulnerable to complacency. Because of that, my life took a much-needed forward progression out of the confines of the regeneration process. I suppose I could learn to forgive James, however, he would first have to freely discuss the situation with me and be willing to accept my father as part of my life. I doubt this will ever happen. Unfortunately, James never dreamed that I would unveil the plan, especially to expose it for all to see in this writing. For all the brother Jameses out there who are insisting on secrecy regarding someone's biological parents, "Get a life!"

Rose Mary and I have grown farther apart from each other than we've ever been. She is extremely distraught that I have decided to write this story, and has expressed this to me on more than one occasion. During one conversation she made the mistake of saying, "If you hurt one hair on any member of my family, you're in big trouble, buster!"

It was only after she said that, and the way she said it, that she realized the impact. On another occasion she stated, "You better be prepared for all the lawsuits if you insist on writing that book!" I have this weird feeling inside me that all of these people are afraid of the truth being exposed. What will be the grounds of the suit? "On the grounds he insists upon telling the truth?"

My father recently visited again. We had much to discuss, including this book. He requested that he be allowed to write an Epilogue II. I told him I didn't see a problem with that. He can write whatever he likes regarding the situation and I'll accept it. Perhaps there is yet another parallel between us, that we both express ourselves much better in our writing than verbally.

We have to work several things out if we are to have a relationship based on friendship, some bigger than others. Although his daughter, Kathi, treated me amicably in our early conversations, we haven't spoken in a long time. Bill states they absolutely refuse to discuss me, especially his sons, my half-brothers. They try to treat me as a nonentity, and this is unfair to everyone involved. As Jan said regarding this issue, "How can they say you're an asshole until they've had a chance to meet you. Then they can call you an asshole!"

It's obvious that they are holding my father accountable for this situation, "guilty" if you will. I wonder if they ever stop to think that, if Bill had decided to marry Rose Mary and accept me as his family, they wouldn't be on the face of this earth today. I asked Bill if he could arrange for me to fly in and meet with them. He didn't think that would ever be possible.

When we met for the second time, he asked if I noticed how he never refers to me as "son," although I call him "Dad" most of the time. He went on to inform me that he believes these titles should be "earned," not given. "I agree, Bill. Don't you think I've earned the right to call you 'Dad' after having to search for you for fourteen years?" Besides, I frequently refer to men whom I respect and admire as "Dad" because, over the course of the years until I found him, many of my role models emerged as people I hoped my father would be like. Hell, I can name at least twenty people I refer to as "Dad" due to my respect for them.

I really have no idea where this is going to go from here. I hope Bill realizes that he has another family in Jan, Linsey, and me. Like it is with any of the people I have finally been able to trust and call my friend, "I'd give the shirt off my back for him!" I said earlier that anything which is rightfully ours and we want it bad enough—go for it. *You're part of something I want desperately, Bill, and it's rightfully mine, too.* With his wife of twenty-five years gone, and all the kids grown up, I can become that friend he now needs, if he so chooses.

I have been able to exorcise many animosities within me, and this has strengthened my marriage. God only knows it's been a bumpy road and I pray the worst is behind us. I do believe counseling is a good idea, since there is so much I want to say to my wife about this situation and other issues which I have not been able to do before. However, I would like a competent arbitrator there to analyze the situation and offer guidance, if that's possible to do when analyzing a marriage. I hope someday to build Jan's trust in me once again, although considering the circumstances, that's an awful lot to ask. I don't know what path this is going to take, but I do hope Jan and

Linsey realize that I truly do love them, regardless of my inability to display this openly.

****

It's really weird how songs appear in my life which have a great deal of impact. I first heard the song, "I'm Just An Old Chunk Of Coal, But I'm Gonna Be A Diamond Someday," that first day back in 1978 when I began writing this book, back when this whole sordid mess entered my life and I was forced to deal with it. As I was writing that first night, with all those emotions spilling out of me, the song came on a country station I happened to be listening to. The sheer amusement of the title as it related to my circumstances made me realize that I would make a positive statement out of the situation, rather than having to endure "Shattered Dreams" for the remainder of my life. For the first time in my life, I feel good about myself and who I've become. I no longer see myself as a bastard son, prodigy of a mistake. I view myself as a success, considering the circumstances and the odds I've been battling since I was a kid.

The future remains to be seen, but I'm going to accept its challenge and roll with any punches which may be dealt. In any event, my writing is not finished, it has just begun. With a little luck and a guardian angel supplied by The Man, I will continue to spread the word about the moral of this story.

As we say down in the southland, down in Texas, U.S.A., "Shure Hite Ta Say Bah," or in coal country, "Yooz Guyz be good, O.K.! Or what? Ain't!"

ABOUT THE AUTHOR

Pat Miller currently resides in Spring, Texas. This is his first published work, but by no means his last. He is still working in an executive position with the Chrysler Credit Corporation and savors those free moments away from the crazy world of the automobile business when he can write and create works which make people believe in themselves, feel good about themselves. Although writing has become a focal point in his life, the word "family" has taken on a new meaning for him and he puts this first, above all others. Because of this book, he fully intends to pursue a support group for anyone who has had to experience firsthand the feeling of being cheated, lied to, or both. Because of this support group, further books concerning "the truth" are inevitable.